The Morphology of Dutch

To the memory of Albert Sassen

THE MORPHOLOGY OF DUTCH

Geert Booij

OXFORD
UNIVERSITY PRESS

Great Clarendon Street, Oxford OX2 6DP

Oxford University Press is a department of the University of Oxford.
It furthers the University's objective of excellence in research, scholarship,
and education by publishing worldwide in

Oxford New York

Athens Auckland Bangkok Bogotá Buenos Aires Cape Town
Chennai Dar es Salaam Delhi Florence Hong Kong Istanbul Karachi
Kolkata Kuala Lumpur Madrid Melbourne Mexico City Mumbai Nairobi
Paris São Paulo Shanghai Singapore Taipei Tokyo Toronto Warsaw
with associated companies in Berlin Ibadan

Oxford is a registered trade mark of Oxford University Press
in the UK and in certain other countries

Published in the United States
by Oxford University Press Inc., New York

© Geert Booij 2002

The moral rights of the author have been asserted
Database right Oxford University Press (maker)

First published 2002

All rights reserved. No part of this publication may be reproduced,
stored in a retrieval system, or transmitted, in any form or by any means,
without the prior permission in writing of Oxford University Press,
or as expressly permitted by law, or under terms agreed with the appropriate
reprographics rights organizations. Enquiries concerning reproduction
outside the scope of the above should be sent to the Rights Department,
Oxford University Press, at the address above

You must not circulate this book in any other binding or cover
and you must impose the same condition on any acquirer

British Library Cataloguing in Publication Data

Data available

Library of Congress Cataloging in Publication Data

Data applied for

ISBN 0-19-829979-6 (hbk.)
ISBN 0-19-829980-x (pbk.)

10 9 8 7 6 5 4 3 2 1

Typeset in Minion
by Peter Kahrel
Printed in Great Britain
on acid-free paper by
TJ International Ltd, Padstow, Cornwall

CONTENTS

List of Tables and Figures — viii
Abbreviations and Symbols — ix
Preface — xi

1. PRELIMINARIES — 1
   1.1. Introduction — 1
   1.2. The nature of morphological rules — 3
   1.3. Paradigmatic word formation — 6
   1.4. Productivity — 9
   1.5. Lexicon and lexicalization — 13
   1.6. Overview of the book — 18

2. THE INFLECTIONAL SYSTEM — 19
   2.1. Introduction — 19
   2.2. The inflection of nouns — 21
      2.2.1. Number — 21
      2.2.2. Possessor marking — 34
      2.2.3. Gender — 36
   2.3. Adjectival inflection — 39
      2.3.1. Degree forms — 39
      2.3.2. The inflection of prenominal adjectives — 43
      2.3.3. The suffix -*e* as nominalizing suffix — 50
      2.3.4. Partitive constructions — 52
   2.4. Verbal inflection — 54
      2.4.1. Finite forms — 55
      2.4.2. Periphrasis and aspect — 66
      2.4.3. Infinitives and participles — 70
   2.5. The boundary and interaction between inflection and word formation — 80

3.	DERIVATION	86
	3.1. Introduction	86
	3.2. Theoretical preliminaries	86
	3.2.1. Input restrictions	91
	3.2.2. Stratal restrictions	94
	3.2.3. Competition between derivational processes	101
	3.2.4. Derivation and semantics	105
	3.3. Prefixation	110
	3.3.1. Verbal prefixes	113
	3.3.2. Nominal prefixes	117
	3.4. Suffixation	119
	3.4.1. Verbal suffixes	119
	3.4.2. Nominal suffixes	121
	3.4.3. Adjectival suffixes	130
	3.4.4. Adverbial suffixes	133
	3.5. Conversion	134
4.	COMPOUNDING	141
	4.1. Introduction	141
	4.2. Nominal compounds	142
	4.2.1. The left constituent of nominal compounds	145
	4.2.2. The semantic interpretation of nominal compounds	151
	4.3. Adjectival compounds	153
	4.3.1. The semantic interpretation of adjectival compounds	155
	4.3.2. Synthetic compounds	158
	4.4. Verbal compounds	161
	4.5. Numeral compounds	165
5.	THE INTERFACE OF MORPHOLOGY AND PHONOLOGY	167
	5.1. Introduction	167
	5.2. Morphological and prosodic domains	168
	5.2.1. The phonological make-up of affixes	169
	5.2.2. Prosodic gapping	171

5.3. Allomorphy	174
5.3.1. Affix allomorphy	174
5.3.2. Stem allomorphy	176
5.3.3. Allomorphy and paradigmatic relations	178
5.4. Phonological constraints on word formation	182
6. THE MORPHOLOGY–SYNTAX INTERFACE	**187**
6.1. Introduction	187
6.2. Syntactic valency effects	188
6.2.1. Deverbal nouns and inheritance	194
6.3. Constructions	202
6.4. Separable complex verbs: syntax or morphology?	204
6.4.1. The syntactic nature of SCVs	205
6.4.2. Lexical properties of SCVs	208
6.4.3. SCVs as constructional idioms	213
6.4.4. Grammaticalization	216
6.4.5. SCVs with adjectives and nouns	220
7. CONCLUSIONS: THE ARCHITECTURE OF THE GRAMMAR	**225**
References	229
Index of Subjects	243
Index of Authors	248
Index of Affixes	251

LIST OF TABLES AND FIGURES

2.1.	Survey of inflectional categories of Dutch	19
2.2.	The plural form *kánons*	26
2.3.	The plural form *kanónnen*	26
2.4.	The plural forms *kades* and *kaden*	27
2.5.	Determiner selection	33
2.6.	The inflection of *open*	46
2.7.	The indicative verbal paradigm of *koken*	55
2.8.	Regular past tense and participle formation	57
2.9.	Stem-alternating verbs	60
2.10.	Stem-alternating verbs with vowel-length alternation	60
2.11.	Stem-alternating verbs with consonantal alternation	61
2.12.	Stem-alternating verbs with schwa-less infinitives	61
2.13.	Semi-regular verbs	61
2.14.	The paradigms of *hebben* and *zijn*	62
2.15.	The paradigms of *kunnen, mogen,* and *willen*	62
3.1.	Non-native suffixes	97
3.2.	Non-native root suffixes	98
3.3.	Borrowed prefixes with native bases	99
3.4.	The formation of female personal nouns	102
3.5.	Relational adjectives	108
3.6.	Denominal nominal suffixes	110
3.7.	Category-neutral native prefixes	111
3.8.	Verbal category-changing prefixes	113
3.9.	Verbal prefixes which correspond to a word	116
3.10.	Native suffixes for personal nouns	121
3.11.	Nomina actionis	125
3.12.	Native adjectival suffixes for qualitative adjectives	131

Figure 5.1. The prosodic structure of *beadem*   170

ABBREVIATIONS AND SYMBOLS

A	Adjective
Adv	Adverb
AP	Adjectival Phrase
attr.	attributive
D	Determiner
def.	definite
Det	Determiner
dim.	diminutive
DP	Determiner Phrase
e	empty category
F	Foot
fem.	feminine
ICV	Inseparable Complex Verb
indef.	indefinite
intr.	intransitive
IPP	Infinitivus pro Participio
LCS	Lexical Conceptual Structure
lit.	literally
n	neuter
N	Noun
NP	Noun Phrase
Num	Numeral
OCP	Obligatory Contour Principle
OT	Optimality Theory
P	Preposition/Postposition
PAS	Predicate Argument Structure
pers.	person
pl.	plural
PP	Prepositional Phrase
Q	Quantifier
RHR	Righthand Head Rule
S	Sentence
SC	Small Clause
SCV	Separable Complex Verb
sg.	singular

SOV	Subject Object Verb
SUBJ	Subject
SVO	Subject Verb Object
t	trace
tr.	transitive
V	Verb
VP	Verb Phrase
X	variable for lexical categories
σ	syllable
ω	prosodic word
<	derives from
→	direction of derivation, 'consists of'
*	not well-formed
?	of questionable status
>	changes into
.	syllable boundary
!	violation of a condition
☞	optimal candidate
/ /	phonological representation
[ ]	phonetic representation

PREFACE

This book on the morphology of Dutch has two aims. First, it is meant as an internationally accessible description of the morphology of Dutch. So far, a full-fledged description of the Dutch morphological system has not been available in English. The availability of such a description, that is, of a theoretically informed reference work on Dutch morphology appeared to be a desideratum among colleagues working on descriptive, typological, theoretical, or computational issues in linguistics. This became especially clear when I participated in a seminar on the morphology of Dutch organized by Professor Greville Corbett and his colleagues at the University of Guildford in June 1999. Moreover, it is now possible to write such a reference work because there are a lot of detailed studies of Dutch morphology, both with a descriptive and a theoretical orientation, on which it can be based. This book can also be used to gain access to these detailed studies which can be found in the references. The list of references is a selection only from the vast number of publications on the morphology of Dutch, with a focus on publications in English. References to detailed morphological studies in Dutch can also be found in de Haas and Trommelen (1993).

The second ambition of this book is to show that the morphology of Dutch poses many interesting descriptive and theoretical challenges, and that its detailed analysis can contribute substantially to the ongoing discussion on theoretical issues such as the nature of word-formation processes, the relation between the syntagmatic axis and the paradigmatic axis of language structure, the interaction of morphology with phonology, syntax, and semantics, rule-based versus constraint-based grammar, and the balance between storage and computation. Therefore, this book can also be used in advanced courses in morphology for the clarification and illustration of theoretical issues.

Some years ago I wrote a Dutch text book on the morphology of Dutch with my colleague Ariane van Santen of the University of Leiden (Booij and van Santen 1995 (1998)). That textbook has functioned as a source of data, specific analyses, and inspiration for the present book. Hence, the present book owes a lot to Ariane van Santen, who also gave very helpful comments on a previous draft. I would also like to thank my colleagues Ad Foolen, Jack Hoeksema, and Jaap van Marle, who were also willing to function as critical readers of the manuscript.

This book is dedicated to the memory of Professor Albert Sassen (1921–1999), Professor of Dutch at the University of Groningen, and my first teacher of morphology when I was a student in Groningen. Throughout the years, I have profited greatly from his comments on my work, from his insights into the morphology of Dutch, and from the many discussions we had, which I remember with gratefulness.

1

Preliminaries

1.1. INTRODUCTION

Since the beginning of the seventies of the past century, the insight has re-emerged that morphology is a central part of grammar. In traditional grammar, and in historical and typological linguistics, morphology has always been in the focus of interest, but it lost this position, at least in theoretical linguistics, in the early days of generative grammar, with its focus on syntax and phonology, and its attempt to reduce morphology as much as possible to syntax on the one hand, and phonology on the other. However, morphology is in full swing again, and forms an exciting area of present-day linguistic research. It deserves a central role, because, as Spencer and Zwicky (1998: 1) put it in their introduction to *The Handbook of Morphology*: 'Morphology is at the conceptual centre of linguistics. This is not because it is the dominant subdiscipline, but because morphology is the study of word structure, and words are at the interface between phonology, syntax and semantics.'

Dutch is a Germanic language spoken by more than twenty million people in the Netherlands, Belgium, and some overseas areas such as Surinam. The kind of Dutch described is standard Dutch as spoken in the Netherlands, of which the author is a native speaker. Dutch is the national language of the Netherlands, and in Belgium it is one of the three national languages. So far, a full-fledged description of the Dutch morphological system has not been available in English.[1]

---

[1] The only Dutch handbook of morphology is de Haas and Trommelen (1993). However, this book does not deal with inflection in a systematic way. Moreover, it has a strongly descriptive orientation, and tends to neglect the semantic aspects of word formation. Another important source of information on the morphology of Dutch is the second edition of the *Algemene Nederlandse Spraakkunst* (Haeseryn et al. 1997), a general reference grammar of Dutch. The only textbook on the morphology of Dutch is Booij and van Santen (1995, revised edition 1998). Furthermore, there is a short introduction to generative morphology, Don et al. (1994).

What is morphology about? Morphology is a subdiscipline of linguistics that has two basic tasks. First, it has to define the notion 'possible complex word' for each language. Thus, it will account for the fact that the native speakers of a language are not only able to make new sentences, but also to make new words. In other words, the morphological module of a grammar will indicate how the lexicon, the set of existing words of a language, can be extended by the native speaker by making new words. In short, morphology deals with word formation. Second, morphology deals with the form of words in different syntactic contexts. This is the inflectional part of morphology.

Morphology does not only deal with the creation of new words and word forms. Complex words, once formed, can be memorized and will thus often form part of the mental lexicon of the native speaker. Lexical listing of complex words is even unavoidable when the complex word has idiosyncratic formal and/or semantic properties. The lexicon of a language contains thousands of complex words. Therefore, the rules of the morphological module also have to function as redundancy rules with respect to the existing complex words of a language (Jackendoff 1975, Aronoff 1976, Booij 1977).[2] However, this is not an exclusive property of morphological rules. For instance, the syntactic rule that an English NP may consist of an adjective followed by a noun cannot only be used to create new NPs, but also functions as a redundancy rule with respect to existing, lexically listed NPs such as *big toe*, *hard disk*, *sour cream* that have a conventionalized, not completely compositional meaning (Jackendoff 1997a).

What kind of morphological operations do we find in Dutch? The main formal mechanisms used are affixation (used in inflection and derivation) and compounding. In addition, conversion is also used for creating new words, but it is of course a matter of debate whether conversion belongs to word formation (cf. Chapter 3). The mechanism of vowel change (Ablaut or metaphony) is not used any more in a productive way.

---

[2] Jackendoff's (1975) conception of morphological rules as redundancy rules is that they can be used to compute the amount of independent (i.e. unpredictable) information in each lexical entry of the lexicon. Another formalization, which is compatible with my interpretation of morphological rules as morphological templates or constructions can be found in Riehemann (1998), who makes use of multiple lexical inheritance hierarchies that express the predictable properties of a complex word.

1.2. THE NATURE OF MORPHOLOGICAL RULES

Before going into the details of the morphology of Dutch, I will first discuss a number of theoretical preliminaries. The basic assumption of this book is that of word-based morphology: morphological operations apply to words. Native speakers will discover the existence of a morphological process in their native language on the basis of the comparison of a number of words with systematic form–meaning differences. For instance, Dutch has the following pairs of words:

(1)   *Verb*   *Noun*
       denk 'to think'   denker 'thinker'
       fiets 'to cycle'   fietser 'cyclist'
       zoek 'to search'   zoeker 'searcher'

On the basis of such pairs of words the native speaker can conclude a word-formation rule: 'add -*er* to a verb to form a noun that refers to the subject of the verb'. The rule can then also be used productively, for the creation of new words such as *zapper* derived from the (borrowed) verb *zappen* 'to zap' (note that the citation form of Dutch verbs is the infinitival form, stem + -*en*; the citation form will be used in running text, the stem form in the numbered lists of examples).

This example shows that in morphology, the paradigmatic and the syntagmatic dimension of language structure are strongly interwoven. The starting point is a paradigmatic one: we compare a set of verbs with a set of formally and semantically related nouns. On the basis of this comparison, we can conclude the existence of a syntagmatic operation, a word-formation process in which an affix is attached to a word.

It is clear then that morphology must be word-based because it is the comparison of words that forms the starting point of the coming into existence of a word-formation process. The notion 'word-based', which plays a prominent role in Aronoff (1976), the first monograph on morphology within the framework of generative grammar, has given rise to some misunderstanding. What is meant by 'word-based' is not that a word in its surface form is the basis of the word-formation process. The formal basis of a morphological operation on a word, its stem form, does not necessarily occur as a surface word. In many languages, a stem always has to be supplemented by overt inflectional endings before it can appear as a concrete grammatical word. In this respect languages such as English and Dutch differ from morphologically richer languages such as the Slavonic languages: English and Dutch do not require the addition of overt forms to the stems of words in order for them to be usable.[3] In other words, it is the stem form of a lexeme that is the basis for word formation. Moreover, the phonological form of a stem is not necessarily a form that also occurs as a phonetic form: it is the underlying phonological form of the stem that is the input for morphological operations. For instance, the plural form *hoeden* [hudən] 'hats' for the word *hoed* 'hat' [hut] shows that it is the more abstract underlying and as such unpronounceable form /hud/ that forms the basis for the morphological operation of pluralization. Therefore, as pointed out by Aronoff (1994: 7), it might be better to use the term 'lexeme-based morphology' instead of 'word-based morphology'. A lexeme is a word in the abstract sense, the lexical unit 'that is entered in dictionaries as the fundamental element in the lexicon of a language' (Matthews 1991: 26), with which one or more grammatical words, such as the different forms of a verb, correspond.

There is an additional reason why we want to say that even in Dutch and English, morphology is based on stems, and not on words. Consider, for instance, the Dutch compound *boekverkoper* and its English equivalent *bookseller*. In these compounds, the first constituents should not be interpreted as concrete words, because the words *boek* and *book* are singular nouns whereas no singular meaning should be attached to these constituents: a *boekverkoper* is someone who sells books in general, not just a single book. That is, *boek* is a lexical stem here, a stem that happens to be usable as a concrete word form (the singular form) as well. This means that we have to state explicitly for Dutch that stems can also function as word forms. For instance, a noun stem can also function as the singular form of that noun (cf. Chapter 2).

How do we formalize morphological rules? In Aronoff (1976), the format of rewriting rules is used. For instance, the formation of deverbal agent nouns is formalized as follows:

---

[3] That is why Bloomfield (1933: 225) stated that English morphology is word-based, and qualifies German morphology as stem-based. Note, however, that in my view all morphology is stem-based, i.e. morphology applies to the stem form of lexemes. That is, Bloomfield's notion 'word-based morphology' refers to languages in which the phonological shape of words and stems can be identical.

1.2. THE NATURE OF MORPHOLOGICAL RULES

(2) N → V + -er

What this notation expresses is that a noun can consist of a verbal stem followed by the suffix -er. This way of formalizing morphological rules also functions to distinguish between lexical morphemes and affixes, which are bound morphemes: whereas lexical morphemes are listed individually in the lexicon, affixes are not: they only exist as part of these rewriting rules.

Another formalism has been proposed in Lieber (1980): both lexical morphemes and bound morphemes are listed in the lexicon. In the case of bound morphemes, their boundness is indicated by their being subcategorized for appearing in combination with words of a specific lexical category. For instance, the deverbal suffix -er will be categorized as a noun that is subcategorized for appearing after a verb. Morphology itself then consists of only one operation: 'concatenate'. Properties of the complex word, once it has been constructed by concatenation, will be computed by percolation mechanisms such as the Righthand Head Rule (Williams 1981) that states that the syntactic category of a complex word is identical to that of its head, the rightmost constituent. This will assign the category N to deverbal words in -er once the category N has been assigned to the suffix -er.

In this book, I will take a position similar to that of Aronoff (1976): affixes should not appear as lexical entries because they have no existence of their own. The specific format of rewriting rules, however, is perhaps not very insightful. What a rewrite rule such as (2) is meant to express is that there is a class of words of the form $[V + er]_N$ in which the V-slot is open, and can in principle be filled by any verb. Templates of this form, with one or more open slots, are constructions: configurations with specific meanings (in this example the meaning 'one who Vs'). More specifically, these constructions are morphological constructions (as we will see in Chapters 2 and 6, there are also syntactic constructions). In other words, I assume that the morphological module contains a number of these templates, one for each productive morphological process, with an open slot for the base. In the case of compounding, there will be even more than one open slot: nominal and adjectival compounding are productive in Dutch, and hence, we have a template $[[X][Y]]_Y$ for nominal and adjectival compounds (where X stands for N, A, V, and Y stands for N, A).

1.3. PARADIGMATIC WORD FORMATION

So far, we have concentrated on the syntagmatic dimension of morphology, the concatenation of words and affixes into (more) complex words, although it was clear that morphological operations are based on (generalized) paradigmatic relations between words. The insight that paradigmatic relations between words form the foundation of morphology is a hallmark of the Dutch tradition of morphological research.[4]

We will now see that there are certain kinds of word formation that cannot be accounted for in terms of attachment of an affix to a stem, and require a paradigmatic account. Consider, for instance, the formation of nouns in -*ster* that mention female agents. At first sight, they may be characterized as deverbal nouns, just like their sex-neutral counterparts in -*er* (cf. van Marle 1985):

(3) | Verb | Deverbal noun | Deverbal noun |
|---|---|---|
| arbeid | arbeid-ster | arbeid-er |
| 'to labour' | 'female labourer' | 'labourer' |
| spreek 'to speak' | spreek-ster 'female speaker' | sprek-er 'speaker' |
| werk 'to work' | werk-ster 'female worker, charwoman' | werk-er 'worker' |
| zwem 'to swim' | zwem-ster 'female swimmer' | zwemm-er 'swimmer' |

However, it is also possible for the native speaker to conclude that female nouns of this kind are formed by replacing the suffix -*er* with the suffix -*ster*. One reason for assuming that this analysis is sometimes the more adequate one is that when a deverbal noun in -*er* has a particular semantic idiosyncrasy, this semantic property recurs in the corresponding female noun, as is illustrated by the following examples (van Santen and de Vries 1981, van Marle 1985):

(4) betweter '*lit.* better knower, pedant'   betweetster 'female pedant'
     oproerkraaier '*lit.* revolution crower, ring leader'   oproerkraaister 'female ring leader'

---

[4] Cf. van Marle (1985) and Schultink (2000) for a historical survey of Dutch morphology. The role of paradigmatic relations in Dutch morphology is also discussed in van Marle (2000*a*).

1.3. PARADIGMATIC WORD FORMATION

padvinder '*lit.* path finder, boy scout'   padvindster 'girl scout'
strooplikker '*lit.* syrup licker, toady'   strooplikster 'female toady'

Note that the common semantic idiosyncrasy of these word pairs cannot be explained in terms of a common verbal base because Dutch does not have the verbs *betweten, oproerkraaien, padvinden*, or *strooplikken*.

Moreover, there are also nouns in *-er* without a verbal base that exhibit the same correlation (there are no verbs *reizigen* and *rederijken*):

(5)   rederijk-er 'rhetorician'   rederijk-ster 'female rhetorician'
      reizig-er 'traveller'   reizig-ster 'female traveller'

Third, deverbal sex-neutral nouns have the allomorph *-der* after a verbal stem ending in /r/ in order to avoid the sequence [rər] (cf. Booij 1998*a*). The extra /d/ before *-er* often appears also before the suffix *-ster* (in written Dutch) even though the attachment of this suffix does not create the sequence [rər] (van Santen and de Vries 1981):

(6)   aanvoer-der 'captain'   aanvoerd-ster 'female captain'
      bestuur-der 'driver'   bestuurd-ster 'female driver'
      woordvoer-der 'spokesman'   woordvoerd-ster 'spokeswoman'

On the basis of these observations we have to conclude that the paradigmatic relations between coderivatives may lead to new patterns of word formation, in this case the substitution of one affix with another. That is, this is a case of paradigmatic word formation. Note, however, that this does not mean that nouns in *-ster* are always coined in the paradigmatic way. The noun *huishoud-ster* 'female house-keeper', for instance, has been derived by directly attaching the suffix *-ster* to the verbal stem *huishoud* 'to house-keep', since there is no noun *huishouder* 'male housekeeper'.

Another case of paradigmatic word formation is back formation. In that case, a non-existing base is created on the basis of other word pairs. For instance, Dutch has no productive process of creating verbal compounds. Yet, there are a number of such verbs, created on the basis of paradigmatic relations. An example is the verb *stofzuigen* 'to vacuum-clean' formed on the basis of the nominal compound *stofzuiger* 'vacuum cleaner', parallel to the word pair *zuigen* 'to suck', *zuiger* 'sucker' (Booij 1989). This coinage is parallel to English formations, such as *to caretake* and *to baby-sit* from *caretaker* and *babysitter* respectively.

Another argument for the role of paradigmatic relations in morphology are so-called bracketing paradoxes such as *transformational grammarian*. In this phrase, the adjective *transformational* does not modify the whole complex noun *grammarian*, but only the part *grammar*: a transformational grammarian is a person who deals with transformational grammar. Clearly, such phrases are based on a parallel with the word pair *grammar–grammarian* (Spencer 1988, Becker 1994).[5]

Paradigmatic relations also play a crucial role in the analysis of the non-native lexicon of Dutch that consists partially of words borrowed (directly or indirectly) from Greek and Latin, the pan-European lexicon, and of words formed on the basis of the paradigmatic relations between such words. For instance, Dutch has many pairs of words ending in *-isme* and *-ist* for which no lexical base exists:

(7) bolsjewisme   bolsjewist   bolsjewistisch
    'bolshevism'   'bolshevist'   'bolshevistic'
    communisme   communist   communistisch
    'communism'   'communist'   'communistic'
    luminisme   luminist   luministisch
    'luminism'   'luminist'   'luministic'
    pacifisme   pacifist   pacifistisch
    'pacifism'   'pacifist'   'pacifistic'

The basic idea is that, once one of the three forms exists, the other two are also possible. As soon as we know the word *pacifisme*, we can also use the words *pacifist* and *pacifistisch* although there is no lexical base for these words. In formal terms this means that these are cases of affix substitution (Sassen 1981). Even the words in *-istisch* can be formed directly on the basis of corresponding word in *-isme*, without the word in *-ist* playing a role: a Dutch speaker may know the words *mechanisme* and *mechanistisch* without knowing the word *mechanist*. Moreover, we also find the adjective *amateuristisch* 'amateurish' that is derived directly from *amateur* 'id.' since *amateur-*

---

[5] As Beard (1991) pointed out, we find similar semantic patterns for all kinds of relational adjectives, for instance, also for *transformational linguist* for which there is no corresponding NP *transformational lingu-* available, and therefore no explanation in terms of paradigmatic relations. Although this is a correct observation, it does not mean that paradigmatic relations do not play a role in those cases where there are corresponding conventionalized NPs like *transformational grammar*.

ist is neither an existing nor a possible noun of Dutch. This confirms the idea that the suffix sequence *-istisch* functions as a suffixing unit (called a 'synaffix' by Bauer 1988).

Affix substitution is not restricted to the non-native lexicon, as is clear from the data concerning the suffix *-ster* discussed above, but occurs on a much larger scale than in the native lexicon since it is in the non-native lexicon that many complex words have been borrowed from other languages without the corresponding base words. An example from the native lexicon is the formation of *heroveren* 'to recapture' on the basis of *veroveren* 'to capture'.

The role of paradigmatic relations is also crucial in understanding the relation between non-native words of the following kind:

(8)   filosofie 'philosophy'   filosoof 'philosopher'
      fonologie 'phonology'   fonoloog 'phonologist'
      morfologie 'morphology'   morfoloog 'morphologist'
      theologie 'theology'   theoloog 'theologian'

The meanings of the nouns in the right column are a compositional function of the meaning of the nouns in the left column. For instance, a *morfoloog* is someone who is occupied with *morfologie*. Yet, formally, the inverse seems to be the case since a word such as *morfoloog* is shorter than its semantic base *morfologie*. This seems to imply that there are also morphological operations in Dutch that consist of deletion of segments of the base word. It is indeed the case that native speakers do coin words, such as the word *chaoot* 'chaotic person' from the adjective *chaot-isch* 'chaotic' (Sassen 1981). However, we should realize that this kind of word formation (affix extraction) is rather exceptional.

1.4. PRODUCTIVITY

A central issue in present-day morphology is whether all morphological patterns and their extension to new cases can and should be described in terms of rules (or similar mechanisms such as templates of the kind proposed above). The basic division is that between productive and unproductive processes. Together, productive processes define the set of possible complex words of a language, and specify how the lexicon of a language can be extended in a systematic way. Productive processes, such as compounding or the formation of deverbal nouns in -*er* give rise to new coinings, to words that are not yet listed, not yet stored in the mental lexicon of the native speaker. On the other hand, the formation of past tense forms by means of Ablaut is unproductive in modern Dutch, and therefore all past tense forms with Ablaut have to be listed in dictionaries and grammars of Dutch, and stored by the native speaker. Retrieval of stored forms is the only source of such words in actual language use. This is the basic idea of the dual mechanism theory of Pinker (1998, 1999) and Clahsen (1999). This theory claims that there are two sources of complex words for the language user: the outputs of unproductive processes are stored in the mental lexicon, and retrieved from the lexicon, whereas the outputs of productive processes are not stored: such complex words are created by rule when the language user needs them. If a morphological process is unproductive, and hence all its outputs must be listed, that does not mean that the native speaker is completely unable to discover regularities in the relevant formal patterns (Clahsen 1999, Pinker 1998, 1999). Speakers of Dutch, for instance, command a kind of associative patterning in the set of past tense forms which enables them to occasionally extend this pattern to new cases, or to apply these patterns to non-existing words of similar phonological composition (van Santen and Lalleman 1994, van Santen 1997, Jordens 1998).

However, the dual mechanism theory cannot be completely right. If a morphological process is productive, this does not mean that its outputs are never stored. In particular, complex words with a high frequency will normally be stored in the mental lexicon because this will speed up the processing of utterances (Baayen, Dijkstra, and Schreuder 1997). In other words, listing is possible even for the outputs of productive processes. This means that the crucial point of the dual mechanism theory is not that there is never storage of the outputs of productive morphology but rather that the native speaker does not have to rely on the storage of such words, unlike what is the case for words of unproductive categories.[6]

The notion 'productivity' is primarily a qualitative notion: a morphological pattern is productive, if in principle new words can be formed according to that pattern, in an unintentional way (Schultink 1961; see also Booij 1977, Plag 1999), and a pattern is unproductive if new words of that type

---

[6] As pointed out in Booij (1999a), storage of frequent regular forms is also something we have to allow for in order to be able to explain that the effects of once regular phonological rules can survive after the loss of such rules.

cannot be formed, unless intentionally, on the basis of analogy with existing words of that type. However, the quantitative productivity of morphological patterns, the actual number of new words coined, differs from pattern to pattern, because they differ enormously in the kind of restrictions that they are subject to.

First, the different kinds of complex words differ in their semantic and pragmatic usability: diminutive nouns can be used more often than inhabitant names, to give just one example. Second, there might be all kinds of restrictions on the lexical bases for a morphological process: phonological, morphological, syntactic, and semantic (cf. Rainer 2000 for a survey). For example, suffixes of non-native origin nearly always attach to bases that are also non-native, whereas native, i.e. Germanic, suffixes attach to all kinds of bases (Chapter 3). These restrictions will be discussed in detail in the following chapters. Consequently, the number of available bases can differ substantially from one process to another (Booij 1977, Plag 1999). Third, a particular type of complex word may have a stylistic value that makes it unsuitable in certain registers or speech situations, which will restrict the number of new coinings of that type.

Another kind of impediment on the quantitative productivity of morphological processes is the phenomenon of blocking. As pointed out by Rainer (1988) we should distinguish between type-blocking and token-blocking. In the case of type-blocking the actual use of a morphological process is impeded by one or more competing morphological processes. For instance, Dutch has a number of processes for the formation of agent nouns. Therefore, the quantitative productivity of the individual processes of that kind will be reduced by that competition.

In the case of token-blocking, the existence of a word with a particular meaning blocks the formation of a new complex word with the same meaning. A classical example is that speakers of English will not coin the agent noun *stealer* because of the existence of the word *thief* with the same meaning. This kind of blocking is never absolute, however. This is already shown by the fact that in Dutch the equivalent of *stealer*, the word *steler*, has been coined, for reasons of rhyme, in the proverb *De heler is niet beter dan de steler* 'The receiver is as bad as the thief' even though Dutch does have the word *dief* 'thief'. The degree of blocking force of an existing word appears to depend on its frequency. For instance, as is well known, past tense verbal forms with Ablaut have a high frequency, and will therefore easily block the coinage of regular, suffixed past tense forms. If a word is less established, it is still possible to coin a synonymous complex word according to a productive pattern. For instance, the coinage of a noun in *-heid* '-ness' is never blocked by its coderivative in *-iteit* '-ity', although the two words are synonymous: both *absurditeit* and *absurdheid* 'absurdity' are possible words in Dutch.

Blocking might also be caused by the existence of competing syntactic possibilities (de Caluwe 1991, Heynderickx 1992). For instance, in Dutch it is possible to coin adjective–noun compounds. However, we may also use NPs of the A+N type as names for certain entities, as in English, and it is this pattern that is the more popular one.

(9) *A+N compounds*: edelman 'nobleman', hoogbouw 'high rise construction', roodhuid 'redskin', witbrood 'white bread'

(10) *A+N phrases*: rode kool 'red cabbage', groene zeep 'green soap', zwarte markt 'black market'

In this respect Dutch differs from German, which exhibits a more frequent use of A+N compounds, where Dutch uses A+N phrases (compare Dutch *harde schijf* with German *Festplatte* for 'hard disk', or Dutch *oude stad* with German *Altstadt* for 'old (part of the) town').

From this discussion it will be clear that there is a quantitative difference in productivity among the productive morphological processes of Dutch. The next question then is how we can measure the degree of productivity of a process. It is obvious that this cannot be executed by counting the number of words of the relevant type in a dictionary or corpus, because this number does not tell us to what extent the relevant set has been and can be expanded. An interesting measure of productivity, based on large corpora, has been proposed in Baayen (1991, 1992), Baayen and Neijt (1997); cf. also Plag (1999). The basic idea is that the hallmark of productive processes is their creating hapax legomena, i.e. word types instantiating the relevant morphological process for which there is only one token in a given corpus. The number of hapax legomena in a corpus for an unproductive process will be very low, since these are mostly word types of high frequency, whereas a productive process will create a much higher number of words with frequency 1. In this way, morphological processes can be ranked on a scale of productivity.[7]

---

[7] Cf. van Marle (1992) and Plag (1999).

1.5. LEXICON AND LEXICALIZATION

The lexicon of a language consists primarily of the simplex words of a language, and those morphologically complex words that have one or more idiosyncratic (formal or semantic) property. In addition, the lexicon will consist of syntactic chunks that have unpredictable properties, the idioms of a language. This notion 'lexicon' refers to an abstract component of the grammar, and should not be equated with the individual mental lexicon of the native speaker. The individual lexicon will contain fewer lexical entries than the lexicon of a language, whereas the native speaker may also memorize completely regular complex words with a certain frequency, simply because this will speed up language processing (cf. Baayen, Dijkstra, and Schreuder 1997).

The lexicon is not a fixed list, and it is a major function of morphology to expand the fund of lexical items. That is, morphological operations take words (simplex or complex) as their inputs, and create (more) complex words. Most of these words are existing ones, listed in the lexicon, but it is also possible to use possible words as input for word-formation processes. For instance, we may first derive the word *koolachtig* 'cabbage-like' from *kool* 'cabbage', and this complex word can then be suffixed with the deadjectival suffix *-heid* '-ness', thus providing *koolachtigheid* 'cabbagelikeness', without *koolachtig* necessarily being an existing word.

The operations that create complex words of Dutch are affixation and compounding. In addition, conversion, the change of word class of a word without overt phonological effect, is also used to create new words. I will discuss conversion in Chapter 3, the chapter on derivation, because conversion is functionally similar to derivation although there is no attachment of phonological material involved.

There are other means of extending the lexicon as well. For instance, the creation of acronyms, clipping, and blending are also ways of creating of new words:

(11)   acronym: bh 'bra' < bustehouder 'bra'
        clipping: ordi 'vulgar' < ordinair 'vulgar'
        blending: botel 'floating hotel' < boot 'boat' and hotel 'id.'

The crucial difference with the morphological operations of affixation and compounding is that in these cases there is no systematic form–meaning correspondence between the base word and the newly created one. That is, they are not created by morphology in the strict sense, and therefore they will not be dealt with in this book.

Another important source of complex words is the diachronic development of lexicalized word sequences into words. Examples of such lexicalizations are:

(12)   blootshoofds 'bare-headed', onverrichterzake 'in vain', tegelijkertijd 'simultaneously', terwijl 'while', tevreden 'content'

For instance, *tegelijkertijd* is originally a PP, consisting of the preposition *te*, the inflected adjective *gelijker* 'same', and the noun *tijd* 'time'.

Secondly, complex words of lexical categories (N, V, A, Adv) can develop into words of non-lexical categories such as conjunctions and prepositions, the process referred to as grammaticalization (Hopper and Traugott 1993):

(13)   gedurende 'during', gezien '*lit*. seen, because of', hoewel 'although'

The preposition *gedurende* derives from the present participle of the no longer existing verb *geduren* 'to last', *gezien* is the past participle of the verb *zien* 'to see', and *hoewel* is a combination of the words *hoe* 'how' and *wel* 'well'. Similarly, Dutch acquired a number of complex prepositions through the reinterpretation of preposition sequences as complex prepositions:

(14)   [[achter]$_P$ [[aan]$_P$ de wagen]$_{PP}$]$_{PP}$ > [[achteraan]$_P$ de wagen]$_{PP}$
       'at the back of the cart'
       [[rond]$_P$ [[om]$_P$ de mensen]$_{PP}$]$_{PP}$ > [[rondom]$_P$ de mensen]$_{PP}$
       'around the people'

The important theoretical point of these observations is that not all words that consist of more than one morpheme have to be accounted for by the morphological module of the grammar of a language. Moreover, the general hypothesis that word-formation operations only affect lexical categories (V, N, A, or Adv) is thus not refuted by the existence of complex prepositions such as *achteraan* and *rondom*.

A third non-morphological source of new words is borrowing. In the course of history, Dutch borrowed lots of words from Greek, Latin, and French. Many of these words have the appearance of complex words since their roots, morphemes such as *oper-*, *duc-*, and *not-*, occur in sets of formally related words. The roots themselves, however, may not have been borrowed

1.5. LEXICON AND LEXICALIZATION

as words. This applies to the following words with complex appearance:

(15) noteer 'to note'   notatie 'notation'
     opereer 'to operate' operatie 'operation'
     produceer 'to produce' productie 'production'

The native speakers may even expand this pattern to new cases, for instance by substituting the suffix *-eer* with the suffix *-atie*, a pattern of word formation that has indeed become productive in Dutch. This is the kind of word-formation pattern for which Aronoff (1976) introduced the notion 'truncation rule': a rule that deletes a morpheme before another morpheme. For instance, we could claim that first *-atie* is added to the verb in *-eer*, and subsequently *-eer* is deleted. It will be clear, however, that such truncation rules are only neccessary if we want to push all kinds of productive word formation into the normal pattern of the addition of an affix to a base word.

When such roots have also been borrowed as words, they may have received a different shape. In the latter case, the native speaker will be able to see a relation between complex word and base, but with allomorphy involved. This is the case for word pairs like

(16) Calvijn 'Calvin'   calvin-ist 'calvinist'
     filter 'filter'   filtr-eer 'to filtrate'
     orkest 'orchestra' orkestr-eer 'to orchestrate'

An important effect of the lexicalization of complex words is the creation of a set of words that are only formally complex because the original base words of these complex words have been lost in the course of history. Dutch has an abundance of such words. For instance, there are many verbs that begin with a prefix, but contain a root that does not exist as an independent word. Nevertheless, we consider them complex because they behave as such. In particular, prefixed verbs have perfect participles without the prefix *ge-*, and this also applies to formally prefixed verbs:

(17) *Formally complex verb*   *Perfect participle*
     begin 'to begin'   begonnen
     genees 'to cure'   genezen
     ontgin 'to develop'   ontgonnen
     vergeet 'to forget'   vergeten

If the first syllable has no prefix status, the participle will get the prefix *ge-*, as illustrated by the verb *verbaliseren* 'to book' with the participle *geverbaliseerd*: here, the syllable *ver* is part of the root *verbal-*.

There are also many suffixed words without a lexical base, for the same reason: once a complex word has been coined, it can be stored in the lexicon, and it will survive even though its base is lost. The suffix still tells us the syntactic category of the word, and in the case of nominal suffixes its gender:

(18) dier-baar 'precious', huid-ig 'present', beslommer-ing 'chore' (non-neuter), meis-je 'girl' (neuter), moei-lijk 'difficult', arge-loos 'unsuspecting', moei-zaam 'painful'

Compounds are subject to the same fate, and there are therefore many compounds of which one or both of the constituents no longer exist as independent words. Such constituents have been called 'cranberry morphs', cf. Aronoff (1976):

(19) *Compound* *Constituent that is not a lexeme*
aard-bei 'strawberry' -bei 'berry'
stief-vader 'stepfather' stief- 'step-'
oor-zaak 'cause' oor- 'original'
sperzie-boon 'green bean' sperzie- 'asparagus'

Such words still behave as compounds as far as their phonological properties such as stress pattern are concerned. Moreover, if the right constituent is an existing word, the syntactic category of the complex word and part of its meaning is predictable.

Since lexemes form the basis for morphological operations, the idiosyncratic properties of listed complex words will recur in more complex words of which they form the base. For instance, since the passive participle *gesloten* with the literal meaning 'closed' also has the meaning 'introvert', this psychological meaning of *gesloten* will recur in the derived noun *geslotenheid* 'introvertedness'.

However, as pointed out above, that does not mean that it is only existing lexemes that form the input for word formation: possible but non-existing words might also feed word formation.

Although possible but not necessarily existing words may thus form an intermediate step in the derivation of multiply complex words, the conclusion that this is the case cannot always be drawn if the intermediate step does not exist. Consider the following cases:

(20) | Adjective | Complex adjective | Deadjectival noun |
|---|---|---|
| vies 'dirty' | viezig 'filthy' | viezigheid 'filthyness' |
| zoet 'sweet' | zoetig 'sweetish' | zoetigheid 'sweets' |
| gemeen 'mean' | gemenig 'somewhat mean' | gemenigheid 'dirty trick' |
| naar 'unpleasant' | narig 'somewhat unpleasant' | narigheid 'trouble' |
| stom 'stupid' | stommig 'somewhat stupid' | stommigheid 'stupid act' |

The last three adjectives in -*ig* listed in (20) do not exist in Dutch, but they are possible adjectives that can function as intermediate steps. However, the meaning of the nouns in -*igheid* is not completely predictable on the basis of the meanings of the adjective in -*ig* and of the suffix -*heid*: the suffix sequence -*igheid* has become a suffix of its own with the meaning 'substance having the property expressed by the simplex adjective'. In other words, in these cases the noun appears to have been derived directly from the simplex adjective. Such affix sequences functioning as one affix can arise through reinterpretation, on the basis of the paradigmatic relationship between simplex adjectives and nouns ending in -*igheid*. The rise of such a suffix sequence may have been reinforced by the fact that both -*ig* and -*heid* take adjectives as their bases, and hence the base of the adjective in -*ig* can be reinterpreted as the base of the sequence -*igheid* (cf. van Marle 1990a and Haspelmath 1995 for discussion).

It is not even necessary for the affix combination to consist of two linearly adjacent affixes. It is a well-known observation that negative adjectives prefixed with *on-* 'un-' often lack a positive counterpart that exists as an independent lexeme. This may mean that a possible but non-existing lexeme has been used as an intermediate step in the derivation, but it may also be the case that both affixes have been added simultaneously on the basis of paradigmatic relationships:

(21) | Verb | Adjective | Negative adjective |
|---|---|---|
| aanraak 'to touch' | ?aanraakbaar 'touchable' | onaanraakbaar 'untouchable' |
| betaal 'to pay' | betaalbaar 'affordable' | onbetaalbaar 'unaffordable' |

uitstaan	?uitstaanbaar	onuitstaanbaar
'to tolerate'	'tolerable'	'intolerable'
verdedig	verdedigbaar	onverdedigbaar
'to defend'	'defensible'	'indefensible'
verwoest	?verwoestbaar	onverwoestbaar
'to destroy'	'destroyable'	'indestructible'

Although the affixes might have been added simultaneously, this does not mean that there is no hierarchical morphological structure involved: the prefix *on-* does not attach to verbs, only to adjectives; it is the suffix *-baar* that turns the verbal base into an adjective. Therefore, formally, the suffix *-baar* is attached before the prefix *on-*; the morphological structure of an adjective like *onverwoestbaar* is $[on[[verwoest]_V baar]_A]_A$. Thus, we see how the syntagmatic and the paradigmatic dimensions of morphology coexist, and may both play a role when a new complex word is coined.

1.6. OVERVIEW OF THE BOOK

The next three chapters deal with the three components of the morphology of Dutch: inflection (Chapter 2), derivation (Chapter 3), and compounding (Chapter 4). The following chapters are devoted to interface issues: the interface of morphology with phonology (Chapter 5) and with syntax (Chapter 6). Chapter 7 presents a short survey of the theoretical conclusions that we can draw from an analysis of the Dutch morphological system. The book ends with a list of references, which will give the reader access to more detailed studies of the morphology of Dutch, with emphasis on publications in English.

2

The Inflectional System

2.1. INTRODUCTION

The inflectional system of Dutch can be qualified as in between English and German on the scale of morphological complexity: it is more complex than English, and less complex than German. Before discussing the details of the inflectional system, I will first present a survey of the inflectional categories of Dutch. In this survey, I make use of the distinction between categories and features (Matthews 1991: 39). For instance, Number is a morphosyntactic category, i.e. a morphological category with potential syntactic relevance. Singular is a particular value for that morphosyntactic category, and hence it is a morphosyntactic feature.

As argued in Booij (1994, 1996), and following an old tradition in Indo-European morphology (cf. Kuryłowicz 1964), I will distinguish between inherent and contextual inflection. Inherent inflection is that kind of inflection that adds morphosyntactic properties with an independent semantic value to the stem of the word. Contextual inflection, on the other hand, is

TABLE 2.1. *Survey of inflectional categories of Dutch*

Syntactic category	Inflectional category	Feature
Noun	Number	Singular, Plural
Adjective	Degree	Comparative, Superlative
	Attributive use	
Verb	Tense	Present, Past
	Aspect	Perfect
	Mood	Indicative, Imperative, Conjunctive
	Participle	Present, Past
	Infinitive	
	Number	Singular, Plural
	Person	First, Second, Third

that kind of inflection that is required by syntactic context, but does not add information. Examples of contextual inflection in Dutch are the categories Number and Person for finite (tensed) verbal forms: these categories have to be present because of the condition that a finite verb form has to agree in the features for Number and Person with the subject of its clause. Another case of contextual inflection in Dutch is the inflection of the adjective in attributive position (Section 2.3). All other kinds of inflection in Dutch (the plural forms of nouns, the degree forms of adjectives, and the tense, aspectual, infinitival, and participial forms of verbs) are cases of inherent inflection since they add a property that is not exclusively dictated by the syntax.

The distinction between inherent and contextual inflection plays an important role in a range of phenomena. The basic observation is that inherent inflection is more similar to derivation than contextual inflection is. Like derivation, inherent inflection adds information to that expressed by the base, exhibits gaps in its paradigms, may not have an existing word as its base, and tends to lexicalize, that is, to acquire idiosyncratic properties. Like lexemes, inherent inflection patterns may be borrowed from other languages, as is the case for Dutch plural nouns. As to the order of morphemes, derivational morphemes are internal to inflectional ones, and likewise, inherent inflection is internal to contextual inflection. For instance, markings for number and person on verbs are peripheral to markings for tense. Thus, the general order of morphemes at the end of a word is stem – derivation – inherent inflection – contextual inflection. The difference between inherent and contextual inflection also manifests itself in the fact that inherent inflection may occasionally feed word formation, whereas this is never the case for contextual inflection (cf. Section 2.5).

Another difference between contextual and inherent inflection is that contextual inflection is lost more easily. For instance, Romance languages such as French and Italian, and Germanic languages such as English and Dutch have lost their case system. And in American Dutch, it is contextual inflection that is primarily subject to erosion (Smits 1994). This is to be expected since contextual inflection does not express independent information.

From this survey, we can conclude that the Dutch inflectional system is richer than that of English because it exhibits (a restricted form of) adjectival inflection and has a slightly richer verbal paradigm. On the other hand, it is poorer than German inflection because the category Case is absent, and the inflection of adjectives is far less elaborate.

2.2. THE INFLECTION OF NOUNS

The main inflection of nouns is that for the category Number. In addition, there are also relics of a case system, but, generally, Dutch has lost morphological case, just like English. The relics of the case system will be discussed in Sections 2.2.2 and 2.3.3.

2.2.1. *Number*

Dutch is similar to English in that it has no morphological expression for the feature 'singular' of nouns: the form of the nominal stem and that of the singular form coincide. Therefore, I will assume a lexical default rule that will assign the feature value 'singular' to a noun stem used as a word or as the head of a nominal compound. A similar rule can be assumed for verbal stems used as words: they will receive the features [first sg. present tense] by default. Thus, there is no need to assume a zero-suffix in such cases.

There are two plural suffixes, *-s* and *-en* /ən/. These are two competing suffixes, and the principles for selection of the correct one is the main topic of this section. In addition, there is a closed set of nouns that have plural forms in *-eren* /ərən/, and a number of borrowed nouns that have the plural form of the language of origin.

The pluralization of nouns is considered as a form of inflection here, and this is the traditional position. However, that does not mean that there is a plural form for every noun of Dutch. The reasons why we nevertheless consider pluralization a form of inflection is (*a*) that the plural form of a noun is felt to be a form of the same lexeme, and not another lexeme, and (*b*) because normally, it does not feed derivation: except in special cases (cf. Section 2.5) one cannot use plural forms as inputs for derivation, as would be expected if plural nouns were fully independent lexemes.

As pointed out by Sassen (1992), there are many nouns that lack a plural form, for instance: *aandacht* 'attention', *antiek* 'antiques', *aplomb* 'id.', *arbeid* 'labour', *genade* 'grace', *goud* 'gold', *hooi* 'hay', *Maart* 'March', *verzekerdheid* 'assuredness'. The reason for the absence of these plural forms is usually semantic: it does not make sense to have more than one of the referents of these nouns. In other cases a plural form is not impossible but never used for pragmatic reasons. The noun *Nederlands* 'the Dutch language', for instance, has no plural form, unlike the English counterpart *English* because there are not so many varieties of Dutch around the world, as there are for English. It is typical for inherent inflectio/n to exhibit holes in its paradigms (Booij 1994).

On the other hand, there are also many nouns that exist in the plural form only, the so-called pluralia tantum. Examples are the following:

(1) Alp-en 'Alps', hersen-en 'brains', contrei-en 'areas', hurk-en 'haunches', ingewand-en 'intestines', kapsone-s 'airs', notul-en 'minutes of a meeting', Pyrenee-ën 'Pyrenees'

The form of these plural nouns is completely regular, but nevertheless they have to be stored in the (mental) lexicon because they have no corresponding singular form.

There is a set of fifteen nouns that is traditionally said to have a special plural form in *-eren* /ərən/. The set comprises the following words:

(2) | *Singular* | *Plural* |
| --- | --- |
| been 'bone, leg' | beenderen 'bones'/benen 'legs' |
| blad 'leaf, sheet' | bladeren 'leaves'/bladen 'sheets' |
| ei 'egg' | eieren |
| gelid 'rank' | gelederen |
| gemoed 'mind' | gemoederen |
| goed 'commodity' | goederen |
| hoen 'hen' | hoenderen |
| kalf 'calf' | kalveren |
| kind 'child' | kinderen |
| kleed 'cloth, carpet' | klederen[1] 'clothes'/kleden 'carpets' |
| lam 'lamb' | lammeren |
| lied 'song' | liederen |
| rad 'wheel' | raderen |
| rund 'cow' | runderen |
| volk 'people' | volkeren/volken |

As indicated some of these nouns also have a regular form. Moreover, the special plural form is not always used for all meanings of a word, as shown by the pair *bladeren* 'leaves' – *bladen* 'sheets'. The plural form *beenderen* has an

---

[1] The form *klederen* is archaic, the normal form is the contracted form *kleren*.

2.2. THE INFLECTION OF NOUNS

extra stem-final /d/, which reflects the fact that the word *been* is a homonym in which two different words have merged phonologically.

Historically, the sequence *-eren* is a sequence of two plural morphemes, *-er* and *-en*. Unlike German, Dutch no longer has the plural suffix *-er*, and therefore there are two possible synchronic interpretations for this sequence. One interpretation (the traditional one) is that of a third plural suffix *-eren*; the other one is that these nouns exhibit stem allomorphy, and have a special stem allomorph to be used in the plural form. This is the interpretation that I would like to defend. The main argument for this stem choice is that the stem allomorph also occurs in non-plural contexts, both within derivation and compounding, as the following examples illustrate:

(3) beender-lijm 'gelatine'
 blader-deeg 'puff pastry', ont-blader 'to defoliate'
 eier-dop 'egg shell'
 hoender-ei 'hen's egg'
 kalver-liefde 'calf love'
 kinder-wagen 'pram', kinder-lijk 'childish', kinder-achtig 'childish'
 kleder-dracht 'traditional dress'
 lammer-gier 'lammergeier, bearded vulture'
 runder-lap 'braising steak'

Moreover, the stem allomorph *kinder* also occurs before the suffix *-s* since the plural noun *kinders* 'children' is an existing (informal) variant of *kinder-en*. If *-eren* were interpreted as a plural suffix, we would have to assume a fourth plural suffix *-ers*.

As we will see below, words ending in an unstressed syllable normally take *-s* as their plural suffix. In this respect, the stem allomorphs in *-er* behave exceptionally, like a number of other nouns that end in an unstressed syllable. This does not pose a descriptive problem since these plural forms have to be stored lexically anyway because they unpredictably select this special allomorph.

The historical source of the *s*-suffix is West Germanic: this suffix was used in Germanic dialects along the North Sea coast, and may thus be qualified as Ingvaeonic. The English plural suffix is a reflex of this situation. The suffix *-en*, on the other hand, can be qualified as more continental Germanic (compare present-day German that has a variety of plural suffixes with schwa). In the course of time both suffixes became part of the morphological system of Standard Dutch, and thus a division of labour between the two suffixes developed.

The basic generalization as to the choice between these two competing suffixes can be formulated as follows (cf. van Haeringen 1947):

(4) *-s* after an unstressed syllable, *-en* after a stressed syllable

The following examples illustrate the role of the stress pattern in the suffix selection:

(5) *Unstressed final syllable*   *Stressed final syllable*
    kánon 'canon'   kánon-s   kanón 'gun'   kanónn-en
    kánton 'canton' kánton-s   japón 'dress'   japónn-en
    hóstie 'host'   hóstie-s   maníe 'mania'   maníe-en

The obvious consequence of this generalization is that monosyllabic words, which by definition always end in a stressed syllable, select the suffix *-en*; this is indeed—with some exceptions to be discussed below—the case:

(6)   boek 'book'   boek-en
      boon 'bean'   bon-en
      deur 'door'   deur-en
      paal 'pole'   pal-en

The generalization given in (4) is stated in terms of input conditions: what is specified is the form of the input to the suffixation processes. However, there are good reasons for expressing the selection principle in terms of an output condition on the form of the resulting plural noun, as follows:

(7)   A plural noun ends in a trochee

In Dutch, the syllables of a word are preferably parsed into disyllabic left-headed feet, i.e. trochees. That is, both unparsed syllables and monosyllabic feet are less optimal than disyllabic feet. Therefore, it will come as no surprise that if there is a choice in the morphology as to the prosodic form of plural nouns, the optimal prosodic form will be selected. For instance, if the word *kánon* 'canon' had the plural form *kánonnen*, the last syllable could not be parsed into a foot, and would remain unparsed; the plural form *kánons*, on the other hand, forms a trochee, and is therefore the optimal form. Similarly, the incorrect plural form *kanóns* 'guns' ends in a monosyllabic foot, whereas the correct plural form *kanónnen* ends in a trochee (Booij 1998*a*).

2.2. THE INFLECTION OF NOUNS

By formulating the selection principle as a prosodic output condition we do not only describe the relevant facts, but also explain them: if we used a formulation like that in (4), we would not express the driving force behind this pattern, and it would make no difference for the complexity of the grammar if Dutch were just the other way round, that is, if -s occurred after stressed syllables, and -en after unstressed ones.

A number of nouns ending in /ə/ have two plural forms, one ending in -s and one in -n. This applies, for example, to the following nouns:

(8) bode /bo:də/ 'messenger'   bodes, boden
     kade /ka:də/ 'quay'   kades, kaden
     lade /la:də/ 'drawer'   lades, laden
     methode /me:to:də/ 'method'   methodes, methoden

Both plural forms end in a trochee, because the stem-final schwa of the nominal stem disappears before the schwa-initial plural suffix -en due to the phonological rule of Prevocalic Schwa-Deletion (Booij 1995: 68). However, it appears that for such nouns, the preferred choice is -s (van Haeringen 1947), in particular in spoken language, although there are still a number of established plurals in -en. In this connection, it is a relevant fact that in Afrikaans, a daughter language of Dutch with strong creolization effects, nouns in -e systematically select -s: this systematization of plural suffix selection suggests that speakers of Dutch in South Africa grasped the basic principle behind this selection, and were not influenced by the lexical conventions of the mother language.

The selection between these two competing plural suffixes can be very well accounted for in the theoretical framework of Optimality Theory, henceforth OT (McCarthy and Prince 1993, 1994, Kager 1999). The basic idea of this theory is that the grammar of each language is to be seen as a set of universal violable output conditions that are ranked on a language-specific base. The selection of the proper form of a word, in this case the proper form of a plural noun, is performed by choosing that possible form ('candidate') that incurs the least severe violations of the conditions. The higher a condition is ranked, the more severe a violation of that condition is. The prosodic conditions involved are the following:

(9) ParseSyll   syllables must be parsed into feet
     FootMin   feet are minimally disyllabic
     FootMax   feet are maximally disyllabic

Let me illustrate this with the selection of the plural forms *kánons* and *kanónnen* (Tables 2.2 and 2.3).

TABLE 2.2. *The plural form* kánons

kánon + Plural	FootMax	ParseSyll	FootMin
☞(kaːnɔn-s)_F			
(kaːnɔn)_F(n-ən)		*!	
(kaːnɔnn-ən)_F	*!		

TABLE 2.3. *The plural form* kanónnen

kaːnón + Plural	FootMax	ParseSyll	FootMin
(kaː)(nɔn-s)_F		*!	*
(kaː)_F(nɔn-s)_F			**!
(kaː)(nɔn-nən)_F		*!	
☞(kaː)_F(nɔn-nən)_F			*

In these tables ('tableaux') the relevant conditions are given in their order of ranking; the highest ranked condition is the leftmost one. The subscript F indicates the parsing of syllables into feet (a double *n* indicates an /n/ that is ambisyllabic). If there is no subscript added to a constituent, we have to deal with an unparsed syllable. The pointed finger indicates the form that incurs the least severe violations, and that must therefore be chosen as the correct form. In the case of *kánon* the forms with *-en* lead to either a final syllable (*nen*) that is not parsed into a foot, or into a trisyllabic foot. Both cases lead to non-optimal prosodic structure. Therefore, the proper form is *kánons*. In the case of *kanón*, the forms with *-s* lead to word-final monosyllabic feet, which can be avoided by the selection of *-en*. Therefore, the form *kanónnen* should be selected.

Note that this computation presupposes that it is not possible to select a candidate in which the location of the main stress in the plural form is different from that of the stem: Dutch inflectional morphology is normally stress-neutral (exceptions are given in (11)).

As mentioned above, there is a number of nouns with two possible plural forms, both of which have the trochaic form, whereas in the OT-analysis given above it is always one form that is the most optimal. In the case of *kade*, for instance, the form *kades* will be chosen as the optimal one, because the form *kaden* can only be derived by deleting the stem-final schwa of the

2.2. THE INFLECTION OF NOUNS

stem *kade*. Deletion of a segment of an underlying form is a violation of the general Faithfulness Condition of OT that states that the underlying form should appear in the surface form. Therefore, it is this condition that is crucial in making a choice between the two candidates (see Table 2.4).

TABLE 2.4. *The plural forms* kades *and* kaden

kade + Plural	*PrevocSchwa	Faithfulness	FootMax	ParseSyll	FootMin
☞ (kaːdə-s)_F					
(kaːd-ən)_F		*!			

The forms in *-en* are lexicalized forms dating from a period of Dutch in which *-en* was apparently the regular form. We find this exceptional choice of *-en* also in archaic plural forms such as *appelen* 'apples' and *oliën* 'oils' that occur besides the now regular plural forms *appels* and *olies*.

Nouns that end in an unstressed syllable in /s/ select the plural suffix *-en* instead of the expected *-s*. Examples are the following nouns:

(10) cursus 'course'   cursuss-en
      dreumes 'toddler'   dreumes-en
      lobbes 'big dog'   lobbes-en

The explanation for this pattern is as follows. Adding a suffix *-s* to a stem in /s/ means that the distinction between singular and plural will get lost, because Dutch does not have geminate consonants, nor does it have epenthesis in these cases, unlike English plurals of words ending in sibilants. That is, underlying /s-s/ will be pronounced as [s], and hence there will be no overt phonetic realization of the plural suffix. Therefore, the suffix *-en* has to be chosen. In the OT-framework as presented above, this means that there is a condition Morpheme Identity, ranked above the three prosodic conditions involved in the selection of the plural suffix. This condition requires that each morpheme receives its own phonetic expression. If we formed a plural noun like *dreumes-s*, the plural morpheme would not receive an independent phonetic expression since Degemination is an automatic phonological process of Dutch, and hence ranked very high as a constraint.

The effect of the trochaic output constraint (7) can also be seen in a number of nouns that have two plural forms. The relevant nouns are borrowings that end in *-ol*, *-on*, or *-or*:

(11) eléctron 'id.'   eléctron-s, electrón-en
    fénol 'phenol'   fénol-s, fenól-en
    néutron 'id.'   néutron-s, neutrón-en
    proféssor 'id'   proféssor-s, professór-en
    radiátor 'id.'   radiátor-s, radiatór-en

As the examples show, the main stress of the noun shifts one syllable to the right if the suffix *-en* is chosen. Thus, the plural noun always ends in a trochee. The vowel quality also changes when the stress shifts rightward: the [ɔ] is lengthened to [oː]. That is, these nouns have an allomorph ending in stressed [oːl], [oːn], or [oːr] that appears with the plural suffix *-en*. This long stem allomorph is also used in derivation (cf. Section 5.3.2 on stem allomorphy).

Noun pluralization has a number of complications which we will now discuss. First, we find alternations between short and long vowels in the stem, as in (12), in a closed set of nouns and one suffix, which is a reflex of the early Germanic process of vowel-lengthening in open syllables. Some examples are:

(12) ɪ/e: schip 'ship'   schep-en
    ɛ/e: weg 'road'   weg-en
    ɔ/o: hol 'hole'   hol-en
    ɑ/a: bad 'bath'   bad-en
    ɑ/e: stad 'town'   sted-en
    ɛi/e: -heid '-ness' -hed-en

The last two of these alternations are unique for the word *stad* and the suffix *-heid*. The stem allomorphs that are used in the plural forms also play a role in derivation (cf. Section 5.3.2).

Furthermore, there are a number of monosyllabic nouns that end in a vowel, and therefore are predicted to take *-en* but yet take *-s*:

(13) p /pe:/ 'p'   p's
    pa 'dad'   pa's
    po 'chamber pot'   po's

This does not apply to all vowel-final nouns, though; for instance, the noun *ree* 'deer' has the plural form *reeën*, in accordance with constraint (7).

There are two other cases in which non-prosodic factors overrule the prosodic selection mechanism. First, there is a number of nouns borrowed from English and French that select the suffix *-s* where *-en* would be expected because they end in a stressed syllable (monosyllabic nouns carry word-final stress by definition):

(14) *English*
    flat [flɛt] 'apartment'   flat-s
    jeep [dʒip] 'id.'   jeep-s
    test [tɛst] 'id.'   test-s
    tram [trɛm] 'id.'   tram-s
   French
    bureau [byˈroː] 'desk'   bureau-s
    café [kaːˈfeː] 'id.'   café-s
    expért [ɛkˈspɛːr] 'id.'   expert-s

In other words, these are exceptional plural forms that reflect the pluralization patterns of the borrowing languages. There is a number of other words that keep the plural form of the source language. The languages involved are not only French and English, but also Latin, Greek, and Italian. In some cases both the original and the Dutch plural form are possible. If the Dutch plural form is possible, this indicates a higher degree of integration of such a word into everyday standard Dutch.

(15) *Latin*
    collega 'colleague'   collegae, collega's
    corpus 'id.'   corpora
    doctorandus 'MA'   doctorandi, doctorandussen
    matrix 'id.'   matrices, matrixen
    museum 'id.'   musea, museums
    rector 'id.'   rectores, rectors
    tentamen 'examination'   tentamina, tentamens
    universale 'universal'   universalia
   Greek
    dogma 'id.'   dogmata, dogma's
    prolegomenon 'id.'   prolegomena
   Italian
    porto 'postage'   porti
    saldo 'balance'   saldi, saldo's

It should be clear that these facts do not mean that Dutch has borrowed inflectional processes from other languages. What is at stake here is that the plural forms as such have been borrowed, and these plural forms are stored in the lexical memory of the speakers of Dutch. This lexical storage also explains why people coin double plurals such as *musea's*: the plural form *musea* has been stored in lexical memory, and to this form the regular plural suffix is added. Italian borrowings such as *spaghetti* 'id.' and *macaroni* 'id.' are no longer experienced as plural forms at all. Such words take singular finite verbal forms when used in subject-NPs, whereas in Italian these words still require plural verbal forms when they occur in subject position.

Facts of language acquistion and language variation provide independent evidence for the generalizations proposed so far. First, children create forms like *trammen* and *flatten* instead of the conventional but exceptional *flats* and *trams*. This is exactly what we expect given the prosodic selection mechanism proposed above. Secondly, speakers of Southern Dutch in Belgium use plural forms such as *testen* and *experten* instead of *tests* and *experts*, which suggests that in this variety of Dutch these words are no longer experienced as borrowings, and hence take the expected plural suffix.

It is not only borrowings that complicate the choice of the correct plural suffix: there is also a morphological factor that complicates the picture. Let us first observe that in most cases morphologically complex words behave like simplex words in their choice of plural suffix: if the word-final suffix bears primary or secondary stress, *-en* is selected, and if the final suffix bears no stress, *-s* is selected:

(16) Suffixes with primary stress
august-íjn 'Augustinian'   augustijn-en
calvin-íst 'id.'   calvinist-en
Chomsky-áan 'Chomskyan'   Chomskyan-en
leeuw-ín 'lioness'   leeuwinn-en
produc-ént 'producer'   producent-en
voogd-és 'fem. guardian'   voogdess-en
voogd-íj 'guardianship'   voogdij-en
Suffixes with secondary stress
hértog-dòm 'duchy'   hertogdomm-en
stóor-nìs 'disturbance'   stoorniss-en
twée-lìng 'twin'   tweeling-en

2.2. THE INFLECTION OF NOUNS

víez-erìk 'dirty person'   viezerikk-en
wáar-hèid 'truth'   waarhed-en
wáter-schàp 'watership'   waterschapp-en

Since all nominalizing non-native suffixes bear final stress, nouns ending in such suffixes (e.g. *-ist*) will always select *-en* as their plural suffix. This also applies to nouns with those native suffixes that always bear secondary stress because they form prosodic words of their own, such as the nominalizing suffixes *-dom*, *-heid*, *-ling*, *-nis*, and *-schap*. (A prosodic word is a phonological unit: an independent domain of stress assignment and syllabification, with at least one syllable with a full vowel, i.e. no schwa, and never beginning with a schwa, cf. Chapter 5. Words of the categories N, A, V, and Adv consist of at least one prosodic word.) In the case of *viezerik* the suffix bears a rhythmically governed secondary stress.

Similarly, nouns ending in a suffix with schwa will normally select the suffix *-s*, as expected on the basis of the stress pattern (a schwa cannot bear stress). This is the case for suffixes such as *-er*, *-erd*, *-sel* and *-ster*:

(17) bákk-er 'baker'   bakker-s
      léid-sel 'rein'   leidsel-s
      víez-erd 'dirty person' viezerd-s
      wérk-ster 'charwoman'   werkster-s

There is a number of nominalizing suffixes that end in schwa; hence we expect them to take *-s* as plural suffix, just like the simplex nouns that end in schwa. For a number of types of complex nouns this appears indeed to be the case. The exception is the deadjectival suffix /ə/:

(18) *Always* -s
      -age /aːʒə/   rapportage-s 'reports'
      -e /ə/ (female)   studente-s 'female students'
      -ette /ɛtə/   maisonette-s 'id.'
      -tje /tjə/   traantje-s 'tears', dim.
      Always -en
      -e /ə/ (deadjectival) goed-en 'good persons'

This implies that, whereas normally both plural suffixes are made available by the morphology and the choice between the two suffixes is made by the set of ranked phonological conditions discussed above, we have to make the special proviso that words ending in the deadjectival nominalizing suffix /ə/ only allow for the suffix -en (for some speakers of Dutch this also applies to nouns in -isme '-ism'). These facts also show that morphological processes sometimes require access to the internal morphological structure of a word. This is of direct relevance for Anderson's (1992) theory of A-morphous Morphology. This theory claims that, once a derived word has been formed, its internal morphological structure is no longer visible to further morphological operations. Pluralization of deadjectival nouns ending in schwa is therefore a counterexample to this claim.

In addition, there are certain kinds of complex nouns for which the choice of plural suffix varies, and sometimes both plural suffixes can be used (the italic form is the plural form that is in conformity with the trochaic output constraint):

(19) -aar /aːr/   díen-aar 'servant'   *dienaar-s*, dienar-en
                     lúister-àar 'listener'   luisteraar-s,
                                                *luisterar-en
     -aard /aːrd/   lúi-aard 'sluggard'   *luiaard-s*, *luiaard-en
                     Spánjaard 'Spaniard'   *Spanjaard-s,
                                                Spanjaard-en
     -enaar /ənaːr/ klúiz-enàar 'hermit'   kluizenaar-s,
                                                *kluizenar-en
                     Útrecht-enàar   Utrechtenaar-s,
                     'inhabitant of U'   *Utrechtenar-en*
     -eur /øːr/   dìrect-éur 'director'   directeur-s, *directeur-en*
                     mont-éur 'technician'   monteur-s, *monteur-en
     -ier /iːr/   hèrberg-íer 'inn-keeper'   herbergier-s,
                                                *herbergier-en
                     schol-íer 'pupil'   *scholier-s, *scholier-en*

From this pattern of data we can conclude that in particular nouns that refer to persons can take -s instead of the regular -en. The choice of -s over -en for personal nouns also manifests itself quite clearly in the following minimal pair:

(20) portíer 'doorkeeper'   portier-s (pl.)
      portíer 'door (of a car)'   portier-en (pl.)

These data imply that a substantial number of plural nouns have to be stored in the lexicon because they do not conform to the trochaic output constraint, i.e. they are irregular. In this respect, pluralization of nouns, a case of inherent inflection is similar to derivation.

The number of nouns plays a role in some syntactic configurations. Subject-NPs have to agree in number and person with finite verbal forms (cf. Section 2.4). Second, within NPs determiners (articles and demonstratives) and adjectives agree in number and gender with the head noun. Table 2.5 summarizes the pattern of determiner selection (adjectival agreement is discussed in Section 2.3.2). As is clear from this table, it is only in the singular forms for the definite article and the demonstratives that gender makes a difference.

Although I qualified the pluralization of nouns as a case of inherent inflection, there are a few cases in which it appears to be required by a specific syntactic context. The most important one is that of NPs with a quantifying expression as modifier. If the cardinality of the quantifying expression is higher than 1, the plural form of the noun has to be used:

(21) twee boeken 'two books'
      een aantal boeken 'a number of books'
      een kudde schapen 'a herd of sheep'
      drie soorten boeken 'three kinds of book(s)'

However, some quantifiers can be used with singular mass nouns, as in *een kudde kleinvee* 'a herd of small stock'.

This agreement is not a matter of semantics: there are many languages in which the head noun is not pluralized after such quantifying expressions

TABLE 2.5. *Determiner selection*

			Common	Neuter
indef.		sg.	een	een
		pl.	Ø	Ø
def		sg.	de	het
		pl.	de	de
demonstr.	'this'	sg.	deze	dit
		pl.	deze	deze
	'that'	sg.	die	dat
		pl.	die	die

(for instance, Hungarian and Turkish). The plural suffix of the noun does not express independent information in these cases: *twee boeken* does not mean two sets of more than one book. Hence, there is an agreement condition involved here that requires that both the quantifier and the head noun have a cardinality higher than 1. The cardinality of the whole NP will then be computed by means of the unification of the specifications for this property of the constituents. The only exceptions to this agreement condition are some nouns that function as measure phrases, and not as referring entities (Klooster 1972):

(22) drie gulden 'three guilders'
      vijf liter 'five liters'
      acht kilometer 'eight kilometres'

This pattern also has exceptions, as shown by the following data: *twee jaar/ maand/*week/*dag/uur* 'two years/months/weeks/days/hours'.

As the reader will notice, Dutch and English differ here, which underscores the point that this kind of agreement is not just a matter of semantics. It also shows that the same morphological process can function as both inherent and contextual inflection. In this respect nominal pluralization is similar to nominal cases which can also be used in both ways (Booij 1994).

2.2.2. *Possessor marking*

Dutch nouns do not exhibit morphological case marking; this system disappeared in the transition from Middle Dutch to present-day Dutch. There are, however, relics of the case system; one of them is that -*s* (historically the genitive singular case marker) can be used for a number of nouns in the specifier position of a noun phrase:

(23) Jan-s hoed 'John's hat'
      Amsterdam-s rijke verleden 'Amsterdam's rich history'
      vader-s fiets 'father's bicycle'
      jouw moeder-s kamer 'your mother's room'
      dominee-s studeerkamer 'reverend's study'
      ieder-s huis 'everybody's house'
      iemand-s vriend 'someone's friend'
      niemand-s schuld 'nobody's fault'

These nouns with -s function as determiners. The only nouns that can be used with this kind of possessor marker are proper names and nouns that can be used as forms of address, like *vader* and *dominee*, that is, words functioning as proper names with an inherent referential value, and some pronouns. Since a noun like *directeur* cannot be used as a form of address, unlike a noun such as *dominee*, the phrase *directeurs kamer* 'director's room' is ill-formed. These *s*-marked nouns cannot be preceded by an article if they are marked as a possessor by means of -*s*. A phrase like **de dominees fiets* 'the minister's bicycle' is therefore ill-formed. The only prenominal modifiers that are allowed are possessive pronouns. Moreover, the form with -*s* can only be used in prenominal position: a sentence like *Deze hoed is Jans* 'This hat is John's' is ungrammatical.

Unlike the phrasal affix -*s* in English, the Dutch -*s* has a very restricted distribution, as shown above. This kind of grammatical pattern is therefore best qualified as a construction (in the sense of Goldberg 1995): the pattern [(possessive pronoun) + proper name + s]$_{Det}$ functions as a determiner. It is a grammaticalized pattern that is productive to the extent that the slot for proper names is an open one, into which all proper names can be inserted.

The possessive pronoun *zijn* [zɛin] 'his' and its feminine counterpart *haar* 'her' can also be used as a possessor marker for specifier-NPs; in spoken language this will usually be the weak form of this pronoun.

(24) Jan z'n hoed 'John's hat'
      De directeur z'n kamer 'the director's room'
      De professor haar kamer 'the professor's room'

This construction is partially complementary to the previous one: here, a determiner can appear in the specifier-NP, and its head need not be a proper name. On the other hand, the head noun of the specifier is subject to another restriction: it has to be animate: **Amsterdam zijn grachten* 'Amsterdam's canals'.

The weak form of the pronoun *zijn* is *z'n* [zən]/[sən], or even [zə]/[sə] in colloquial Dutch. This pronoun functions as a resumptive possessive pronoun, but in its weak form, it might also be considered a phrasal affix, comparable to the possessor morpheme -*s* in English that also functions as a phrasal affix (as in *the king of England's hat*). This interpretation of the weak form of the possessive pronoun is furthered by the syntax since we do not expect a full NP and a possessive pronoun to co-occur in the pre-head position of an NP. There is also a similar weak form of the feminine singular possessive pronoun *haar* 'her', the form *d'r* [dər] as in *Haar moeder d'r boek* 'Her mother's book'. In colloquial Dutch the form [sə] tends to be overgeneralized and to be even used with female nouns: *Haar moeder se boek*, in particular by children (Weerman and de Wit 1999).² The possessor marker is not the only relic of the case system; there are many frozen, idiomatic expressions that still have case marking. Some examples are:

(25) met dien verstande 'with the understanding'
ten eeuwigen dage 'to all eternity'
de Vader des Vaderlands 'the father of one's country, pater patriae'

However, these are all lexicalized expressions without implications for the synchronic analysis of the morphological system of Dutch.

2.2.3. Gender

Dutch nouns belong to one of two gender classes, common gender or neuter gender. However, gender is not a morphological category since there is no direct morphological expression of gender. Gender manifests itself indirectly, in the choice of determiners (that is why in most grammars of Dutch the nouns are classified into *de*-nouns (common nouns) and *het*-nouns (neuter nouns), and in the form of prenominal adjectives and quantifiers (cf. Section 2.3). Moreover, it determines the selection of the singular relative subject/object pronoun forms: *die* (common gender) versus *dat* (neuter gender); there is no gender distinction for the plural form of relative pronouns, which is always *die*. In short, we base our distinction of two gender classes for Dutch on formal patterns of agreement.

Gender does not play a role in the selection of personal and possessive pronouns; in that case the selection is based on semantic criteria, and it is a case of semantic agreement. This is illustrated by the following sentences, in which the NPs *het meisje* and *het jongetje* have neuter gender, and thus select the relative pronoun *dat*, whereas semantically they are feminine and masculine respectively, and hence select the third person singular feminine and masculine possessive pronoun *haar* 'her' and *zijn* 'his':

---

² See Norde (1997) for a survey of the relevant historical developments in the Germanic languages.

(26) Het meisje, *dat* was gevallen, pakte *haar* auto op 'The girl, who had fallen, picked up her car'
Het jongetje, *dat zijn* moeder zag, was blij 'The boy who saw his mother, was glad'

(It is only for the third person singular forms of pronouns that such a semantic distinction between feminine and masculine is available.) This distinction between the possessive pronouns *haar* and *zijn*, and the subject personal pronouns *hij* 'he' and *zij* 'she' and the corresponding object pronouns *hem* 'him' and *haar* 'her' plays a clear role only for nouns that refer to human beings. For other nouns, the masculine pronouns function as default pronouns. For instance, a dog will usually be referred to with *hij* even though it is of the female sex. There is a tendency, however, to use the possessive pronoun *haar* in relation to nouns that designate institutions. An example is the noun *bestuur* 'board' which has neuter gender; nevertheless, many speakers of Dutch use the possessive pronoun *haar* in referring to this noun. This shows that indeed semantic agreement is quite distinct from gender agreement.

These sentences also demonstrate another property of gender in Dutch, because the heads of the subject-NPs are diminutives: the gender of a complex noun is usually determined by its final suffix. For instance, the diminutive suffix always creates a neuter noun even if the diminutive noun refers to a human being (cf. Chapter 3). This implies that in most cases the gender of complex nouns is predictable on the basis of its final suffix.

This raises the question to what extent the gender of nouns is predictable on the basis of other than morphological properties, i.e. semantic or phonological properties. Cross-linguistically, such properties appear to play a role (Corbett 1991). Semantic properties clearly play a role in determining the gender of simplex nouns in the case of nouns that refer to human beings: almost all of them belong to the common gender (exceptions are *het kind* 'the child', *het wijf* 'the bitch', *het mens* 'the bitch'). However, as we saw above, morphological properties will then overrule this semantic classification in the case of morphologically complex nouns. As far as phonological properties are concerned, it is sometimes possible to predict gender class on the basis of the phonological form of the noun. For instance, all nouns ending in *-ing* are of common gender, whether they are simplex or complex nouns. This applies, for instance, to the following words:

(27)　háring 'herring', kóning 'king', páling 'eel', ring 'id.', sering 'lilac'

(the only exception is the noun *ding* 'thing' which is neuter).[3]

Such observations on the relation between semantic or phonological properties and the gender of a noun (cf. also Steinmetz and Rice 1989) can only be made for a subset of nouns. The fact that there are many nouns that are used as both *de*-noun and *het*-noun also shows that there can be at most subregularities, and that in most cases the gender of simplex nouns has to be stored. Examples of nouns that are used in both genders are:

(28)　kaft 'cover', keer 'time', liniaal 'ruler', matras 'mattress', schort 'apron'

As far as simplex nouns are concerned, it appears that about 80 per cent of them are *de*-nouns (van Berkum 1996) which suggests that common gender is the default gender.

Even if the linguist is able to find certain subregularities or tendencies in gender assignment based on semantic or phonological properties, the question remains if native speakers really grasp these generalizations. An obvious way of finding out about this is to study gender assignment for new simplex nouns (Corbett 1991). New simplex nouns enter a language through borrowing, and through the formation of acronyms. As to borrowed words, it is unclear how they acquire their gender; for instance, *computer* is a *de*-word, but *shirt* is a *het*-word. Probably, the assignment is based on the gender of similar words in Dutch (derived nouns in *-er* are all *de*-words, the Dutch semantic equivalent of *shirt* is the *het*-word *hemd*). The gender of the name of a political movement such as *de Hamas* derives from the noun that expresses the concept 'movement', the *de*-word *beweging* (Haeseryn *et al.* 1997: 150). Acronyms take over the gender of the head noun of the phrase for which they stand. Thus, the acronym *VU* (for *Vrije Universiteit* 'Free University') will select *de* because *universiteit* is of common gender. The phrase *het VU*, on the other hand, is used to refer to the academic hospital of the Free University because the Dutch word for hospital, *ziekenhuis*, is a neuter noun. Similar patterns have been observed by Treffers-Daller

---

[3] This brought some linguists (cf. Trommelen 1984) to assume a suffix *-ing* in the polysyllabic nouns in *-ing* with penultimate stress, even though *-ing* is a deverbal suffix, because this nominalizing suffix always creates *de*-nouns, and always selects the diminutive allomorph *-etje*. However, this cannot be accepted as an adequate analysis since there is no independent evidence for the suffix status of the ending *-ing* in these nouns. Instead, we conclude that the phonological form of nouns may play a role in gender assignment.

(1994) for borrowings from French into Dutch by bilingual speakers of Dutch in Brussels.

It is clear then that gender is a burden for the lexical memory of the speaker of Dutch because it has to be memorized for many nouns, and certainly for most simplex nouns. It is therefore remarkable that the system is quite stable, and that there are no indications of a gradual loss of the gender distinctions in Dutch (in Afrikaans, however, the distinction has been lost). In a number of psycholinguistic experiments, van Berkum (1996) tried to find evidence for facilitating effects of gender in language processing, which might explain the stability of the gender distinction. However, such positive effects were not found.

2.3. ADJECTIVAL INFLECTION

Dutch adjectives exhibit two kinds of inflection. First, they have two degree forms, the comparative and the superlative, instantiations of inherent inflection. Secondly, adjectives in prenominal position are inflected. This is a case of contextual inflection, determined by the syntactic configuration in which the adjective occurs. Another type of contextual inflection is the partitive genitive construction. These kinds of inflection are dealt with in the following subsections.

2.3.1. *Degree forms*

Dutch adjectives may have two degree forms, the comparative and the superlative. The comparative suffix is *-er* [ər] or *-der* [dər], the superlative form is *-st*.

(29)
	Comparative	*Superlative*
absúrd 'id.'	absurd-er	absurd-st
delicáat 'delicate'	delicat-er	delicaat-st
lélijk 'ugly'	lelijk-er	lelijk-st
rijk 'rich'	rijk-er	rijk-st
bítter 'id.'	bitter-der	bitter-st
raar 'strange'	raar-der	raar-st
sóber 'id.'	sober-der	sober-st

The allomorph *-der* of the comparative suffix is used instead of *-er* in order to avoid the sequence /rər/ which is generally avoided in Dutch (Booij 1998a). In other words, there is, as in the case of the competition between the plural suffixes, a choice between two allomorphs, the selection of which is governed by the negative output condition 'avoid the sequence r-schwa-r'.[4] There are a number of homonymous suffixes *-er* in Dutch; besides the comparative suffix we find the deverbal agentive and instrumental suffix *-er*, and the denominal suffix *-er* that forms personal nouns (cf. Chapter 3). In all these cases the allomorph *-der* is used after stems ending in /r/. However, unlike the comparative suffix, these other two suffixes also have an allomorph *-aar*, used after stems ending in schwa plus a coronal sonorant consonant, as in:

(30) Diemen 'id.'   Diemen-aar 'inhabitant of D.'
      luister 'to listen' luister-aar 'listener'
      twijfel 'to doubt' twijfel-aar 'doubter'

Unlike verbs ending in *-er*, we cannot coin a comparative form like **bitter-aar* 'more bitter', and have to use *bitter-der* instead. The fact that the different suffixes *-er* have different sets of allomorphs supports the view that we have to deal here with homonymous suffixes, and not with just one suffix *-er*. This position stands in contrast with that of Beard (1995) who claims that there is no relation between form and meaning in morphology, and that consequently there is only one suffix *-er*, which expresses a wide array of different meanings. If this view were correct, we would expect the same allomorphs to be available for all uses of the suffix *-er*.

As may be expected for cases of inherent inflection, we find many gaps in the degree paradigms of adjectives, i.e. there are many adjectives for which degree forms are not available, and cannot be made, mainly on semantic grounds: it is only possible to make such forms for adjectives that express a gradable property. Hence, relational adjectives, and adjectives that express an absolute property do not feed this kind of inflection. As soon as we make degree forms for an adjective, we are forced to give it a gradable interpretation, i.e. the property referred to has to have a certain scale or range:

---

[4] However, some native speakers of Dutch do accept forms like *barrer* (< *bar* 'severe') and *starrer* (< *star* 'rigid') with a short stem vowel.

(31) *Relational adjectives*
  parlementair 'parliamentary'   *parlementair-der – *parlementair-st
  taalkundig 'linguistic'   *taalkundig-er – *taalkundig-st
  Adjectives expressing non-gradable properties
  dagelijks 'daily'   *dagelijks-er – *dagelijk-st
  dood 'dead'   *dod-er – *dood-st
  supermooi 'very beautiful'   *supermooi-er – *supermooi-st

This semantic requirement also explains why complex adjectives like *zeegroen* 'sea-green' that refer to one particular point on the range of colours expressed by the adjectival head, resist comparative formation: a comparative form like *zeegroener* is semantically ill-formed.

However, such degree forms can be used if the language user wants to impose a gradable interpretation on them. The adjective *parlementair*, for instance, can also have the meaning 'civilized, polite', and it is with this meaning that degree forms are possible. A degree form such as *doder* 'deader' can be used in the context of a play in which the actors have to die on the stage, and compete in how they behave as dead. In a sentence like

(32) Mijn tante zag er het Amerikaanst uit van allemaal 'My aunt looked the most American of all'

the superlative form requires an interpretation of the adjectival stem *Amerikaans* that can be paraphrased as 'prototypically American'. This is what has been called type coercion (Pustejovsky 1993, 1995: 111): the function of the superlative suffix requires a particular type of argument, a gradable property, and hence the argument (in this case the adjectival stem) is converted into the required type.

As may be expected for inherent inflection, degree forms of adjectives can feed word formation. In particular, they can be substantivized by means of the nominalizing suffixes *-e* and they can incidentally be used in complex verbs prefixed with *ver-*:

(33) (a) jonger-e 'youngster', ouder-e 'aged person', de mooi-st-e 'the most beautiful (person)', het mooi-st-e 'the most beautiful (thing)'
      (b) ver-erg-er 'to worsen', ver-oud-er 'to become older'

Moreover, the prefix *aller-* 'very' only takes superlative forms as its input:

(34) een *allerlief/allerliefst meisje 'a very sweet girl'

Clearly, the form *allerliefst* cannot be derived from a base **allerlief* since this adjectival base is ill-formed; therefore, *aller-* must have been prefixed to the superlative form *liefst*. Note, however, that the superlative form thus prefixed loses its superlative meaning since we can use it with an indefinite determiner: *een allerliefst meisje/*een liefst meisje* (Hoeksema 1998: 48).

A number of Dutch superlative forms have an exceptional kind of base word, for instance:

(35) boven-st 'uppermost' < boven 'above'
      buiten-st 'outermost' < buiten 'outside, out of'
      onder-st 'lowest' < onder 'under, beneath'

The base words *boven*, *buiten*, and *onder* cannot be used as adjectives, only as prepositions and adverbs.

A few adjectives exhibit stem allomorphy: the stems that are used in the degree forms are used in these forms only. The stem allomorphs can be qualified as suppletive stems since there is no regular relation between the different allomorphs:

(36) goed 'good'   bet-er   be-st
      veel 'much/many'   mee-r   mee-st
      weinig 'few'   min-der   min-st

In the monosyllabic form *meer* there is not even a suffix *-er* present, and therefore it is not a case of stem suppletion, but of suppletion at the level of the word.

The comparative and superlative form may also be expressed in a periphrastic form, by making use of the adverbs *meer* 'more' and *(het) meest* 'most' respectively (*het* is omitted after a determiner). These forms are used when the adjective cannot be used attributively, as is the case for the adjective *bereid* 'prepared' that does not have the forms **bereider* and **bereidst*:

(37) Zij was meer bereid/het meest bereid het probleem aan te pakken
      'She was more willing/most willing to tackle the problem'

This also applies to some present and passive participles that are used as adjectives, but this is not systematically the case:

(38) De meest gelezen/*gelezenste krant van Nederland 'the most widely
      read newspaper of the Netherlands'

De meest berekenende/*berekenendste schurk 'the most scheming crook'

The choice of the periphrastic form of the superlative may also be governed by the phonological form of the adjectival stem: adjectives ending in -e, -s, -sk, -st, or -isch thus avoid phonetically complex and opaque forms:

(39) bruusk 'sudden'   *bruusk-st [brγskst]/meest bruusk
      log-isch 'logical' *logisch-st [lo:ɣist]/meest logisch
      solide 'firm'   *solide-st [so:lidəst]/meest solide
      vast 'solid'   *vast-st [vɑstst]/meest vast

Again, these data show that this kind of inflection does not obey the principle that there is a form for each cell of the paradigm. Empty cells are, as we saw, quite characteristic for inherent inflection.

2.3.2. *The inflection of prenominal adjectives*

As in many Germanic languages, prenominal modifiers (adjectives and quantifiers) in Dutch exhibit agreement with the head of the NP. These modifiers agree with the head noun with respect to number and gender. Moreover, the form of the prenominal modifier also depends on the (in)definiteness of the NP.

As we saw above, Dutch has two genders for nouns, common gender and neuter gender. Gender is not a morphological category, since there is no direct morphological expression of gender. The gender class of a noun manifests itself only indirectly, for instance in the choice of (definite) determiners, and the form of prenominal modifiers.

The basic generalization concerning the inflection of prenominal adjectives is that they have the form 'stem + schwa' unless the NP bears the features [indefinite, singular, neuter]: in that case, the adjectival ending is Ø.

(40) *Neuter nouns*

SG. INDEF.	SG. DEF.	PL.
een mooi boek 'a nice book'	het mooie boek	(de) mooie boeken
mooi hout 'nice wood'	het mooie hout	

Non-neuter nouns

SG. INDEF.	SG. DEF.	PL.
een mooie pen 'a nice pen'	de mooie pen	(de) mooie pennen
mooie wijn 'nice wine'	de mooie wijn	

Both the forms of the determiners and the forms of the adjectives instantiate the cross-linguistic generalization that formal distinctions for certain categories expressed on singular nouns tend to be neutralized in plural forms. The notion 'indefinite' used here should be interpreted as 'undetermined' since we also find the schwa-less adjectives before neuter nouns that are proper names, as in *voormalig president Gorbatsjov* 'former president Gorbatchov' (Blom 1994: 82).

The definiteness of an NP depends on the presence and nature of the determiner; in addition, possessor phrases, quantifiers, and question words also determine the definiteness of an NP, and thus affect the form of the following adjective:

(41) *Indefinite* welk mooi huis? 'which nice house?'
            geen mooi huis 'no nice house'
            ieder mooi huis 'each nice house'
            zo'n groot huis 'such a big house'
     Definite dit/dat mooie huis 'this/that nice house'
            jouw vaders mooie huis 'your father's nice house'
            Piets mooie huis 'Peter's nice house'

These facts suggest that NPs should receive a feature (in)definite on their top node, based on the semantic properties of the preadjectival modifier; this feature can then percolate downward to the prenominal adjective position. Similarly, the gender feature of the head noun can be assumed to percolate upward to the top node of the NP, and then downward to both the determiner node and the adjectival node. The form of the adjective is then 'stem + ə' unless it possesses the features [indefinite, neuter, singular], in which case the form is 'stem + Ø'. We only have to assign these specific features to adjectives without inflectional schwa; adjectives with an inflectional schwa will remain unspecified for (in)definiteness, gender, and number, and will only be assigned the feature [attributive].

It is not only adjectives that are inflected in prenominal position: this also applies to a number of grammatical words that function as modifiers and are inflected as prenominal adjectives: *ons/onze* 'our', *welk/welke* 'which', *ieder/iedere* 'every', *elk/elke* 'each', *sommige* 'some'. The quantifiers *veel* 'much' and *weinig* 'few' exhibit a slightly different pattern: they usually have the 'stem + Ø' form (*veel, weinig*) in the plural indefinite. The form *vele* 'many' can be used with plural nouns in order to stress the individuality of the members of the set, as in *vele boeken* in (42). In the singular the only possible forms are *veel* and *weinig* whatever the gender. On the other hand, after definite determiners they have the regular schwa-final form:

(42)   veel/vele boeken 'many books'   de vele boeken 'the many books'
        weinig mannen 'few men'   de weinige mannen 'the few men'

The quantifier *alle* 'all' does not have the regular schwa-less form *al* before singular common nouns like *hout* 'wood' (*alle hout*/*al hout); the form *al* is also used before a definite singular form in pre-determiner position: *al het geld* 'all the money', *al de wijn* 'all the wine'.

In a number of cases, the prenominal form of the adjective does not end in a schwa-suffix, although it bears the relevant features. In some cases, there is a phonological explanation for this fact: if the adjectival stem ends in schwa, this schwa will be deleted before the inflectional schwa by the phonological rule of Prevocalic Schwa-Deletion (Booij 1995: 68), and thus it looks on the surface as if no inflectional schwa has been added. This applies to schwa-final adjectives such as *oranje* 'orange' and *stupide* 'stupid'.

A more interesting pattern is that the inflectional schwa does not appear after a stem ending in /ən/. This also applies to past participles and infinitives that are used as adjectives (most of these words end in /ən/):

(43)   het opən boek 'the open book'
        het hout-ən paard 'the wooden horse'
        de geslot-ən deur 'the closed door'
        de te nem-ən maatregelen 'the measures to be taken'

As these examples show, it does not make a difference whether *-en* is a suffix, or part of a morpheme, as in *open*. The absence of a final schwa cannot be explained here by phonology: there is no phonological rule of Dutch that deletes a schwa after the sequence /ən/. As pointed out in Booij (1998a), the schwa only 'disappears' in this case of contextual inflection, where the schwa has no independent informational value. On the other hand, the schwa that is used to nominalize adjectives, as in *het opene* 'the open', always shows up. Thus, these data confirm the conclusion by Kiparsky (1971) [1982: 67] that it is contextual inflection that gets lost first.[5]

No doubt the driving force behind this absence of inflectional schwa is

---

[5] More detailed information about the history of this pattern, and its fate in Afrikaans and American Dutch can be found in Raidt (1968), Lass (1990), van Marle (1995), and Smits (1994, 1996). See Booij (in press) for a diachronic study of this schwa-loss phenomenon.

the same as we have also seen active in the selection of the plural suffixes. The addition of a schwa to a stem that itself ends in a schwa-syllable creates a rhythmic lapse: two unstressed syllables after a stressed one. In other words, the last syllable of a form like *opene* cannot be parsed as part of a trochee, and is therefore less optimal. We can therefore account for this pattern in terms of selection of one of two competing allomorphs by means of an output constraint: the inflectional schwa of prenominal adjectives has a competing allomorph Ø that is selected as the most optimal after a stem that already ends in a schwa-headed syllable. I illustrate this (Table 2.6) with the adjective *open* as in *de open deur* 'the open door'. The relevant constraints have already been introduced in Section 2.2.1.

TABLE 2.6. *The inflection of* open

	FootMax	ParseSyll	FootMin
☞(oːpən-Ø)$_F$			
(oːpən-ə)$_F$	*!		
(oːpə)$_F$ nə		*!	

Both candidates with an inflectional schwa are less optimal; on the second line, we get a foot consisting of three syllables, and on the last line we get a candidate with the final syllable unparsed. The first candidate does not violate any of the three conditions. As predicted, the zero-allomorph is also chosen after the few Dutch adjectives that end in an unstressed vowel such as *prima* 'fine' and *séxy* 'id.'.

It is not the case that all inflected adjectives with a sequence of two schwa-syllables are avoided. Such sequences do appear in adjectives with a stem ending in /ər/ and /əm/, for instance [lɛkərə] in *een lekkere cake* 'a nice cake', and *goocheme* [ɣoːxəmə] 'smart' in *een goocheme jongen* 'a smart boy'. This implies that we still have to subcategorize the zero-allomorph for specific phonological contexts, in particular for appearing after a stem in /ən/, and after vowels.[6]

A number of adjectives in *-er* are traditionally called uninflectable because

---

[6] The restriction of the zero-allomorph to words in *-en* might be related to the effect of apocope of /n/; this results in forms such as [oːpə] for *open*, in which the final schwa could be interpreted as an inflectional schwa (Jack Hoeksema, personal communication). The conclusion that we still need subcategorization for the selection of allomorphs can also be found in Lapointe (2000).

they do not have the schwa-ending. This applies to locative adjectives in *-er* such as *Groninger* 'from Groningen', as in the noun phrase *Groninger koek* 'cake from Groningen'; it also applies to some other adjectives in *-er* such as *rechter* 'right', and *linker* 'left', all of them adjectives that can be used in prenominal position only. This is probably the right interpretation because the alternative of assuming a zero-allomorph for these cases raises the problem that normal adjectives in *-er* such as *lekker* do not allow for this zero-allomorph. Moreover, there are also some material adjectives that can only be used prenominally, and also do not exhibit inflection, even though they do not end in *-en*: adjectives such as *plastic* 'id.' and *aluminium* 'id.'.

A second complication in the inflection of prenominal adjectives is that we also find schwa-less adjectives in positions where the form with schwa is expected (Schultink 1962: 66, Blom 1994, cf. Odijk 1992 for a formal analysis). In those cases, semantic factors are involved. The absence of the schwa here is optional although there might be cases where convention prefers the schwa-less variant. There are three cases to be distinguished. First, the schwa is always absent in adjective–noun combinations that mention a specific profession or function, both in the singular and the plural:

(44) een/de controlerend geneesheer   controlerend geneesheren
                                         'medical officer'
      een/de toegepast taalkundige   toegepast taalkundigen
                                         'applied linguist'

In these cases, the adjective–noun combinations function as a name; formally such combinations can be interpreted as AN-compounds, which then implies that the adjective is not inflected. The only phrasal aspect of such compounds is that their stress pattern (main stress on the noun) is that of nominal phrases, and not that of AN-compounds, which have main stress on the left constituent. This category can be extended, in particular if names for professions have to be coined. In other words, it is not simply a matter of lexicalization of specific word combinations, but rather the grammaticalization of a particular pattern of word combination.

There are also adjectives where the expected inflectional schwa is only absent in the singular forms. The first category of nouns that allow this are personal nouns; if the noun is female, nouns with an overt morphological marking for being feminine are preferred (hence the last example is rejected as ungrammatical by most speakers of Dutch):

(45) een wijs man 'a wise man'
een Frans filosoof 'a French philosopher'
een slecht docent 'a bad teacher' = someone who teaches badly
een goed vader 'a good father' = someone who performs his duties as a father well
een goed docent-e 'a good female teacher' = a woman who teaches well
een begenadigd violist-e 'a gifted violinist' (fem.)
?een goed moeder 'a good mother'

As argued in Blom (1994), the semantic difference between the use of a schwa-less adjective and its counterpart with a schwa is that in the first case, the property mentioned by the adjective is not a property of the individual referred to by the head noun, but modifies the stereotype associated with that noun. For instance, *een goed vader* refers to someone who performs his role as a father well, it does not refer to a person, who is a father and is also good.

Secondly, the inflectional schwa is also absent in AN-combinations with *het*-nouns as heads that function as names such as

(46) het oudheidkundig museum 'the archaeological museum' (*compare*: *de oudheidkundig afdeling 'the archaeological department')
het bijvoeglijk naamwoord 'the adjective' (*compare*: *de bijvoeglijk bijzin 'the attributive clause')

Here, it is impossible to omit the inflectional schwa in the plural: *de oudheidkundig museums*. Many of these AN-combinations are lexicalized names, but this set of names can be extended. This use of the schwa-less adjective can again be understood from the perspective that the adjective gives a further specification of the function mentioned by the head noun.

Most adjectives can also be used as adverbs. If the adverb modifies a prenominal adjective, its adverbial nature appears from the absence of an inflectional schwa, since adverbs are not inflected. Thus we get minimal pairs such as

(47) een echte flinke jongen 'a real tough boy'
een echt flinke jongen 'a really tough boy'

This formal distinction between adverb and adjective might, however, be obliterated through reinterpretation: adverbs that also function as adjectives are formally reinterpreted as adjectives as shown by the presence of the inflectional schwa, although the semantic interpretation of these words is still adverbial. For instance, the following words function both as adjectives and adverbs, but with different meanings:

(48)   *Adjectival meaning*   *Adverbial meaning*
    echt   real   very
    erg   dreadful   very
    geweldig great   very
    heel   whole   very

Due to this reinterpretation, we find phrases like the following in which the adverb that modifies the adjective is inflected:

(49)   een echt/echte flinke jongen 'a very tough boy'
       erg/erge warme soep 'very hot soup'
       heel/hele aardige mensen 'very nice people'
       geweldig/geweldige hoge bomen 'very tall trees'

As expected, adverbs that do not have an adjectival counterpart and therefore cannot be reanalysed as adjectives never exhibit the inflectional schwa. This applies to the adverbs *helemaal*, *vaak*, and *zeer*:

(50)   helemaal/*helemale doorgedraaide lui 'absolutely mad people'
       vaak/*vake afwezige collega's 'often absent colleagues'
       zeer/*zere aardige mensen 'very nice people'

This formal reinterpretation of adverbs as adjectives can also be seen in the phrase

(51)   een zo groot mogelijke opkomst 'an attendance as large as possible'

In this phrase, the adjective *groot* is embedded in the discontinuous adverbial phrase *zo ... mogelijk*. Dutch adjectival phrases are subject to the Head-Final Filter (Hoekstra 1984): in prenominal position, the head of an AP with complements should occur at the right periphery. Therefore, Dutch speakers are inclined to interpret the adverb *mogelijk* in (51) as an adjective, hence the inflectional schwa. This is again possible because there is an adjectival counterpart *mogelijk* 'possible'. This is not possible for an adverb like *genoeg* 'enough' that cannot be used as a prenominal adjective, and this explains why definite phrases like the following are avoided, unlike the indefinite counterpart:

(52) *het groot genoege glas/een groot genoeg glas 'a big enough glass'

These facts suggest that reanalysis is not only a diachronic mechanism, but also a synchronic one: these words are simultaneously treated as adverbs from the semantic point of view, and as far as syntactic position is concerned, but morphologically they behave like adjectives.[7]

2.3.3. *The suffix -e as nominalizing suffix*

Adjectives ending in schwa also occur without a following noun as in

(53) een zwarte fiets en een rode 'a black bicycle and a red one'
      een oud boek en een nieuw 'an old book and a new one'

These are cases where apparently the head noun can be gapped under identity with a noun in a parallel construction: *een rode* is interpreted as *een rode fiets*, and *een nieuw* as *een nieuw boek*. In addition, it is also possible to omit the head noun by making use of deictic identification of the head noun, as in

(54) Dit zijn hele mooie 'These are very beautiful ones'

In the case of gapping under deictic identification some Dutch speakers appear to be reluctant to omit the (neuter) noun after an adjective without overt inflectional ending, as in *Geef mij maar een zwart* 'Give me a black (horse)'; however, such a sentence is possible if context and/or situation permit identification of the intended referent.

It is also possible to use adjectives in *-e* without a following head noun, but without a contextual or deictic antecedent being available, as in

(55) een/de blinde 'a/the blind person', sg.
      het goede 'the good (thing)'

If used with the common determiner *de*, such adjectives always refer specifically to a human person; if used with *het*, the neuter singular article, the noun always refers to an abstract noun. Hence, the cases in (55) cannot be

---

[7] The idea that reanalysis is a synchronic phenomenon can also be found in van Marle (1990*a*).

2.3. ADJECTIVAL INFLECTION

interpreted as cases of gapping of a head noun under identity. This suggests that we have to deal here with two derivational affixes -*e* that derive nouns from adjectives. This conclusion is supported by the fact that the common deadjectival words in -*e* can form inputs for pluralization, and thus lead to plural NPs such as *de blinden* 'the blind (persons)'. It is also supported by the fact that this schwa appears after stems in -*en*, as in *de besprokene* 'the discussed (person)' and *het besprokene* 'the discussed matter', whereas adjectives select a zero-allomorph after -*en*.

These affixes thus serve to create so-called transcategorial constructions (cf. Lefebvre and Muysken 1988), that is, constructions that exhibit properties of more than one syntactic category. Such affixes keep the syntactic valency of the base although they have the effect of transposing the bases to another syntactic category. The following examples (cf. Kester 1996: 232–3) illustrate this for the suffix under discussion here:

(56) de zeer rijke 'the very rich person'
      de twee miljoen gulden rijke 'the two-million-guilder-rich person'
      de nog ziekeren 'the yet sicker, the people that are even sicker'
      de hiervan volkomen afhankelijken '*lit.* the here-on completely
          dependent, the persons completely dependent on this'

For instance, in the first example the word *rijke* is preceded by the adverb *zeer* that cannot occur before nouns. Hence, it is the adjectival nature of the base *rijk* that must license the occurrence of the adverb in this position, since normally an adverb does not occur in between a determiner and a noun in Dutch. On the other hand, the use of the determiner, and the occurrence of the nominal plural suffix on the head word in the two last examples in (56) indicate the nominal character of these words.

One possible interpretation of these facts is that some affixes may occur as constituents of syntactic structure, i.e. they are syntactic affixes (cf. Hoekstra 1986*a*,*b*). In such an interpretation, the structure of *de zeer rijke* will be as follows:

(57) [de [[zeer rijk]$_{AP}$ [e]$_N$]$_{N'}$]$_{NP}$

That is, we may assume that the bound morpheme -*e* is a noun, the head noun of the NP. On the surface, this -*e* then will be combined prosodically with the preceding adjective, because it is part of the (phonological) word *rijke* at the surface level.

A second possible analysis is that the (inflected) adjective *rijke* licenses an empty noun in the head position of the NP. This is the analysis advocated in Kester (1996). It is in line with the lexicalist position because it does not assume that bound morphemes play direct syntactic roles. A problem for this analysis is that it does not explain why these kinds of words can be pluralized, just like nouns, as in the last two examples in (56).

The third position, which will be taken in this book, is that affixes such as *-e* are attached to their bases by non-syntactic, lexical rules, but exhibit inheritance: certain combinatorial possibilities of the base, in particular the modifiers and complements they allow for, are inherited by the derived word. That is, this *-e* is a nominalizing suffix, but inherits the set of possible complements from its adjectival base.[8] Thus, the suffix *-e* discussed here can be seen as a derivational suffix with inheritance properties (cf. Section 6.2.1).

Finally, note that there is also conversion of adjectives to nouns without the addition of overt phonological material (cf. Schultink 1962: 66). This phenomenon will be discussed in Section 3.5.

2.3.4. Partitive constructions

Noun phrases can have the surface form Quantifier Adjective + *s*, as is illustrated by the following examples (taken from van Marle 1996: 73):

(58) iets groen-s 'something green'
      niets waar-s 'nothing true'
      wat leuk-s 'something nice'
      veel mooi-s 'a lot of nice stuff'
      weinig prachtig-s 'little/not much splendid'
      meer fraai-s 'more fine things'
      allerlei heerlijk-s 'all sorts of lovely things'
      een heleboel lief-s 'a lot of sweet things'
      een massa goed-s 'a lot of good things'

In addition, the *wat voor* 'what kind of' construction also allows for these combinations of adjective + *s*:

---

[8] As we will see in Section 2.4, participial and infinitival sufffixes of Dutch behave similarly: they derive adjectives and nouns respectively which still exhibit verbal combinatorial properties. That is why infinitives and participles are classified in Haspelmath (1996) as category-changing inflection.

(59) Wat voor moois heb je gezien? 'What kind of beautiful things did you see?'

Since this construction is productive, and applies to all kinds of adjectives, this seems to be a case of contextual inflection in which the quantifier requires the adjective to carry the genitive ending -s. On the other hand, there exists a number of deadjectival nouns in -s, which seems to imply that words like *groens* have the status of nouns. These are words like *nieuw-s* 'news', *lekker-s* 'sweets', *fraai-s* 'nice things', and *mooi-s* 'beautiful things', which can be used as the head of an NP:

(60) Het nieuws verbaasde ons 'The news surprised us'

The noun status of these adjective + s words (the position defended in van Marle 1996) would also be in harmony with the fact that most of these quantifiers can modify (mass) nouns:

(61) wat soep 'some soup'
      allerlei rommel 'all sorts of rubbish'
      een massa snoep 'a lot of sweets'

However, this does not hold for the quantifiers *iets* 'something', *niets* 'nothing', and *niks* 'nothing', which cannot occur before a mass noun, but do occur before adjective + s.

As was the case for the suffix -e discussed in the preceding section, these words in -s still have the syntactic valency of the adjective in that they occur with modifiers and complements that occur before adjectives, but normally not before nouns:

(62) iets heel lastig-s 'something very difficult'
      niets in het oog vallend-s '*lit.* nothing in the eye falling, nothing that catches the eye'

A problem for the hypothesis that this suffix -s always creates nouns is that many of them cannot occur with a determiner, unlike a noun like *nieuws* 'news': noun phrases such as *het lastigs, het in het oog vallends* are impossible. In this respect, the suffix -s differs from the suffix -e discussed in the preceding section, since these words can always be used as NPs, with the determiner *de*, and also allow for nominal pluralization. Therefore, Hoeksema (1998) proposed analysing this construction as a determiner phrase with a quantifier in the determiner position, and an empy head noun. For instance, the phrase *iets lastigs* would have the following structural analysis (Hoeksema presupposes a DP analysis of noun phrases):

(63)   [[iets]$_D$ [[lastig-s]$_{AP}$ [e]$_N$]$_{NP}$]$_{DP}$

where *e* stands for 'empty'. The *-s* is then considered a case of contextual inflection, and will be formally marked as licensing an empty noun in the head position of the NP. This analysis has the advantage of explaining why these words do not behave like normal nouns, and differ in this respect with words in *-e* as discussed above. Those cases where the adjective + *s* combination clearly behaves as a noun, as is the case for *nieuws* 'news', can then be seen as cases of a nominal reinterpretation of the adjective on the basis of the surface structure in which an overt noun is lacking.

However, the problem of this analysis remains that the appearance of the *s* is not a normal case of contextual inflection, since it is restricted to a specific construction with quantifiers and empty nouns. Moreover, unlike what is presupposed in Hoeksema's analysis, adjectives do not bear case in present-day Dutch. Therefore, I prefer to interpret this structure as a construction, a grammaticalized pattern [Quantifier [Specifier [A-*s*]$_N$]$_{NP}$]$_{NP}$ with an open slot for the adjective. The combination A+*s* functions as a derived mass noun, which means that cardinal numbers cannot be used as quantifiers here. The suffix *-s* thus functions as a derivational suffix that only occurs in a specific syntactic configuration. Like the suffix *-e* discussed in Section 2.3.3, it triggers inheritance: the combinatorial possibilities of the adjectival base are transferred to the derived noun. Such a construction is similar to the possessor-marker construction discussed in Section 2.2.2 in that in both constructions a bound morpheme *-s* only occurs in specific syntactic configurations.

2.4. VERBAL INFLECTION

The basic division in verbal inflection is that between finite and non-finite forms. The finite forms of the indicative mood express the categories Tense, Number, and Person. There are three non-finite forms: the infinitive, the perfective/passive participle, and the present participle.

2.4.1. Finite forms

The paradigm for the indicative mood of a regular verb such as *koken* 'to cook' (the infinitive form in *-en* is the citation form) is based on the stem, in this case *kook* (Table 2.7).

The letter *e* in the plural ending and in the past tense suffix stands for the schwa. Due to Prevocalic Schwa-Deletion, the allomorph of the past tense suffix before *-en* is *-t*.

The expression of number and person in these finite verbal forms is a case of contextual inflection: finite forms have to agree in person and number with the subject of the clause in which the finite forms appears. Tense, on the other hand, is a case of inherent inflection: the choice of the correct tense form is not determined by the syntactic structure in which it appears. It is the role of Tense to locate the state or event referred to on the time axis with respect to the time of speaking. Contextual inflection is peripheral to inherent inflection (Booij 1994, 1996), and the forms in Table 2.7 are in conformity with this generalization.

As Table 2.7 shows, the inflectional suffixes can be used for more than one slot in the paradigm. For instance, the plural suffix *-en* can be used both in the present and past tense, and for all three persons. Hence, this suffix will only be specified as [Number: Plural]. The suffix *-t* will be specified as [Number: Singular; Person: not-1, in the context Tense: Present]. We do not need to postulate zero-suffixes for cases in which a particular value is not marked morphologically. Instead, we can assign the relevant properties by means of default rules that specify a verbal stem used as a word or as the head of a verbal compound for those categories for which it has no value by means of overt marking. We need this mechanism for marking verbal forms

TABLE 2.7. *The indicative verbal paradigm of* koken

		Present	Past
Sg.	1	kook	kook-te
	2	kook-t	kook-te
	3	kook-t	kook-te
Pl.	1	kok-en	kook-t-en
	2	kok-en	kook-t-en
	3	kok-en	kook-t-en

as Present Tense. In addition, singular forms also lack explicit marking for Number, and some of them also for Person. Thus we get the following default rules for verbal forms (where [ ] indicates lack of specification):

(64) Tense: [ ]   →   Tense: Present
      Number: [ ]   →   Number: Singular
      Person: [ ]   →   Person: 1 Condition: Tense: Present

This formalization implies that verbal forms may not be completely specified with respect to all relevant morpho-syntactic categories. For instance, plural forms are not specified for Person. This does not pose any problem for subject–verb agreement that requires a finite form to agree in Number and Person with the subject of its clause. Agreement is a checking procedure that checks if there is any contradiction between the features of the subject and that of the verb. For instance, since the finite form *koken* has no specification for Person, it will never contradict the value for Person of the subject, and hence be able to co-occur with subjects of all three persons (cf. Pollard and Sag 1994: chapter 2).

We should realize that categories such as Present Tense and Past Tense, as used here, are formal, morphological categories, and still require semantic interpretation rules. For instance, the present tense forms can be used to refer to events in the past: this is the use as so called 'praesens historicum', in order to create a particular narrative mode. Similarly, past tense forms may not necessarily refer to the past, since they can be used in complex sentences due to the 'sequence of tense' effect that induces agreement in tense form between the verbal form of the main clause and that of the embedded clause, as in:

(65) Ik hoopte dat je morgen zou koken 'I was hoping that you will cook tomorrow'

The need for semantic interpretation of specific morphological forms also applies to Person and Number. For instance, in Italian the third person singular form of a verb is also used as the polite form for a second person singular subject; in German the third person plural pronoun *Sie* and the corresponding finite verbal form are used as polite forms. In Dutch, we find only one relic of this politeness use of third person forms: the personal pronoun *U*, the polite form of 'you', can take the third person singular verbal form. In most cases there is no formal distinction between second and third person; the exceptions are the verbs *hebben* 'to have' and *zijn* 'to be' and the modal verbs (see below). Thus we may get the polite forms *U heeft* 'you have' and *U is* 'you are', with the third person singular forms. However, the second person forms *U hebt* and *U bent* are nowadays the preferred options. In particular *U is* has an archaic flavour, more than *U heeft*.

The past tense suffix *-te* has an allomorph *-de*; the two allomorphs are in complementary distribution: *-te* when the stem ends in a voiceless segment (i.e. a voiceless fricative or stop), and *-de* elsewhere, i.e. when the stem ends in a voiced segment (vowel, sonorant consonant, or voiced obstruent). The examples in Table 2.8 illustrate this (for ease of exposition, I have also added the phonetic form of the obstruent cluster, and the form of the perfect participle).

According to Booij (1995), there is no straightforward fully phonological account of the alternation between *-de* and *-te* (by assuming a common underlying form /də/) because there is no independently motivated phono-

TABLE 2.8. *Regular past tense and participle formation*

Verb	Stem	Past tense sg.	Perf. participle
tob 'to toil'	/tɔb/	tob-de [bd]	ge-tob-d
voed 'to feed'	/vud/	voed-de [d]	ge-voed
roof 'to rob'	/roːv/	roof-de [vd]	ge-roof-d
nies 'to sneeze'	/niz/	nies-de [zd]	ge-nies-d
veeg 'to sweep'	/veːɣ/	veeg-de [ɣd]	ge-veeg-d
rem 'to brake'	/rɛm/	rem-de	ge-rem-d
ban 'to ban'	/bɑn/	ban-de	ge-ban-d
meng 'to mix'	/mɛŋ/	meng-de	ge-meng-d
vel 'to fell'	/vɛl/	vel-de	ge-vel-d
stuur 'to steer'	/styr/	stuur-de	ge-stuur-d
aai 'to caress'	/aːj/	aai-de	ge-aai-d
duw 'to press'	/dyw/	duw-de	ge-duw-d
echo 'to echo'	/ɛxoː/	echo-de	ge-echoo-d
olie 'to oil'	/oːli/	olie-de	ge-olie-d
kap 'to cut'	/kɑp/	kap-te [pt]	ge-kap-t
vat 'to seize'	/vɑt/	vat-te [t]	ge-vat
paf 'to puff'	/pɑf/	paf-te [ft]	gepaf-t
pas 'to fit'	/pɑs/	pas-te [st]	ge-pas-t
poch 'to boast'	/pɔχ/	poch-te [xt]	ge-poch-t

logical rule of (progressive) voice assimilation that could derive the correct surface forms. The generalization that there is agreement with respect to voice between the last segment of the stem and the suffix-initial consonant can be expressed by assuming an underlying form for the past tense suffix with an initial coronal consonant that is not specified for voice; we then have to assume a process (Laryngeal Spreading) that spreads the voice specification of the stem-final segment to that suffix-initial coronal. This is the analysis given in Booij (1995: 62). Alternatively, we may account for this alternation by assuming two lexically given competing allomorphs, *-de* and *-te*. Such an analysis would be similar to that proposed for the selection of the correct plural suffix given in Section 2.2. The choice between these two allomorphs can then be made by an output condition Agree that requires two adjacent segments to agree in voice. This condition will select *-te* after voiceless obstruents, and *-de* elsewhere.[9]

In addition to the indicative forms, there is also an imperative/adhortative form that is identical to the second person singular form, for instance *fiets* 'cycle!'; this form is used both for singular and plural addressees. The infinitive form can also be used for giving commands.

In archaic Dutch, there is an additional plural form 'stem + *t*' such as *fietst!* 'cycle', pl. In this kind of Dutch one may also find the conjunctive form 'stem + *e*', as used in cookery books (e.g. *men nem-e een lepel suiker* 'one should take one spoon of sugar').

The second person singular present form exhibits syntactically conditioned allomorphy: if the subject pronoun (*jij* or *je* 'you') follows the verb form, the ending is Ø instead of *t*. This is not a matter of phonology (for instance, the effect of a phonological process of /t/-deletion, a process that does exist in Dutch), as is shown by the following examples, in which the verb is followed by words of the same phonological form:

(66) Loop je? 'Do you walk?'
      Loopt je broer? 'Does your brother walk?'

As in all Germanic languages, the verbs can be divided into a class of regular, and a class of irregular verbs. The regular verbs take the past tense

---

[9] A phonological alternative within OT-phonology is defended in Borowsky (2000). She argues that a condition of stem-identity that is ranked higher than that of affix-identity will force the suffix-initial consonant to change with respect to voice instead of the last consonant of the verbal stem, and thus the effect will be progressive assimilation.

2.4. VERBAL INFLECTION

suffix *-de/-te*, whereas the irregular forms express the past tense by means of stem alternation (mostly vowel alternations, but there are also some cases where consonants are involved in the alternation between present stem and past tense stem). The terms 'regular' and 'irregular' are not fully adequate, however, since these terms suggest that there is no regularity whatsoever involved in stem-alternating verbs. This is not correct, as we will see below. One might therefore prefer the historical terms weak and strong verbs: weak forms form their past tense by means of suffixation, strong (or Ablauting) verbs form their past tense stems by means of vowel alternation. The problem for this latter classification is that there are also irregular verbs that do not fit into the historical class of Ablauting verbs, because they have more complex stem alternations in which consonants also play a role. Therefore, the best distinction is that between suffixing verbs (the default class), and stem-alternation verbs. For ease of exposition, however, I will also use the term 'regular or irregular verb'.

Most of the stem alternation verbs can be classified according to the kind of vowel alternation in the stem. Since the formation of perfect participles involves the same classification of verbs, I also list them in the examples of stem-alternating verbs below. These participles exhibit stem alternation, and select the suffix *-en*, whereas the suffixing verbs take the suffix /d/. All participles have a prefix *ge-* /ɣə/ as well, except when the verbal stem begins with an unstressed prefix. In the list in Table 2.9 I give one example of each vowel-alternation pattern. Most of these patterns are either of the form ABB or of the form ABA. For each pattern the number of verbal roots with that pattern is indicated (based on Haeseryn *et al.* 1997). In some cases the root is used in both simplex and complex verbs, and thus the actual number of verbs with vowel alternation is higher.

There is also a set of verbs in which the past tense stem itself exhibits an alternation: the singular stem has the short vowel /ɑ/, whereas the plural stem has the long vowel /a:/. This alternation between short and long vowel is a reflex of the early Germanic process of open syllable lengthening which is due to Prokosch's Law (stressed syllables must be heavy). This process was lost in early Middle Dutch, and hence this alternation became lexicalized. As we saw in Section 2.2, this lexicalized alternation between short and long vowels can also be seen in the pluralization of nouns.

The third set of stem-alternating verbs (a total of twenty-two roots) consists of those verbs that also have consonantal alternations; there is quite

TABLE 2.9. *Stem-alternating verbs*

Alternation pattern	n	Present tense stem	Past tense stem	Perf. participle
A–B–B				
/ɛi–eː–eː/	51	knijp 'to pinch'	kneep	ge-knep-en
/i–oː–oː/	12	schiet 'to shoot'	schoot	ge-schot-en
/ʌy–oː–oː/	23	buig 'to bend'	boog	ge-bog-en
/eː–oː–oː/	4	weeg 'to weigh'	woog	ge-wog-en
/ɪ–ɔ–ɔ/	25	bind 'to bind'	bond	ge-bond-en
/ɛ–ɔ–ɔ/	17	zend 'to send'	zond	ge-zond-en
A–B–A				
/aː–u–aː/	3	draag 'to carry'	droeg	ge-drag-en
/aː–i–aː/	4	blaas 'to blow'	blies	ge-blaz-en
/ɑ–i–ɑ/	2	val 'to fall'	viel	ge-vall-en
/ɑ–ɪ–ɑ/	2	hang 'to hang'	hing	ge-hang-en
/oː–i–oː/	2	loop 'to walk'	liep	ge-lop-en
/ɔ–ɛ–ɔ/	1	word 'to become'	werd	ge-word-en
/u–i–u/	1	roep 'to call'	riep	ge-roep-en
A–B–C				
/ɛ–i–ɔ/	6	help 'to help'	hielp	ge-holp-en
/ɛ–i–aː/	1	schep 'to create'	schiep	ge-schap-en
/eː–u–oː/	1	zweer 'to swear'	zwoer	ge-zwor-en

some variation here. Six of these verbs with consonantal alternation, the verbs *doen, gaan, slaan, staan, zien,* and *zijn* have the additional property that the plural present tense forms and the infinitive do not take -*en*, but -*n* as their ending; the suffixes of the present and perfect participles also lack the schwa in their suffixes, except the perfect participle *geslagen* (see Table 2.12). The last of these, the verb *zijn* 'to be' has suppletive stems throughout its paradigm (cf. below).

TABLE 2.10. *Stem-alternating verbs with vowel-length alternation*

Alternation pattern	n	Present tense stem	Past tense stem	Perf. participle
A–B–A				
/eː–ɑ; aː–eː/	7	lees 'to read'	las/lazen	ge-lez-en
/eː–ɑ; aː–oː/	6	neem 'to take'	nam/namen	ge-nom-en

2.4. VERBAL INFLECTION

TABLE 2.11. *Stem-alternating verbs with consonantal alternation*

Infinitive	Past tense stem	Perf. participle
brengen 'to bring'	bracht	ge-brach-t
eten 'to eat'	at	ge-get-en
komen 'to come'	kwam	ge-kom-en
kopen 'to buy'	kocht	ge-koch-t
moeten 'to have to'	moest	ge-moet-en
verliezen 'to lose'	verloor	verlor-en
weten 'to know'	wist	ge-wet-en

TABLE 2.12. *Stem-alternating verbs with schwa-less infinitives*

Infinitive	Pres. stem	Pres. participle	Past stem	Perf. participle
doen 'to do'	doe	doend	deed	ge-daa-n
gaan 'to go'	ga	gaand	ging	ge-gaa-n
slaan 'to hit'	sla	slaand	sloeg	ge-slag-en
staan 'to stand'	sta	staand	stond	ge-staa-n
zien 'to see'	zie	ziend	zag	ge-zie-n
zijn 'to be'	zij	zijnd	was/war	ge-wees-t

There are also verbs that are partially irregular in that the past tense stem is formed by means of stem alternation, whereas the perfect participle is formed in the regular way, through addition of the suffix /d/, or, vice versa, it is the participle only that is irregular (see Table 2.13). Note that in the last example there is also a vowel alternation involved in the participial form.

A number of irregular verbs deserve special mention. First, the verbs *zijn* 'to be' and *hebben* 'to have' that also function as auxiliaries in periphrastic constructions have special paradigms (Table 2.14). The modal verbs *kunnen*

TABLE 2.13. *Semi-regular verbs*

Verb	Stem	Past tense stem	Perf. participle
jaag 'to hunt'	/jaːɣ/	joeg	ge-jaag-d
vraag 'to ask'	/vraːɣ/	vroeg	ge-vraag-d
zeg 'to say'	/zɛɣ/	zei	ge-zeg-d
bak 'to bake'	/bɑk/	bak-te	ge-bakk-en
lach 'to laugh'	/lɑx/	lach-te	ge-lach-en
wreek 'to revenge'	/ʋreːk/	wreek-te	ge-wrok-en

'can', *mogen* 'may', and *zullen* 'will' have stem alternations within the present tense paradigm, and in addition the special property that the third person singular present tense has the zero-ending, like the first person singular. The modal verb *willen* has both a regular and an irregular past tense stem (*wilde/wou*) (Table 2.15).

The default conjugation (the class of regular verbs) is that in which the past tense stem is formed by means of suffixation, and the participle by means of the suffix /d/ (and the prefix *ge-*). This is not just because most verbs have this kind of conjugation, but also because new verbs take this con-

TABLE 2.14. *The paradigms of* hebben *and* zijn

The paradigm of *zijn*

	Pres. sg.	Pres. pl.	Past sg.	Past pl.	Perf. participle
1	ben	zijn	was	waren	ge-wees-t
2	bent	zijn	was	waren	
3	is	zijn	was	waren	

The paradigm of *hebben*

	Pres. sg.	Pres. pl.	Past sg.	Past pl.	Perf. participle
1	heb	hebben	had	hadden	ge-had
2	hebt	hebben	had	hadden	
3	heeft	hebben	had	hadden	

TABLE 2.15. *The paradigms of* kunnen, mogen, *and* willen

	Pres. sg.	Pres. pl.	Past sg.	Past pl.	Perf. participle
1	kan	kunnen	kon	konden	ge-kun-d
2	kunt/kan	kunnen	kon	konden	
3	kan	kunnen	kon	konden	
1	mag	mogen	mocht	mochten	ge-mog-en
2	mag	mogen	mocht	mochten	
3	mag	mogen	mocht	mochten	
1	wil	willen	wilde	wilden	ge-wil-d
2	wil	willen	wilde	wilden	
3	wil	willen	wilde	wilden	

2.4. VERBAL INFLECTION

jugation. New verbs might be borrowed (mainly from English), or derived through suffixation or conversion:

(67) *Borrowings*
    mail 'to mail'   mail-de   ge-mail-d
    surf 'to surf'   surf-te   ge-surf-t

    Conversions
    computer 'to use the computer'   computer-de   ge-computer-d
    echo 'to echo'   echo-de   ge-echoo-d
    prijs 'to put price labels on'   prijs-de   ge-prijs-d

    Suffixed verbs
    kanal-iseer 'to channel'   kanaliseer-de   ge-kanaliseer-d
    ruïn-eer 'to ruin'   ruïneer-de   ge-ruïneer-d

The verb *prijzen* mentioned above is derived from the noun *prijs* 'price'. Therefore, it contrasts in its conjugation with the strong verb *prijzen* 'to praise' that is phonologically identical, but inflected by means of stem alternation: *prijzen – prees – geprezen*. Similar pairs are:

(68) behang 'to wallpaper'   behang-de   behang-d
        < behang 'wallpaper'
      behang 'to hang with'   behing   behang-en
      pluis 'to give off fluff'   pluis-de   ge-pluis-d
        < pluis 'fluff'
      pluis 'to search'   ploos   ge-ploz-en
      zweer 'to ulcerate'   zweer-de   ge-zweer-d
        < zweer 'ulcer'
      zweer 'to swear'   zwoer   ge-zwor-en

If the weak conjugation is the default one, we expect that verbs of the irregular set might shift to the weak conjugation. It is indeed the case that a lot of verbs have become weak, for instance

(69) scheer 'to shave'   schoor/scheerde   ge-schor-en
      waai 'to blow'   woei/waaide   ge-waai-d
      klief 'to split'   kloof > kliefde   ge-klief-d
      spuw 'to spit'   spoog > spuugde   ge-spuug-d

(cf. van Haeringen 1940 for more examples). In the first two examples, both past tense forms are in use, in the second two examples the suffixed form has become the only acceptable one. On the other hand, Dutch appears to preserve most of the stem-alternating verbs, and this is why van Haeringen (1940) spoke about 'de taaie levenskracht van het sterke werkwoord' ('the tough vitality of the strong verb'). As pointed out by Schultink (1962: 37) and van Santen (1997), this has to do with the high token frequency of many of these verbs. This high frequency implies that the past tense forms are stored and retrieved from the lexicon. The high activation level of these stored forms will block the formation of the regular past tense forms. This does not mean that it is never possible for a weak verb to become a strong one. In the course of history, some Dutch verbs shifted from weak to strong, e.g. *belijden* 'to confess' and *vermijden* 'to avoid'. There are also verbs derived from nouns through conversion that have irregular inflection, verbs such as *fluiten* 'to play the flute, whistle' < *fluit* 'flute'. This shows that native speakers have been able to discover the vowel-alternation patterns in the set of strong verbs, and to extend these patterns to new cases. That is why the term 'irregular' might be slightly misleading (cf. van Santen and Lalleman 1994, van Santen 1997, Jordens 1998).

Prefixed verbs derived from verbs with stem alternation keep the stem-alternation pattern of their verbal base, and do not get the default inflection (as pointed out above, their perfect participles do not have the prefix *ge-*):

(70) be-lijd 'to confess'   beleed   beled-en
      be-roep 'to call upon'   beriep   beroep-en
      ont-loop 'to evade'   ontliep   ontlop-en
      ont-val 'to elude'   ontviel   ontvall-en
      over-kom 'to happen to'   overkwam   overkom-en
      over-lijd 'to die'   overleed   overled-en
      ver-drijf 'to chase away'   verdreef   verdrev-en
      ver-schijn 'to appear'   verscheen   verschen-en

This kind of inheritance of irregularities can also be observed for similar verbs in English (*stand – stood/understand – understood*), German (*schreib – schrieb/beschreib – beschrieb*), and in Romance languages like French (*venir – viens/devenir – deviens*). Moreover, we also see this in Dutch plural formation: if a noun selects a long allomorph in *-er* as its plural stem, the same stem occurs in compounds headed by that noun: *kleinkind* 'grandchild' – *kleinkinderen* (cf. Section 2.2).

This raises the question of how to account for the inheritance of the stem-alternation patterns of base verbs by their derivatives. The solution advocated in Lieber (1980, 1989, 1992: 85) is to list the past tense stems in the lexicon, in addition to the present tense stems. These past tense stems can then also feed word formation, in particular prefixation. For instance, the past tense form *ontliep* 'evaded' is formed by prefixing *ont-* to the past tense stem *liep*. At first sight, the problem with this solution seems to be that it creates a bracketing paradox since semantically a form like *ontliep* is the past tense stem of the verb *ontlopen*. Thus, the following structures are assigned to *ontliep*:

(71) morphological structure: ont[loop + Past]
      semantic structure: [ontloop] + Past

In order to avoid such bracketing paradoxes, Hoeksema (1984) proposed the concept of morphological head operation: certain morphological operations, such as past tense formation and noun pluralization are qualified as head operations: they are formal operations on the head, and since the head requires a particular stem, this stem will also occur in the derived verb and the plural noun. The advantage of such an analysis is that bracketing paradoxes can be avoided and that the semantic interpretation of such morphological structures obeys the principle of compositionality. The obvious disadvantage is that a new type of formal operation has to be added to the repertoire of formal operations in morphology.

A third option is the more traditional approach of diacritic feature percolation: for each subclass of stem alternations we posit a diacritic feature that triggers a particular stem change. This diacritic feature is then percolated from the verbal base to the dominating verbal node of the complex verb, and thus it will also trigger the stem change in past tense forms of such prefixed verbs. This solution presupposes that each stem-alternating past tense form is created through spell-out rules for the past tense forms that are conditioned by specific diacritic features, or by specific lexical items (as in Halle and Marantz 1993).

Although this solution can provide a techically correct account of these patterns, it raises the question of whether these stem alternations should really be expressed in terms of spell out rules for past tense rather than being listed as such in the lexicon. The latter option is more in line with psycholinguistic findings (cf. Clahsen 1999, Pinker 1999).

What is, in my opinion, at stake here is paradigmatic word formation, a phenomenon introduced in Chapter 1. As we saw, morphology cannot be equated with the concatenation of morphemes; words can also be formed through the actuation of paradigmatic relations. The formation of the past tense forms and participles of prefixed verbs can be seen as an instantiation of paradigmatic word formation, for which there is much more evidence. I will discuss the role of paradigmatic relations in stem allomorphy patterns more extensively in Chapter 5. Here, it suffices to observe that the creation of irregular prefixed verbs can indeed be seen as the actuation of existing paradigmatic relations between lexically listed stems:

(72)   loop – liep – gelopen = ontloop – ontliep – ontlopen

Note that this analysis presupposes, like Lieber's, that the different stem verbs of irregular simplex verbs are listed in the lexicon, and not generated by rule. The difference from Lieber's analysis is that there is no bracketing paradox implied since the prefixation is seen as applying to the whole set of paradigmatically related stems that together form the verbal lexeme involved in the prefixation process.[10]

2.4.2. Periphrasis and aspect

The present and past tense forms of verbs are usually referred to as the simplex tenses, because there are also complex tenses, periphrastic forms consisting of the finite form of an auxiliary verb and the perfect participle of a main verb. These forms, with the auxiliary *hebben* 'to have', or in some cases *zijn* 'to be', are referred to as the perfect forms. For example, the following third person singular forms are available for the verb *fietsen* 'to cycle' and the verb *struikelen* 'to stumble' respectively:

(73) *Present*   fietst   struikelt
      Past   fietste   struikelde
      Present perfect heeft gefietst   is gestruikeld
      Past perfect   had gefietst   was gestruikeld

---

[10] Similar observations have been made for English. For instance, the comparative form of *unhappy*, *unhappier*, should be seen as derived from the comparative form *happier* and not from *unhappy* because the comparative suffix *-er* does not attach to bases of more than two syllables. At the phrasal level, the same applies: the phrase *transformational grammarian* is coined on the basis of the pattern *grammar – grammarian = transformational grammar – X* (cf. Spencer 1988, Beard 1991).

The auxiliary *hebben* is the default choice; *zijn* is chosen if the verb has the inherent property of telicity, i.e. expresses an inherently bounded event. A good test for telicity is the impossibility of such verbs co-occurring with a durational phrase like *urenlang* 'for hours'. Verbs of movement, although inherently atelic, may also function as telic verbs in combination with a directional expression; in such cases they also select the auxiliary *zijn* (cf. Zaenen 1993).[11]

(74)   De koningin is overleden 'The queen has died'
       *De koningin is urenlang overleden 'The queen has died for hours'
       De koningin heeft een uur gefietst 'The queen cycled for an hour'
       De koningin is naar Amsterdam gefietst 'The queen cycled to Amsterdam'

As these examples show, in main clauses the finite form of the auxiliary may be separated from the perfect participle, due to the rule of Verb Second that requires finite verbal forms to occupy the second position in main clauses. In subordinate clauses the verbal complex appears in clause-final position (Koster 1975). The order of finite form and participle is variable: the auxiliary either precedes or follows the participle. The first of these orders is common in Western varieties, the second one is used in Eastern varieties (and also in German). As we will see below, this variation in word order has relevance for morphology since it can be used to determine the categorial status of words with a participial form: if such words do not allow for this variation, they have lexicalized into adjectives.

The traditional terms for these periphrastic verbal forms, present perfect and past perfect, suggest that they do not only express tense, but also aspect. This is indeed the case. What we mean by aspect here is 'grammatical aspect'. Perfective aspect presents a situation as completed, whereas imperfect aspect presents the situation as ongoing. This kind of aspect is to be distinguished from another kind of aspect: Aktionsart or lexical aspect, the inherent aspect related to a verb and its arguments. Well-known categories in this respect are durative and telic aspect. For instance, the verb *to read* is inherently durative, but will receive a telic interpretation (with an endpoint of the event implied) in combination with the object argument *a book*. That

---

[11] Cf. also Hoekstra (1984), Lieber and Baayen (1997), and Hoekstra (1999) for detailed analyses and discussion.

is, this kind of aspect is determined compositionally on the basis of the properties of the verb and of its arguments (Verkuyl 1993). A sentence like *John read the book* has the past tense form, perfective aspect, and its Aktionsart is telic. The independence of perfectivity and telicity is clear from the fact that in the sentence *John was reading the book* there is still telicity, but the grammatical aspect is imperfective (Boogaart 1999: 9).

As shown by Boogaart (1999), the simplex tenses of Dutch (present and past tense) are aspectually neutral, i.e. they can have either an imperfective or a perfective aspectual interpretation, depending on context of interpretation and kind of discourse, whereas the English past tense tends to receive a perfect aspectual interpretation. The complex forms, on the other hand, have a specific aspectual value. As the glosses of the sentences (74) show, English and Dutch differ in the precise aspectual values of the corresponding verbal forms. In particular, the simplex past form of English more often has perfective aspect than its Dutch counterpart. As for Dutch, the situation can be characterized as follows: the present perfect form (the marked form) can be used for the semantic category PRESENT PERFECT (the capitals indicate that a semantic category is involved), as in the sentence *Ik heb dat boek gelezen* 'I've read that book'. However, in non-narrative discourse this form can also be used for the category PERFECTIVE PAST (i.e. a bounded situation that happened before the moment of speaking), whereas English uses the simple past for the latter category (Boogaart 1999: 210), as illustrated by the following examples:

(75)   Yesterday, I read that novel
       Gisteren heb ik dat boek gelezen

In narrative discourse, however, where a sequence of events is related, it is possible to use the past tense as in English:

(76)   Gisteren ging ik naar de bibliotheek, en las dat boek uit
       Yesterday I went to the library, and finished reading that book

This shows again that there is no one-to-one correspondence between formal morphological categories such as those of Tense and Aspect, and the specific semantic interpretation of these formal properties of verbal forms.

There are no simplex passive forms: passive verbal forms are expressed by means of the auxiliary *worden* 'to become' in combination with the passive participle, which is formally always identical to the perfect participle. The perfect form of these passive forms is created by means of the verb *zijn* 'to be' (the verb *worden* is one of those verbs that take *zijn* as the auxiliary for perfect forms), and the participle of the main verb, whereas the participle of the verb *worden* (*geworden*) has to be omitted:

(77) Het boek werd door Jan gelezen 'The book was being read by John'
      Het boek is door Jan gelezen (*geworden) 'The book has been read by John'

Consequently, the perfect participle form of the verb has two functions: together with the relevant auxiliary it serves to express either perfective aspect, or passive meaning.

The formation of passive participles can be seen as conversion of perfect participles: there is no overt phonological change but there is a change in the argument structure of the verb in that the external argument is suppressed, and hence no longer expressed as subject of the clause. Both transitive and intransitive verbs allow for passive participle formation (cf. Section 2.4.3).

Let us now discuss how we formally account for these periphrastic constructions. Our starting point is that these are verbal clusters that together behave as a verbal unit. This can be concluded from the process of 'PP over V' that extraposes a PP across a verb (cf. Reuland 1990, Ackema 1999*a*: 89):

(78) ...dat Jan gedurende een week werkte 'that John for a week worked'
      ...dat Jan werkte gedurende een week
      ...dat Jan gedurende een week gewerkt heeft
      ...dat Jan gewerkt heeft gedurende een week
      *...dat Jan gewerkt gedurende een week heeft

As the ungrammaticality of the last example shows, the main verb and the auxiliary cannot be split by PP over V. We will therefore assume that they form a unit of the type $[VV]_V$. The properties of the V cluster will then be determined compositionally by the operation of unification (Börjars, Vincent, and Chapman 1997). For instance, the words *gewerkt* and *heeft* will be specified as follows:

(79) gewerkt   Predicate: WORK (SUBJ)
      heeft   Aspect: Perfect
                Tense: Present
                Number: Singular
                Person: 3

Unification of these properties will result in a verbal cluster *heeft gewerkt* with the properties specified in (79); thus, such a verbal cluster will function as a finite form of the verb *werken* 'to work', although it has a syntactically complex form since it is a combination of words that is split in main clauses.

There is one construction in which the perfective participle is replaced with the infinitival form of the verb: in so-called raising constructions. Verb-raising is the phenomenon in languages such as Dutch and German that the verb of an embedded clause is raised to the matrix clause and then forms one verbal cluster with the verb of that matrix clause. If the verb of the matrix clause has the perfective form, the infinitive is used instead of the participle, the so-called infinitivus-pro-participio (IPP) effect (cf. Hoeksema 1988 for discussion and analysis):

(80) *Without raising*
dat hij probeerde [een boek te kopen]$_S$ '*lit.* that he tried a book to buy'

With raising
dat hij een boek probeerde te kopen '*lit.* that he a book tried to buy'

IPP-effect
dat hij een boek heeft proberen te kopen '*lit.* that he a book has try to buy, that he has tried to buy a book'

The replacement of the participle with the infinitive is obligatory for those verbs that always trigger raising, such as the modal verbs.

Another category that is often expressed in verbal paradigms of Indo-European languages is that of 'future'. In Dutch, this category is expressed by the modal verb *zullen* 'will'. However, it never has a pure tense value, since it is also possible to refer to future events by means of the simple present form:

(81) Jan komt morgen 'John will come tomorrow'
Jan zal morgen komen 'John will come tomorrow'

Therefore, *zullen* still carries some of its lexical meaning in combination with another verb (unlike *hebben*), and hence cannot be considered as a purely periphrastic form.

2.4.3. *Infinitives and participles*

The number of infinite forms is restricted to three: the infinitive, the past

2.4. VERBAL INFLECTION

participle, and the present participle. Their behaviour is quite interesting because they all occur in transcategorial constructions, and thus pose interesting problems of linguistic analysis.

The form of the infinitive is always 'stem + -*en*' except for the six verbs mentioned in Table 2.12 that have a vowel-final stem followed by the ending -*n*. As mentioned above, the infinitive form can also be used as an imperative or adhortative form.

Characteristic for the infinitive is that it has both verbal and nominal properties. Using the distinction of Haspelmath (1996) between internal and external syntax, we may say that the internal syntax of the infinitive is that of a verb, and its external syntax is that of a noun. Its verbal properties manifest themselves in the fact that the infinitive still has the case-assigning properties of a verb: it can select bare NPs, without a preposition, and also allows for preposition-less dative NPs; on the other hand, its external syntax is that of a noun since it cooccurs with the determiners *een* 'a' and *het* 'the'. These examples all have the meaning 'giving a present to your mother':

(82) (a) het je moeder een cadeautje geven '*lit.* the your mother a present give-INF'
 (b) het een cadeautje geven aan je moeder '*lit.* the a present give-INF to your mother'
 (c) het geven van een cadeautje aan je moeder '*lit.* the give-INF of a present to your mother'
 (d) *het je moeder geven van een cadeautje '*lit.* the your mother give-INF of a present'

As has been observed by Hoekstra (1986*b*), and as shown by these examples, there are different degrees of deverbalization as a consequence of the attachment of the infinitive suffix -*en*. In all cases, the external syntax is that of a noun because the determiner *het* is used. As to the co-occurrence of complements, we see variation. In (82a), the infinitive selects two verbal complements, a bare object-NP and a prepositionless dative-NP. In example (82*b*), the dative-NP with the preposition *aan* has the form that is standard for the complement of a nominal head, i.e. it is case-marked. In (82*c*) both complements have the form of nominal complements, with prepositions. Finally, (82*d*) is ungrammatical because one cannot use the verbal complement form (i.e. a bare NP) for the dative-NP, whereas the lower object-NP *een* *cadeautje* is preceded by the preposition *van*, which implies a nominal interpretation of the infinitive.[12]

Examples like (82a) show that the infinitive form is not a case of category change from V to N because both its verbal properties and its nominal properties are active, in the selection of verbal complements and a determiner, respectively. In this respect it is similar to the suffix *-e* discussed in Section 2.3.3 that adds nominal properties to an adjective, but preserves the adjectival properties as well. That is, this is another example of transcategorial constructions. In this respect there is a difference between the bare infinitive and the infinitive preceded by the particle *te* 'to': the combination *te* + infinitive behaves as a purely verbal category. Therefore, a phrase like **het je moeder een cadeautje te geven* 'lit. the your mother a present to give' is ill-formed (compare 82a).

The nominal character of the bare infinitive can also be seen in its use with the phrase *aan het* 'at the'; this is a construction that functions as the equivalent of the progressive form in English, but has the form of a PP:

(83) De koningin is aan het fietsen *'lit.* The queen is at the cycling, the queen is cycling'

Similarly, the determiner *een* 'a' can also be used before an infinitive, as in

(84) De dief zette het op een lopen *'lit.* the thief put it on a walking, the thief started running away'

These constructions are lexicalized, however: it is only the preposition *aan* that can express the progressive meaning in combination with *het* + infinitive, and the use of *een* + infinitive is restricted to the verb *zetten*.

In a number of cases, the infinitives have lexicalized into words that function as pure nouns and do not have verbal properties anymore. For instance, *eten* is not only the infinitival form of the verbal stem *eet* 'to eat', but also used as a synonym of *voedsel* 'food'. Other examples of such infinitives with a secondary, purely nominal meaning and function are:

(85) bestaan 'existence', drinken 'drinks', wezen 'essence, nature'

Again, this is similar to what we saw for adjectives + *-e*, and to what we will

---

[12] Cf. Hoekstra (1986b), Reuland (1988), and Zubizarreta and van Haaften (1988) for detailed discussion.

see for participles, which are both verbal and adjectival, and can lexicalize into adjectives.

A consequence of the nominal nature of infinitives is that they feed the productive process of nominal compounding (Booij 1989) since they can function as the head of a nominal compound (verbal compounding is unproductive in Dutch). This will be discussed in detail in Section 4.4.

As we have already seen above, the perfect participle of the regular verbs is formed by prefixing the verbal stem with *ge-* and suffixing it with /t/ or with /d/; the /d/ surfaces as [d] in onset position, and as [t] in coda position. Therefore, the difference between the two suffixes is only heard if the participle is inflected as an adjective, in prenominal position, and is then followed by the inflectional schwa. The choice between /t/ and /d/ is governed by the same principle as that of the past tense suffix: /t/ after a verbal stem that ends underlyingly in a voiceless obstruent, otherwise /d/. The participles of irregular verbs also have the prefix *ge-*, but the suffix is *-en*. In addition, as we have seen above, the vowel of the perfect participle stem may differ from that of the present tense.

An interesting complication is that the prefix is omitted before verbs that begin with a prefix that does not bear the main stress of the verb, as the following examples illustrate (it does not make any difference whether the verb is irregular or regular):

(86) *Verb*   *Perfect participle*
     be-proef 'to test'   beproef-d
     be-rijd 'to ride'   bered-en
     er-ken 'to acknowledge'   erken-d
     er-vaar 'to experience'   ervar-en
     ge-loof 'to believe'   geloof-d
     ge-niet 'to enjoy'   genot-en
     her-open 'to reopen'   heropen-d
     her-roep 'to revoke'   herroep-en
     onder-ga 'to undergo'   ondergaa-n
     onder-bouw 'to support'   onderbouw-d
     ont-ga 'to escape'   ontgaa-n
     ont-moet 'to meet'   ontmoet
     mis-draag 'to misbehave'   misdrag-en
     mis-ken 'to ignore'   misken-d

ver-geet 'to forget'	verget-en
ver-ken 'to explore'	verken-d
vol-maak 'to make perfect'	volmaak-t
voor-kom 'to prevent'	voorkom-en

It is crucial that the first unstressed syllable of the stem has the status of prefix, otherwise the prefix *ge-* is added. In this respect, Dutch differs from German where the only condition for the absence of the participial prefix *ge-* is that the first syllable does not bear the main stress of the verb. The verb *verbaliseren* 'to fine', for instance, begins with an unstressed syllable that does not have prefix-status, and hence the participle is *geverbaliseerd*. Verbs with the prefix *her-* are also interesting because a number of verbs with this prefix have main stress on the prefix (Schultink 1964). An example is *hérinterpreteren* 'to reinterpret'. As predicted, the participle is *geherinterpreteerd*, with the prefix *ge-* present, because the stem-initial prefix bears the main stress of the verb.

These facts have direct relevance for Anderson's (1992) theory of A-morphous Morphology mentioned in Section 2.2.1. The fact that the prefixation of *ge-* depends on the internal morphological structure of the verbal stem is a clear counterexample to this claim (cf. Carstairs-McCarthy 1992 for similar phenomena).

The formation of perfect participles also throws light on the issue of when we are justified in considering a verb as complex. There are quite a number of verbs that behave as prefixed verbs with respect to participle formation (that is, these verbs have a perfect participle without the prefix *ge-*), although the root of such verbs does not occur as an independent word, or, if it does occur, it is with a completely unrelated meaning. Hence, there is no semantic compositionality in the meanings of these prefixed verbs. This has to do with the fact that, once complex verbs have been coined, they are stored in lexical memory whereas their bases were lost as independent lexical items in the course of history. A clear example is the verb *vergeten* 'to forget': the root *geet* that corresponds to English *get* does not exist as an independent word. Other examples are:

(87) | *Verb* | *Perfect participle* |
|---|---|
| begin 'to begin' | begonnen |
| beweer 'to claim' | beweerd |
| gedij 'to prosper' | gedijd |

2.4. VERBAL INFLECTION

ontbeer 'to miss'	ontbeerd
ontmoet 'to meet'	ontmoet
verdwijn 'to disappear'	verdwenen
verzuim 'to omit'	verzuimd

In all these examples, a prefix is recognizable, but there is no corresponding base word. Therefore, we consider these verbs as formally complex verbs.

Perfect participles can also be used as passive forms, as pointed out above: they then require the auxiliary *worden* for imperfect tense forms, and the auxiliary *zijn* for the expression of perfect aspect. The semantic operation involved in the passivization of the past participles can be circumscribed as argument suppression (cf. Booij 1992): the subject argument of the active verb forms is no longer expressed as such, but can be expressed in a *door*-phrase analogous to the English *by*-phrase. The original object argument, if any, is expressed as a subject. The passivization effect is to be seen as a property of the participle itself, not of the combination of a passive auxiliary with the perfect participle, because the passive meaning is also there if the participle is used without the auxiliary. This is the case when the passive participle is used prenominally, when it feeds deadjectival word formation, and in combinations with other verbs (for instance, in the sentence *Ik kreeg het boek thuis bezorgd* 'I got the book delivered at home').[13]

Dutch also has impersonal passives for intransitive verbs. In that case the subject position of the clause is filled by an expletive subject pronoun *er*, as in *Er werd enthousiast gedanst* '*lit*. There was enthusiastically danced, there was enthusiastic dancing'. The class of verbs that allow for impersonal passives can be characterized as those verbs that refer to actions/events controllable by the subject, but the syntactic context also plays a role (cf. Zaenen 1993 for details and discussion).

Passive participles of transitive verbs, and perfect participles of the class of verbs that select the perfect auxiliary *zijn* (for instance, telic verbs like *vallen* 'to fall' and *sterven* 'to die') can also be used as adjectives, both in prenominal and predicative position. They occur, like infinitives, in transcategorial constructions; their internal syntax is that of a verb, and their external syntax is that of an adjective.

---

[13] Cf. Ackerman and Webelhuth (1998: ch. 8) for discussion of this issue for German.

(88)   het mij door mijn collega gegeven boek '*lit.* the me by my colleague given book, the book given to me by my colleague'
de gisteren gestorven vriend '*lit.* the yesterday deceased friend'

In the first example, the occurrence of the phrase *door mijn collega* and in particular that of the bare dative NP *mij* that requires a verbal governor shows that the participle has not lost its verbal properties in its adjectival use.

Like the perfect participle, a passive participle by itself does not express a specific aspectual value: it is the passive auxiliaries *worden* and *zijn* that express non-perfective and perfective aspect respectively. However, when a passive participle is used as an adjective, for instance in prenominal position, its semantic aspect is perfective: it expresses a property that is the result of the action or event expressed by the verb. Thus, we get the following chain of conversion operations for participles:

(89)   gegeven: Perfect Participle → Passive Participle → Passive Participle/A [PERFECT]
gestorven: Perfect Participle → Perfect Participle/A [PERFECT]

The participles that can be used as adjectives have the common property that they take non-agentive, theme-like arguments (Zaenen 1993). It is the NP-head of the construction in which these participles are used as adjectives that functions as the theme-argument required by the adjective.[14]

Participles used as adjectives can lose their verbal properties. For instance, the participle *gesloten* 'closed' can also be used for referring to a particular mental disposition, and then has the meaning 'tight-lipped'. Other examples are:

(90)   gehecht 'attached to', gejaagd '*lit.* hunted, nervous', gelaten '*lit.* let, resigned', geslepen '*lit.* sharpened, sly' , gespannen '*lit.* stretched, tense'

The difference between the adjectival and verbal interpretation of such participles manifests itself in word-order differences: in embedded clauses a verbal participle (perfect or passive participle) can either precede or follow the

---

[14] Exceptional cases of perfect, non-passive participles used as adjectives are *bereden* in *de bereden politie* 'the mounted police', and *gestudeerd* in *een gestudeerd persoon* 'a learned person'; in these cases the subject argument of the participle is an agent.

finite verb, whereas participles used as adjectives can only appear where all predicates appear, i.e. before the finite verb:

(91) Ik dacht dat die deur was gesloten/gesloten was 'I thought that that door had been closed'
  Ik vind dat deze jongen *is gesloten/gesloten is 'I find that this boy is tight-lipped'

As pointed out in Booij (1994, 1996), it is inherent inflection that typically exhibits lexicalization. The data concerning participles presented here form a clear illustration of that generalization.

There are two other kinds of adjectives with a participial form that have no verbal properties, so called pseudo-participles. First, we find many adjectives derived by affixing *ge*...*t/d* to a nominal base. Such adjectives have the meaning 'provided with N':

(92) ge-gleuf-d 'grooved'   < gleuf 'groove'
  ge-gom-d 'gummed'   < gom 'gum'
  ge-masker-d 'masked'   < masker 'mask'
  ge-handicap-t 'handicapped' < handicap 'id.'
  ge-marmer-d 'marbled'   < marmer 'marble'
  ge-spier-d 'brawny'   < spier 'muscle'

This pattern has very probably arisen through reanalysis of conversion pairs of nouns and verbs. For instance, since Dutch has both the noun *stroomlijn* 'streamline' and the converted verb *stroomlijnen* 'to stream-line', the participle *gestroomlijnd* can be reinterpreted as being derived directly from the noun *stroomlijn*. Hence, this pattern *ge*-N-*t/d* could be extended to other nouns without a verbal intermediate step. It is then a typical case of paradigmatic word formation (cf. Section 4.3.2 for further discussion of these adjectives).

Since there are participles without *ge*- as well (when the verbal stem begins with an unstressed prefix), we also find pseudo-participles without *ge*- that begin with such a prefix:

(93) bejaard 'aged'   < jaar 'year'
  befaamd 'famous'   < faam 'fame'
  verduiveld 'devilish' < duivel 'devil'
  verkikkerd 'nuts'   < kikker 'frog'

A second source of pseudo-participles is the borrowing and formal adaptation of French participles without their verbal bases being borrowed as well; they end in -*eerd*:

(94)　geraffineerd 'sly', geporteerd 'willing to', gepikeerd 'angry', geflatteerd 'flattering', gedecideerd 'resolute'

This is a case of paradigmatic word formation based on relations between French forms and their Dutch counterparts. For instance, we have patterns like the following:

(95)　　　　　*Verb*　　　　　　　　*Perfect participle*
　　　French　stationner　　　　　stationné
　　　Dutch　 stationeren　　　　　gestationeerd
　　　　　　　'to station, to park'　'stationed, parked'

On the basis of such relations, it can be concluded that an equivalent of a French participle may be created directly by adding the prefix *ge-* and replacing the French ending *-é* with *-eerd*, without also borrowing the verb itself, and this is what often happened, with the effect that there are many pseudo-participles ending in *-eerd*. An example is the adjective *getalenteerd* 'gifted', for which there exists no corresponding verb *talenteren*.

Present participles are formed by adding the suffix *-end* /ənd/ to the verbal stem. They are mainly used in two positions: in prenominal position (in which they have the normal adjectival inflection) and as secondary predicates. Thus, it seems that synchronically they are adjectives rather than verbal forms:

(96)　de mopperende ouders 'the grumbling parents'
　　　Mopperend verliet de leraar de klas 'Grumbling, the teacher left the classroom'

In this respect they are identical to the participles discussed in the previous section. However, most of them cannot be used in predicative position: a sentence such as **De leraar is mopperend* 'The teacher is grumbling' is ungrammatical. It is, however, possible to use some of these present participles in predicative position (Bennis and Wehrman 1990):

(97)　Mijn moeder was lopend 'My mother was on foot'
　　　De ongerustheid was groeiend 'The concern was growing'

2.4. VERBAL INFLECTION

In predicative position, it is also possible to use a longer form of these words, with a final schwa: *Mijn moeder was lopende, De ongerustheid was groeiende*.

Present participles keep their verbal properties, which is clear from the kind of complements they take: bare NPs (direct objects and dative objects), just like finite verbal forms:

(98) De leerlingen vervloekend, verliet de leraar de klas 'Cursing the pupils, the teacher left the classroom'
De mij sprookjes vertellende oma '*lit*. The me fairy tales telling grandmother'

Thus, present participles form another category of verbal forms that occur in transcategorial constructions: they have the external syntax of adjectives since they inflect like adjectives, and have a similar syntactic distribution, but the internal syntax is verbal, because the form of their complements is that of verbal complements.

Like many past participles, a lot of these present participles have lexicalized meanings, and are then to be considered as pure adjectives, without verbal properties, for example:

(99) kwetsend 'grieving', schokkend 'shocking', woedend 'very angry'

That such words have lost their properties as present participles can be concluded from the fact that, unlike most present participles proper, they do occur in predicative position, as shown by sentences like the following:

(100) Deze opmerking is kwetsend 'This remark is offensive'
Deze foto is schokkend 'This picture is shocking'
Ik ben woedend 'I am very angry'

This applies in particular to present participles of psychological verbs. Unlike present participles like *lopend* and *groeiend* that also occur in predicative position, they do not have the longer form ending in schwa in that position; a sentence like **Ik ben woedende* is ill-formed.

Another possible consequence of the lexicalization of present participles into pure adjectives is that of stress shift. For instance, we find the following minimal pairs:

(101) Verb   Present participle   Adjective
       dóeltreffen   dóeltreffend   doeltréffend 'effective'
         'to hit the target'
       nádenken 'to think'   nádenkend   nadénkend 'pensive'
       ópvallen   ópvallend   opvállend 'remarkable'
         'to draw attention'
       úitsteken 'to stick out' úitstekend   uitstékend 'excellent'

Verbal inflection is stress-neutral, and hence the addition of a participial ending will not shift the main stress rightward. Derived adjectives in Dutch, on the other hand, bear their main stress on the last stressable syllable (as mentioned before, a syllable headed by schwa cannot bear stress), hence the stress shift to be seen here is the consequence of the present participles having become full adjectives.

This interpretation of the stress shift as an indication of these words becoming fully adjectival is supported by the observation that the negative prefix *on-* 'un-' that attaches to adjectives, only attaches to the forms with rightward stress: *onopvállend, onnadénkend, ondoeltréffend*. Also, only the forms with rightward stress feed deadjectival comparative formation; for instance, *opvállender* is a well formed comparative, unlike *ópvallender*.[15]

2.5. THE BOUNDARY AND INTERACTION BETWEEN INFLECTION AND WORD FORMATION

So far, we have assumed that there is a clear demarcation of inflection and derivation, and that it is therefore obvious what to deal with in a chapter on inflection. On the other hand, we also saw that in particular inherent inflection is in many ways similar to derivation. The question therefore arises why we would like to maintain the traditional distinction between inflection and derivation. The intuitive idea behind the distinction is that inflected forms are all manifestations of the same lexeme, whereas derivation creates new lexemes. Nevertheless, some morphologists have come to the conclusion that there is no sharp distinction between the two (for instance, Bybee 1985,

---

[15] See Bennis and Wehrmann (1990) for a detailed discussion of Dutch present participles.

Plank 1994), or that the opposition inflection–derivation should be seen as the poles of a continuum, ranging from prototypical inflection to prototypical derivation (Dressler 1989).

As far as I can see, there is one basic reason for maintaining the distinction between inflection and derivation. This reason is that normally (but not always) the formal basis for derivation is the stem of a word, i.e. the word minus its inflectional affixes. For instance, in deverbal word formation it is the bare stem of the verb that is the input form, the forms with all its inflectional affixes stripped off. The same applies to adjectives. As to nouns, it is also the bare stem that normally forms the input for denominal word formation:

(102)	*Stem*	*Derived word*	*Inflected form*	*Derived word*
V	werk 'to work'	werker 'worker'	werk-t 'works'	*werkter
A	rood 'red'	roodheid 'redness'	rod-e 'red', attr.	*rodeheid
N	boom 'tree'	boompje 'tree', dim.	bom-en 'trees'	*bomentje

In the morphological literature we find a number of additional criteria for the distinction between inflection and derivation (cf. Plank 1994, Booij 1998*b*, 2000*b* for surveys) which I will shortly review and comment upon here.

A first criterion is that derivation may change syntactic category, unlike inflection. This is no reliable criterion, since, as we saw in this chapter, infinitives and participles (cases of inherent inflection) also change syntactic category to the extent that these forms get, besides their verbal properties, additional nominal and adjectival properties respectively (see also Haspelmath 1996).

A second criterion is that inflection is obligatory, unlike derivation. For instance, given that Latin nouns are inflected for number and case, each Latin noun must be inflected for these two categories, and has an ending indicating number and case. The problem for this criterion is that it is theory-dependent in its application. For instance, a Dutch singular noun has no inflectional ending, and is singular by default. As long as we do not assume a singular zero-suffix, we might claim that such nouns are not inflected, and that therefore, inflection is not always obligatory.

Full productivity has also been claimed to be characteristic for inflection. As far as Dutch is concerned, this is true for verbal inflection; nouns, however, may not have a plural form, and many adjectives do not have comparative and superlative degree forms. That is, in the domain of inherent inflection there is not always full productivity, just like in the domain of derivation.

As a corollary of the more general and productive nature of inflection it has also been claimed that inflection is semantically more transparent than derivation. This appears nevertheless to be a matter of degree, since, as we saw in this chapter, inherent inflection also lends itself to lexicalization and semantic opacity.

Anderson (1982: 587) proposed the following delimitation of inflection: 'Inflectional morphology is what is relevant to the syntax'. The problem for this criterion is that derivation may also have relevance for syntax. For instance, there are a number of derivational processes that determine the syntactic valency of their output words (cf. Chapter 6). Moreover, we also find agreement patterns among derivational categories. Dutch has a process for the formation of female inhabitatives: the suffix -*se* is added to the noun (for instance: *Amsterdam* – *Amsterdamse* 'female inhabitant of Amsterdam'). In a sentence with a female subject, this form must be used in predicative position (*Amsterdammer* is the unmarked inhabitative):

(103)   Zij is een Amsterdamse/*Amsterdammer 'She is an inhabitant of Amsterdam'

In other words, this looks like a case of derivational gender agreement (cf. van Marle 1996).[16] However, it is not certain that this is a case of syntactic agreement, since we can use the neutral form in a sentence like:[17]

(104)   Zij is net als hij een Amsterdammer 'She is, just like him, an Amsterdammer'

Hence, derivational agreement is not such a strong argument against Anderson's criterion.

Finally, it has been assumed that there are psycholinguistic differences between inflection and derivation: outputs of derivational processes will be readily stored, whereas inflectional forms need not be stored and can be made ad hoc because they are transparent and formed by productive processes. However, there is internal linguistic evidence for storage of certain types of inflectional forms, in particular of plural nouns and of the different stems of the irregular verbs. In this respect inflection and derivation

---

[16] Cf. Christofidou *et al.* (1990) for a similar case of gender agreement.
[17] Jack Hoeksema, personal communication.

2.5. INFLECTION AND WORD FORMATION

appear to differ only gradually. In addition, there is also external, psycholinguistic evidence for storage of regular inflected forms (cf. Baayen, Dijkstra, and Schreuder 1997).

In conclusion, in many respects inflection and derivation form a continuum, and therefore there is no sharp functional distinction between the two. Nevertheless, we do need this distinction because it is the stem form of the lexeme, without the inflectional endings, that normally functions as the basis for derivation.

The necessity of a formal distinction between inflection and derivation has led some morphologists to assume 'split morphology', the hypothesis that inflection and derivation belong to different modules of the grammar (Perlmutter 1988, Anderson 1992). Derivation then belongs to the presyntactic word-formation module, whereas inflectional processes are accounted for in a postsyntactic module of inflectional rules that spell out the morphosyntactic properties of each word. These properties are partially assigned by rules of agreement, on the basis of the syntactic configuration in which the word occurs (for instance, the number feature of verbs is a copy of that of the subject). Note, however, that agreement phenomena do not force us to assume that inflection is post-syntactic. It is also possible to assume that fully inflected words are inserted into syntactic structure. Agreement conditions will then check the compatibility between features in the relevant syntactic positions.

The basic argument in favour of split morphology is that it expresses the generalization that inflection is peripheral to derivation. The peripherality of inflection is one of Greenberg's (1963: 93) universals:

(105)   *Universal 28.* If both the derivation and the inflection follow the root, or they both precede the root, the derivation is always between the root and the inflection.

Although this is a correct generalization, it does not mean that such a generalization has to be expressed by the organization of the grammar. Note that the split morphology hypothesis does not account for the equally important generalization that contextual inflection is peripheral to inherent inflection. There are also more specific tendencies in the order of inflectional morphemes that are not expressed by split morphology. For instance, Bybee (1985: 35) established the following ordering of verbal inflectional markers:

(106)   stem–aspect–tense–mood–number–person

Dutch is in conformity with this generalization, as the data in this chapter show.

A problem for split morphology is that some kinds of inherent inflection do interact with derivation: they feed derivation (and, more generally, word-formation).[18] For instance, participles feed deadjectival word formation such as prefixation with the negative prefix *on-* '-un-'. However, in the case of present participles, it is the subclass of present participles that have lexicalized to adjectives that feed word formation. Therefore, they do not form a clear case of inflection feeding derivation. In the case of passive participles feeding word formation, on the other hand, lexicalization into adjectives is not a precondition. A derivational suffix like *-heid* '-ness' freely takes these participles, and their adjectival interpretation is a matter of type coercion: it is the suffix that requires them to be adjectives. Moreover, regular and transparent comparative forms of adjectives are sometimes used in deadjectival word formation, and plural nouns in *-en* are used as bases for the collective suffix *-dom* 'state of, group of' and the suffix *-achtig* '-like' (and also within compounds, as we will see in Chapter 4). This possibility is excluded by the split morphology hypothesis. The following examples illustrate the claim that certain kinds of inherent inflection may feed word formation:

(107)   *Passive participles*
        aangepast 'adjusted'   aangepast-heid 'adjustedness'
        gesloten 'closed'   gesloten-heid 'closedness'
        gestuurd 'controlled'   on-gestuurd 'uncontrolled'
        verteerd 'digested'   on-verteerd 'undigested'

        Comparatives
        beter 'better'   ver-beter 'to improve'
        erger 'worse'   ver-erger 'to worsen'
        ouder 'older'   ouder-dom 'old age'

        Plural nouns
        boeken 'books'   boeken-achtig 'bookish'
        helden 'heroes'   helden-dom 'heroism'
        leerlingen 'pupils'   leerlingen-dom 'the group of pupils'

[18] For examples and discussion of this phenomenon in other languages, see Booij (1994, 1996), Chapman (1996), Rainer (1996), and Cetnarowska (2000).

2.5. INFLECTION AND WORD FORMATION

Infinitives

nalaten 'to leave'	nalaten-schap 'heritage'
wedden 'to bet'	wedden-schap 'bet'
weten 'to know'	weten-schap 'science'

The infinitival forms in these examples function as nouns, since *-schap* requires nominal bases; this is in conformity with our observation that infinitives have nominal properties.

Contextual inflection never feeds derivation. This follows from its nature: it does not express independent semantic or grammatical information, and hence it makes no sense to include it as part of a complex word. As to the category Tense, which I qualified as inherent inflection, we do not find tensed forms that feed word formation. For instance, we cannot coin the compound *werkte-vrouw* 'former charwoman' besides *werkvrouw* 'charwoman'. This may be related to the deictic nature of Tense: deictic categories never appear inside words, or else lose their deictic properties in such positions. For instance, the Dutch pronoun *wij* 'we' can be used in the compound *wij-gevoel* 'lit. we-feeling, corporate identity'. In this use, *wij* has lost its deictic properties, and therefore a sentence such as

(108) Zij hebben een slecht ontwikkeld wij-gevoel 'They have a badly developed we-feeling'

is well-formed, although the subject of this sentence is third person.

In sum, the interaction between certain kinds of inherent inflection and derivation suggests that the split morphology hypothesis is incorrect. This does not mean, however, that the distinction between inflection and derivation is a matter of degree: there is a functional continuum, but there is a formal reason for maintaining the distinction: it is stems, and not fully inflected words, that normally form the input for word formation.

3

Derivation

3.1. INTRODUCTION

Derivation can be defined as the formation of new lexemes by means of affixation: the attachment of bound morphemes to the stem forms of lexemes. The word classes that can be extended by derivation are the open or lexical classes of a language: nouns, verbs, adjectives and adverbs. In this chapter, I will present a survey and analysis of the derivation patterns of Dutch, a language that makes use of both prefixation and suffixation (but not of infixation). In addition, this chapter will also deal with conversion, the change of word class without any overt phonological change, because, as we will see, conversion is functionally similar to derivation. Before entering upon a more detailed analysis of the different affixation patterns, I will discuss a number of theoretical preliminaries and issues with respect to derivation.[1]

3.2. THEORETICAL PRELIMINARIES

As we saw in Section 2.5, an important property of derivation is that it can change the word class of the input lexeme. The inputs for a particular derivational process are often of one particular lexical category (N, V, or A), and the outputs are also of a specific lexical category. There is also derivation in which the lexical category of the output word is the same as that of the input word. However, in such cases it may still be the case that input and output differ in lexical subcategory. For instance, intransitive verbs can become transitive verbs, and non-neuter nouns may be changed into neuter nouns. Below, the nine possibilities are illustrated:

---

[1] See also Fleischer (2000), Iacobini (2000), and Naumann and Vogel (2000) for a discussion of a number of theoretical issues with respect to derivation.

3.2. THEORETICAL PRELIMINARIES

(1)
A → N	*suffixation*	schoon-heid 'beauty'	< schoon 'beautiful'
V → N	*suffixation*	sprek-er 'speaker'	< spreek 'to speak'
	prefixation	ge-praat 'talking'	< praat 'to talk'
N → N	*suffixation*	moeder-schap 'motherhood'	< moeder 'mother'
N → A	*suffixation*	meester-lijk 'masterly'	< meester 'master'
V → A	*suffixation*	lees-baar 'readable'	< lees 'to read'
A → A	*suffixation*	blauw-ig 'bluish'	< blauw 'blue'
	prefixation	on-gewoon 'uncommon'	< gewoon 'common'
N → V	*suffixation*	analys-eer 'to analyse'	< analyse 'analysis'
	prefixation	ver-slaaf 'to enslave'	< slaaf 'slave'
A → V	*suffixation*	kalm-eer 'to calm down'	< kalm 'calm'
	prefixation	ver-bleek 'to turn pale'	< bleek 'pale'
V → V	*suffixation*	krabb-el 'to scratch'	< krab 'to scratch'
	prefixation	be-rijd 'to ride on'	< rijd 'to ride'

As this survey shows, there is an asymmetry between suffixation and prefixation: suffixation can be used for all types of category change, whereas prefixation is not always available for this purpose. In other words, there is a tendency for prefixation to be category-neutral, whereas suffixation is often category-changing. As to adverbs, they form a restricted category in this respect, since they do not function as inputs, but can be derived from adjectives by means of suffixation, for instance *hog-elijk* 'highly' from *hoog* 'high'.

This asymmetry between prefixation and suffixation has led some students of Dutch morphology to adopt the so-called Righthand Head Rule (RHR), proposed for English by Williams (1981), as a principle that is also valid for Dutch. This rule says that the rightmost constituent of a complex word is the head of that word, and hence determines the syntactic (sub)category of the complex word. Thus, it is predicted that suffixes are category-determing, and prefixes are not.

The RHR presupposes that in a complex word one of its constituents can be qualified as its head, which means that it is this constituent that determines the syntactic category and subcategory of the complex word. For instance, in the adjective *leesbaar* 'readable' it is the deverbal suffix *-baar* that determines the adjectival nature of this word. Hence, *-baar* can be qualified as the head of this word. As far as denominal nominalizing suffixes are concerned, they are category-determining although they do not change the syntactic category. They do determine the syntactic subcategory of their outputs, in particular gender. For instance, diminutive denominal nouns are always neuter, whatever the gender of the base noun, as shown in (1) by the pair *(de) moeder – (het) moederschap*.

There is, however, some doubt if the notion 'head', which is essential in the analysis of syntactic structure, and also has to play a role in a proper account of compounding (cf. Chapter 4), is an insightful notion for the analysis of derivation. In syntax, the notion 'head' is defined quite differently, not in terms of location (left or right), but in terms of structure: the head of an XP is the X^0 of that XP. In the analysis of compounds, the most syntax-like kind of word formation, the notion 'head' has the advantage that a substantial set of properties of the whole compound is predicted on the basis of the independently determinable properties of one of its constituents, its head, which also occurs as an independent word. In the case of affixes, on the contrary, there is no independently given specification of its categorial value, and hence we first have to encode the categorial properties on that affix, which are then percolated (cf. Lieber 1989) to the dominating node of the whole complex word.[2]

As the data in (1) show, there is counterevidence to the RHR: the nominalizing prefix *ge-* and a number of verbalizing prefixes have category-changing power (cf. Sections 3.3. and 6.2).[3] Thus, the RHR is not a valid generalization with respect to affixation. As for compounding, it will be argued in Chapter 4 that it is possible to interpret the location of the head as a parameter, to be fixed for each language, but there is certainly not a universal rule of right-headedness for compounds. What remains true, however, is that in Dutch all suffixes (but not all prefixes) are category-determining. Verbalizing suffixes also determine the syntactic valency of the complex verb,

---

[2] Bauer (1990) gives a critical discussion of the notion 'head' in morphology.

[3] The relevance of the RHR for Dutch is defended by Trommelen and Zonneveld (1986). They are, however, forced to introduce certain ad hoc rules in order to cope with the cases of category-changing prefixation. Another attempt to save the RHR as a generalization for Dutch is Neeleman and Schipper (1993) which also deals with the class of category-changing prefixes. The RHR is also problematic for English since it has category-determining prefixes such as *en-*, as in *to enthrone*. Furthermore, in Italian, there are category-neutral suffixes, contary to what is predicted by a universal interpretation of the RHR. For example, the Italian diminutive suffix *-ino* derives Ns from Ns (*ragazzo* 'boy' – *ragazzino* 'little boy'), and As from As (*bello* 'beautiful' – *bellino* 'nice').

3.2. THEORETICAL PRELIMINARIES

and nominalizing suffixes the gender of the resulting noun, and in some cases the choice of its plural suffix (cf. Section 2.2).

Can each derivational process be defined in term of a unique lexical category for both input and output? As far as input category is concerned, the answer is no. First, there are some very productive affixes that take more kinds of bases, sometimes even from non-lexical categories (van Marle 1981). Such affixes will be referred to as polyfunctional affixes. An example is the diminutive suffix. Although most of its bases are nominal, it may incidentally also take adjectives and verbs as inputs, and even intransitive prepositions (used as adverbs):

(2) | Category | Base | *Diminutive* |
|---|---|---|
| N | vrouw 'woman' | vrouw-tje 'small woman, sweetheart' |
| A | lief 'sweet' | lief-je 'sweatheart' |
| V | dut 'to nap' | dut-je 'nap' |
| Num | tien 'ten' | tien-tje 'ten-guilder note' |
| P/Adv | uit 'out' | uit-je 'outing' |
| NP | twaalf uur '12 o'clock' | twaalfuur-tje 'wrapped lunch' |
| PP | onder ons 'between us' | onderons-je 'private chat' |
| Det | dit en dat 'this and that' | dit-jes en dat-jes 'odds and ends' |

It is only with nominal bases that diminutive formation is very productive (in the quantitative sense), but its productivity also manifests itself in the occasional extension of diminutive affixation to words of other categories. As van Marle (1981) observed, the bases from other lexical categories are typically simplex words: we hardly find diminutives based on complex verbs or adjectives (an exception is *dubbeldikje* 'double thick ice cream' from *dubbeldik* 'double thick' but this example is taken from the creative language used in advertisements, where we often find exceptional formations).

A second source of this kind of polyfunctionality is reinterpretation. The base of an existing complex word may be assigned another lexical category than its original one, and subsequently other complex words are coined according to this new structural interpretation. Thus, the suffix *-baar*, originally denominal, as in *vruchtbaar* 'lit. fruit-bearing, fruitful' < *vrucht* 'fruit', became deverbal through reinterpretation of words like *strijdbaar* 'militant' (where *strijd* 'fight' can be either a noun or a verb), and this is the use in which this suffix is now productive.[4] In other words, in its productive use the suffix -*baar* is monofunctional.

Another example is the suffix -*schap*. This suffix can be attached productively to nouns referring to persons, and creates neuter nouns with the meaning 'the function of being N'. In addition, there are closed sets of non-neuter nouns in -*schap* based on either nouns or adjectives, and with different meanings, 'the set of Ns' and 'the property of being A' respectively:

(3) broeder 'brother'   (het) broederschap 'being a brother'
                           (de) broederschap 'fraternity'
     zwanger 'pregnant'   (de) zwangerschap 'pregnancy'

The fact that the suffix -*schap* creates different subcategories of nouns (neuter and non-neuter nouns) correlating with different meanings of -*schap* suggests that this is not a straightforward case of one polyfunctional suffix. We have to conclude that there are two suffixes -*schap*.

There are also affixes that attach productively to words of more than one category, and this may correlate with differences in meaning contribution of the affix. For instance, the adjectival suffix -*achtig* attaches to nouns, adjectives, and verbs, with different though related meanings. In addition, within its denominal use, -*achtig* allows for different interpretations, that is, it is also a polysemous affix:

(4) Base Meaning
     N   '-like'   aap-achtig 'monkey-like', metaal-achtig 'metal-like'
           'full of'   rots-achtig 'rocky'
           'liking'   pasta-achtig 'pasta liking'
     A   '-ish'   groen-achtig 'greenish', kaal-achtig 'baldish'
     V   'inclined to'   huichel-achtig 'hypocritical', vergeet-achtig 'forgetful'

Another example of polyfunctionality is the nominal suffix -*er* that attaches productively to both verbs and nouns, and creates personal nouns. The difference in meaning is that deverbal -*er* creates specifically subject names,

---

[4] Cf. van Marle (1988) and Hüning and van Santen (1994) on the history of -*baar*, and Fleischmann (1977) for a detailed study of the change in category of the inputs of -*age* in French and English.

nouns that refer to the subject of the base verb, whereas denominal *-er* is used for creating all kinds of personal nouns:

(5) base V   et-er 'eater', lop-er 'walker'
    base N   Amsterdamm-er 'inhabitant of Amsterdam',
             wetenschapp-er 'scientist'

In sum, affixes may exhibit polyfunctionality, and there can be meaning differences that correlate with the difference in lexical category of the base word.[5] However, polyfunctionality and polysemy are independent phenomena; as pointed out by Hüning (1999: 232), an affix can be polysemous across categories, and exhibit the same range of polysemy for all types of base words. The nominalzing suffix *-erij*, for instance, can be used with verbal and nominal bases, but in both uses the resulting noun can be an action noun or refers to the place/institution where the action takes place.

3.2.1. *Input restrictions*

As we saw above, a first formal characterization of a derivation process is the specification of its input and output category. In addition to these word-class restrictions, there might be other kinds of restrictions on the bases that can be used in a derivational process, which thus reduce the number of possible inputs, and hence the quantitative productivity of such a word-formation process. These restrictions can be phonological, morphological, lexical, syntactic, semantic, or pragmatic in nature.

As to phonological restrictions, affixes may impose requirements on the phonological shape of their bases. For instance, the suffix *-aar*' *-er*' can only be attached to stems ending in a coronal sonorant consonant (cf. Section 5.4).

An example of a morphological restriction is that suffixed nouns cannot function as inputs for denominal *-ig* suffixation (Booij and van Santen 1998: 56):

---

[5] These facts seem to pose a problem for the Uniform Base Hypothesis proposed in Aronoff (1976: 48) which claims that each word-formation process has a unique syntactic specification of the base. This hypothesis pertains to productive uses of derivational affixes only. As Aronoff (1976: 48, fn. 3) points out there are ways of defining, for instance, N and A as a single class, by means of the feature [–V], but with such a feature system it is not possible to define N, V, and A as a single class. The only way to maintain the hypothesis is then to assume homophonous affixes, one for each class of input words. This is not a trivial solution because it expresses what is perhaps a correct generalization: the meaning contribution of an affix varies with the class of the words to which it is attached.

(6) nuf 'prim'   nuff-ig 'prim, affected'
    sinterklaas 'Santa Claus' sinterklaz-ig 'Santa Claus-like'
    vijand 'enemy'   vijand-ig 'hostile'
    but:
    held-in 'heroine'   *heldinn-ig
    schol-ier 'pupil'   *scholier-ig
    viol-ist 'violinist'   *violist-ig

Another possible example of an input restriction is that the diminutive suffix -*tje* cannot be attached to nouns ending in certain schwa-final suffixes such as *blind-e* 'blind person' – **blindetje* and *kampioen-e* 'female champion' – **kampioenetje*, *ge-berg-te* 'mountains' – **ge-berg-te-tje* (de Haas and Trommelen 1993: 282), whereas there are other nouns ending in schwa that do allow for diminutive formation, such as *machinetje* 'machine', dim. (although some speakers of Dutch may prefer *machientje*, with deletion of the stem-final schwa). Therefore, this restriction cannot be a phonological restriction. The status of this restriction is, however, not so clear. As to nouns in *-e*, it appears that the suffix *-e* functions generally as a closing suffix, i.e. it blocks further derivational suffixation, and hence the formation of diminutive nouns. Hence, this is probably not a specific restriction on diminutive formation. In other cases, the lack of a diminutive noun may have to do with the semantics or pragmatics of the relevant words. For instance, the semantic appropriateness and pragmatic usefulness of the diminutive noun *gebergtetje* are not very obvious. Therefore, it requires careful argumentation to show that a restriction on input words is really morphological in nature.[6]

A more general tendency concerning the morphological complexity of base words is that derivational processes are not recursive, that is, do not apply to their own outputs. For instance, we do not find adjectives like *groen-ig-ig* 'green-ish-ish'. One might reason that this is not to be seen as a formal

---

[6] As observed by Krott, Schreuder, and Baayen (1999), there is a general tendency for complex words to be underrepresented as bases of (more) complex words. They conclude on the basis of facts concerning Dutch word formation that it is short and highly frequent words that are mostly used in word formation, which generally reduces the chance of complex words occurring as constituents of complex words since they are not so short and frequent as simplex words. In other words, there is also an external, psycholinguistic explanation available for the restriction to morphologically simplex base words, and this makes it hard to determine whether we really need specific morphological restrictions on base words in the grammar of Dutch.

restriction, since it is not clear what kind of meaningful use would be available for such an adjective. This semantic/pragmatic interpretation of the restriction on recursivity seems to be supported by the observation that in languages such as Afrikaans and Polish we do find double diminutives:

(7) *Afrikaans* huis 'house'   huis-ie 'little house'   huis-ie-tjie 'dear little house'
    Polish   kot 'cat'   kot-ek 'pussy-cat'   kot-eč-ek 'dear pussy-cat'

In these cases, the double use of the diminutive suffix makes sense because this suffix can also express endearment, in addition to small size. In Dutch, however, the diminutive suffix can also be used as an endearment suffix, and nevertheless such double diminutives are impossible. This implies that we do need a formal prohibition on recursivity to account for such restrictions.

Semantic restrictions rather than morphological restrictions appear to be at stake when we look at the deadjectival negative prefix *on-* 'un-'; there are different sets of adjectives to which this prefix cannot be attached, for instance colour adjectives, words that denote an absolute, non-gradable property such as *zwanger* 'pregnant' and *dood* 'dead', adjectives with a negative meaning such as *arm* 'poor', and adjectives in *-loos* '-less' (a subset of the adjectives with a negative meaning):

(8) ademloos 'breathless'   *on-ademloos
    diep 'deep'   on-diep 'shallow'
    handig 'dexterous'   on-handig 'clumsy'
    zinloos 'meaningless'   *on-zinloos

It is a semantic restriction that *on-* does not attach to adjectives with a component of negative meaning since this prefix is also not used in combination with simplex adjectives with negative meanings such as *dom* 'stupid, not clever' and *lelijk* 'ugly, not beautiful'. In other words, we do not have to assume a specific morphological restriction that *on-* does not attach to adjectives ending in *-loos*. Note, however, that this remains a semantic restriction on the class of base words that *on-* takes, and does not follow from a general semantic incompatibility of the negative meaning of the prefix *on-* with negative expressions: a phrase like *niet onhandig* 'not clumsy', with a combination of two negative elements, is semantically fully correct. The double negative construction even serves to make a normally unacceptable *on*-adjective usable: *onknap* 'un-handsome' is normally not used, but does occur with *niet*, as in *Mijn buurman is niet onknap* 'My neighbour is not unhandsome'. Moreover, each adjective can be turned into its contradictory counterpart by means of the negative prefix *niet-* 'not', and if it is non-native by means of the prefix *non-* 'id.'.

The classical example for Dutch of a syntactic restriction on derivation is that the deverbal suffix *-baar* '-able' only attaches to transitive verbs, at least in its productive use. This restriction is obviously directly related to the meaning contribution of this suffix, 'being able to be V-ed', a meaning that can only be applied to a base verb that is transitive.

As to pragmatic restrictions: a complex word will not be coined if there is no use for it, although it would be formally possible. For instance, the diminutive of *gevaar* 'danger', *gevaartje*, is not a concept that we will often need, and hence such a word will not be readily coined, though it is a possible diminutive. We might therefore say that it is a possible but not a probable complex word (cf. van Santen (1992*a*) who advocates the distinction between the notions 'possible word' and 'probable word').

The formal and semantic restrictions discussed so far are negative restrictions that seem to be absolute restrictions. If they are indeed absolute, they form part of the definition of the notion 'possible complex word'. However, as argued by Mackenzie (1985*a*), restrictions may also be violable. This means that in that case they define the prototypical cases of a word-formation type only. For instance, Mackenzie observed that deverbal *ge-*nominalization applies preferably to simplex verbs (as in *ge-huil* 'crying'), but that base verbs with a particle or a prefix are not absolutely impossible (for example *opgebel* 'making phone-calls' < *opbellen* 'to phone', *geverhuis* 'moving' < *verhuizen* 'to move'). This also means that the words of the different subsets will differ as to the probability of their use.

Lexical restrictions mainly pertain to the layer of the lexicon from which base words can be taken. They are discussed in the next subsection. As we will see there, they can also be violated, sometimes with special effects.

3.2.2. *Stratal restrictions*

Stratal restrictions are a specific kind of lexical restrictions related to the division of the Dutch lexicon into two layers or strata, a native (Germanic) layer, and a non-native (Romance) one. A general restriction on the use of

3.2. THEORETICAL PRELIMINARIES

suffixes of non-native origin is that they only attach to base words of non-native origin. In this respect, they differ from native suffixes, which can be used for both native and non-native stems.[7] This can be illustrated by the behaviour of the non-native suffix *-iteit* '-ity' that competes with the native suffix *-heid* '-ness':

(9) *Native stem*   blind 'blind'   blind-heid 'blindness'   *blind-iteit

                      doof 'deaf'   doof-heid 'deafness'   *dov-iteit

     Non-native stem   stabiel 'stable'   stabiel-heid 'stableness'   stabil-iteit 'stability'

                      divers 'diverse'   divers-heid 'diversity'   divers-iteit 'diversity'

Occasionally, we find words in *-iteit* derived from native adjectives, such as *stommiteit* 'stupidity' (< *stom* 'stupid') and *flauwiteit* 'silly comment' (< *flauw* 'silly'). Such coinings can also be used to create a jocular effect, or a pejorative effect (as in the use of the non-native suffix *-oot* in *malloot* 'idiot', from the native adjective *mal* 'mad'). Other examples are *arbeiderisme* 'proletarianism' (< *arbeider* 'worker'), *veralgemeniseren* 'to generalize' (< *algemeen* 'general') and *endemolliseren* 'to turn into commercial TV' (< *endemol* 'clipping name of a commercial TV company').

Many of the non-native complex words of Dutch have not actually been coined by means of attachment of a non-native suffix to a non-native stem: they have been borrowed (and sometimes slightly adapted) from the Romance lexicon which has the function of a pan-European lexical stock, used intensively by the different European languages. Such words might also have been created on the basis of analogy to other non-native words. Typically, these complex words belong to a high register of language use in which metalinguistic awareness of word structure plays a role that may lead to new coinings by language users.

In the case of unproductive derivational patterns, the native–non-native distinction also has a role to play, namely in accounting for the distribution of these non-native suffixes. A number of these non-native suffixes can be

---

[7] A similar asymmetry between native and non-native suffixes has been observed for English in Bloomfield (1933: 252): 'Normal roots combine with normal affixes, learned roots with learned affixes.'

used productively, for instance *-eer*, *-esk*, *-iaan*, *-isch*, *-iseer*, *-isme*, *-ist*, and *-iteit*. However, as pointed out above, the use of such derived non-native words is restricted to specific registers of written language. Their productive nature also manifests itself in the fact that they can be attached to proper names of, for instance, scientists, philosophers, writers, and countries. In this case, it does not even matter if the base word is native or non-native, but these words do keep an intentional flavour:

(10) Schultink (Dutch morphologist)   Schultink-iaan 'follower of Schultink'
      Finland 'id.'   Finland-iseer 'to Finlandize'
      Bruegel 'id.'   Bruegel-esk 'Bruegel-like'

In this respect, the denominal adjectival suffix *-isch* has a special status. It is not a suffix of Romance, but of Germanic origin, and used very productively in German. It behaves as a non-native suffix in that it combines very easily with non-native stems. On the other hand, it is also used for making geographical adjectives from geographical nouns with a native shape, for instance *Belgisch* < *België* 'Belgium' and *Normandisch* < *Normandië* 'Normandy'. In this use, the coinings are felt as native words, without a marked status. Hence, the status of the suffix *-isch* appears to be a hybrid one, since it is used in both the native and the non-native domain (Heynderickx and van Marle 1994).

The non-native suffixes play a prominent role in paradigmatic word formation whereby a non-native suffix is replaced with another one, based on a network of relations between non-native complex words (Section 1.3).

The suffixes listed in Table 3.1 also occur in complex words with a base that does not occur as an independent word, i.e. after roots. For instance, the suffix *-aal* occurs after roots, as in *feder-aal* 'federal' and *radic-aal* 'radical'. In addition, there are a number of non-native suffixes that (almost) only co-occur with roots; obviously, the complex words with these suffixes have been borrowed, or created paradigmatically. But this may equally well apply to those complex words for which a corresponding base word happens to exist: the existence of a corresponding base word does not prove that a complex word has been derived directly from this base word in Dutch rather than borrowed directly. A sample of such 'root suffixes' is given in Table 3.2.

In many cases the base of a non-native suffix has a form that is different from the corresponding lexeme. For instance, the adjective *vir-aal* 'viral' can be said to have the lexeme *virus* 'id.' as its base, since *vir-* can be considered

TABLE 3.1. *Non-native suffixes*

Suffix	Base	Base word	Output	Derived word
-aal	N	synode 'synod'	A	synod-aal 'synodical'
-aan	N	parochie 'parish'	N	parochi-aan 'parishioner'
-aat	N	doctor 'doctor'	Nn	doctor-aat 'doctorate'
-air	N	hypotheek 'mortgage'	A	hypothek-air 'mortgage-'
-ant	V	predik 'to preach'	N	predik-ant 'clergyman'
-aris	N	bibliotheek 'library'	N	bibliothec-aris 'librarian'
-ast	N	gymnasium 'grammar school'	N	gymnasi-ast 'grammar-school pupil'
-atie	V	organiseer 'to organize'	N	organis-atie 'organization'
-eel	N	fundament 'fundament'	A	fundament-eel 'fundamental'
-eer	N	parfum 'perfume'	V	parfum-eer 'to perfume'
-ees	N	Taiwan 'id.'	N	Taiwan-ees 'Taiwanese'
-ein	N	republiek 'republic'	N	republik-ein 'republican'
-erie	N	parfum 'perfume'	N	parfum-erie 'perfume shop'
-esk	N	ballade 'ballad'	A	ballad-esk 'ballad-like'
-esse	N	secretaris 'secretary'	N	secretar-esse 'secretary', fem.
-ette	N	opera 'id.'	N	oper-ette 'operetta'
-eur	N	ambassade 'embassy'	N	ambassad-eur 'ambassador'
-eus	N	rancune 'rancour'	A	rancun-eus 'rancorous'
-iaan	N	presbyter 'id.'	N	presbyter-iaan 'presbyterian'
-ide	N	broom 'bromine'	N	brom-ide 'bromide'
-ief	N	agressie 'aggression'	A	agress-ief 'aggressive'
-ier	N	juweel 'jewel'	N	juwel-ier 'jeweller'
-iet	N	metropool 'metropolis'	N	metropol-iet 'metropolitan'
-ieus	N	mode 'fashion'	A	mod-ieus 'fashionable'
-ine	A	blond 'id.'	N	blond-ine 'blonde'
-isch	N	algebra 'id.'	A	algebra-isch 'algebraic'
-iseer	A	banaal 'banal'	V	banal-iseer 'to banalize'
-isme	A	absurd 'id.'	Nn	absurd-isme 'absurdism'
-ist	N	propaganda 'id.'	N	propagand-ist 'id.'
-iteit	A	absurd 'id.'	N	absurd-iteit 'absurdity'
-oir	N	emancipatie 'emancipation'	A	emancipat-oir 'emancipatory'
	N	urine 'urine'	Nn	urin-oir 'urinal'
-oot	N	psyche 'id.'	N	psych-oot 'psychotic'

as an allomorph of *virus* (cf. Section 5.3.2). In other words, in such cases the complex word can still be considered to be lexeme-based.

The term 'non-native' is not meant to suggest that all native speakers of

Dutch know the historical origin of these stems, roots, and suffixes, but suggests that the foreignness of such words is recognizable. There are phonological cues for being non-native: non-native stems contain often at least two full vowels, unlike native stems, and non-native suffixes bear the main stress of the word, always contain a full vowel, and are always vowel-initial (cf. Section 5.3 and van Heuven, Neijt, and Hijzelendoorn 1994). One should realize, however, that it is not always possible to classify a suffix as either non-native or native. This applies, for instance, to the suffix *-age* '-age' which is historically non-native but has been introduced into Dutch at such an early stage that it also combines with native stems (compare *percent-age* 'percent-age', *percent* 'per cent' to *lekk-age* 'leakage', the latter with a native verbal base *lek* 'to leak'). Another example is the suffix *-ier*: *brigad-ier* 'constable' has been derived from the non-native noun *brigade* 'id.', but *winkel-ier* 'shop keeper' from the native noun *winkel* 'shop'.

Prefixes can also be divided in native and non-native ones, but there are only few historically non-native prefixes that attach to non-native bases

TABLE 3.2. *Non-native root suffixes*

Suffix	Output	Example
-abel	A	accept-abel 'acceptable'
-ade	N	seren-ade 'id.'
-ans	N	stimul-ans 'incentive'
-arius	N	ordinar-ius 'full professor'
-asme	Nn	sarc-asme 'sarcasm'
-een	N	Chil-een 'Chilean'
-ement	Nn	rend-ement 'profit'
-ent	N	doc-ent 'teacher'
-et	Nn	kwart-et 'quartet'
-ica	N	fanat-ica 'fanatic', fem.
-icus	N	fanat-icus 'fanatic'
-ie	N	agress-ie 'aggression'
-íe	N	fonolog-ie 'phonology'
-iek	N	fonet-iek 'phonetics'
-iek	A	fanat-iek 'fanatic'
-ijn	N	Argent-ijn 'Argentinian'
-ioen	Nn	vis-ioen 'vision'
-is	N	bas-is 'base'
-itis	N	bronch-itis 'id.'

3.2. THEORETICAL PRELIMINARIES

only. An example is the negative prefix *in-* which can be contrasted to its native counterpart *on-*:

(11) *Non-native bases*
    humaan 'human'   in-humaan 'inhuman'   on-humaan 'inhuman'
    stabiel 'stable'   in-stabiel 'unstable'   on-stabiel 'unstable'
    Native bases
    aardig 'nice'   *in-aardig   on-aardig 'not nice'
    gezond 'healthy'   *in-gezond   on-gezond 'unhealthy'

Other prefixes that behave in this way are the negative prefixes *a-* (as in *a-sociaal* 'anti-social') and *non-* (as in *non-verbaal* 'non-verbal'), and the prefix *de-* 'id.' (as in *de-centraal* 'decentralized'). However, most of the historically non-native prefixes attach to both non-native and native stems. Table 3.3 illustrates this for native base words.

TABLE 3.3. *Borrowed prefixes with native bases*

Prefix	Example
anti- 'id.'	anti-godsdienstig 'anti-religious'
co- 'co-'	co-ouderschap 'shared parentage after divorce'
contra- 'id.'	contra-gewicht 'counterweight'
ex- 'former'	ex-man 'former husband'
hyper- 'id.'	hyper-gevoelig 'hypersensitive'
infra- 'id.'	infra-rood 'infrared'
loco- 'vice-'	loco-burgemeester 'vice-mayor'
meta- 'id.'	meta-taal 'metalanguage'
micro- 'id.'	micro-golf 'microwave'
mono- 'id.'	mono-rail 'id.'
neo- 'id.'	neo-gereformeerd 'neo-protestant'
pre- 'id.'	pre-pensioen 'early retirement'
pro- 'id.'	pro-apartheid 'pro-apartheid'
pseudo- 'id.'	pseudo-wetenschap 'pseudo-science'
semi- 'id.'	semi-overheid 'semi-government'
sub- 'id.'	sub-groep 'subgroup'
super- 'id.'	super-gaaf 'very nice'
turbo- 'super'	turbo-koe 'very productive cow'
ultra- 'id.'	ultra-zacht 'very soft'
vice- 'id.'	vice-voorzitter 'vice-chairman'

The list of prefixes in Table 3.3 is not exhaustive because, in addition to borrowed Greek and Latin prefixes, many non-native roots now function as prefixes (also called 'affixoids' because of their lexical origin), for example *pseudo-* and *macro-*. We might, for instance, consider the roots *euro-* and *tele-* as prefixes, since they productively combine with both native and non-native stems, as in *euro-beleid* 'europolicy' and *tele-ingenieur* 'telecommunications engineer'. Morphemes such as *tele* have also been called 'combining forms' or 'confixes' because they need some morphological complement in order to be usable.

The explanation for this 'promiscuous' behaviour of the non-native prefixes is that they form prosodic words of their own (cf. Section 5.2), and hence have a word-like appearance. Thus, these prefix–word combinations are similar to compounds, which can consist of a non-native and a native word. Some of these prefixes have also developed into lexemes:

(12) Jan is anti *'lit.* John is anti, John does not agree'
 Mijn ex 'my ex, my former husband/wife'
 Deze biefstuk is super 'This steak is super'
 Je moet dit macro bekijken 'You have to consider this at a macro-level'

Non-native prefixes are also found in complex words with a non-native root that is not a lexeme, as in *ex-cuseer* 'to excuse' and *sub-versief* 'subversive'. If non-native affixes are used as root affixes, i.e. without a lexematic base, we consider these words as formally complex words. There are two reasons for assigning them internal morphological structure. First, in the case of suffixed words, the suffix is the determiner of the word class of the word, and hence the word class of such words is predictable if we represent them as complex words. This applies to an adjective such as *subversief* 'subversive' in which the ending *-ief* is a predictor of its adjectival nature. Secondly, their internal structure is revealed by the networks of words in which they participate. For instance, in *reductie* 'reduction' we recognize *re-* as a morphological constituent because the root *ductie* also appears in *productie* 'production', *inductie* 'induction', *deductie* 'deduction', etc. And in *fanat-iek* 'fanatic' we recognize a root *fanat* and hence a suffix *-iek* because the root *fanat* recurs in the related words *fanat-isme* 'fanaticism' and *fanat-icus* 'fanatic'.

When a complex word contains both non-native and native suffixes, the order of these suffixes is always such that the non-native suffix precedes the native suffix. This follows from the fact that non-native suffixes only attach to non-native stems. As we saw above, it is the suffix that determines the subcategory to which a word belongs. Hence, if the last suffix of a complex word is [−native], the whole word will be [−native]. I will assume therefore that this feature is percolated from the suffix to the dominating node of the complex word. When the last suffix is [+native], the whole word will then be [+native], and hence will not be available for non-native suffixation. The important theoretical implication of this account is that we do not need the mechanism of level-ordering (with the level of non-native affixation ordered before that of native affixation) for morphological purposes.[8]

This account can also handle so-called morphological bracketing paradoxes. For instance, the noun *ongrammaticaliteit* 'ungrammaticality' has been derived from the adjective *ongrammaticaal* 'ungrammatical', and this adjective in its turn has been derived from *grammaticaal* 'grammatical'. That is, native affixation has preceded non-native affixation in this case. This is a problem in a theory of level ordering in which all non-native morphology is ordered before all native morphology. In the feature percolation approach outlined above, however, there is no problem: the adjective *ongrammaticaal* remains [−native] because the prefix *on-* is not category-determining, and hence does not make the word *ongrammaticaal* a native word. Therefore, it is still possible to attach the [−native] suffix *-iteit* to this complex adjective.

3.2.3. *Competition between derivational processes*

So far, we have seen that a particular word-formation process may be subject to restrictions on the class of base words. That is, the actual derivational domain of a derivational process may be limited, and the quantitative productivity of a word-formation process (the actual number of ouput words of that word-formation process) is thus inversely proportional to the number of restrictions on the class of input words.

In addition, we also have paradigmatic restrictions on word formation in the form of blocking effects. As pointed out in Section 1.4, there is token-

---

[8] This kind of level-ordering has been defended in early generative studies of English morphology; cf. Spencer (1991: 79 ff.). As shown in Booij (1995) there is also no phonological argument for level ordering of this kind. Other arguments for level ordering are discussed and rejected in Section 4.4. A general discussion of level-ordering can be found in Booij (2000c).

blocking and type-blocking. Here, we will focus on type-blocking, that is, on the competition between different word-formation processes with the same meaning contribution. According to van Marle (1985, 1986), a case of type-blocking in the realm of derivation is the competition between a set of suffixes that are all used for coining female personal nouns. Van Marle argued that all but one of these suffixes have a restricted derivational domain because they impose specific positive requirements on their base words, and that the remaining unrestricted default suffix *-e* applies to those personal nouns that do not belong to the derivational domain of one of the more restricted suffixes. That is, the use of the general suffix is blocked in those cases where a restricted suffix can be used. Some of these suffixes are actually more or less unproductive; the words with these suffixes form closed classes, in particular *-es* and *-in*. The occurrence of some of these female suffixes is directly correlated with the presence of a specific suffix in the base word.

This pattern of derivational possibilities for the formation of female personal names exhibits a number of interesting properties. First, we see that nouns in *-aar* have two possibilities: they allow for both *-es* and *-ster* as female suffix. A similar observation can be made for the choice between *-euse* and *-rice*: both can be used for creating the female counterparts of nouns in *-eur* (*monteur* 'technician' – *monteuse*, *conducteur* 'conductor' –

TABLE 3.4. *The formation of female personal nouns*

Suffix	On bases in	Male noun	Female noun
-e	—	fotograaf 'photographer'	fotograf-e
-es	—	voogd 'guardian'	voogd-es
	-aar	zond-aar 'sinner'	zondar-es
	-er	zang-er 'singer'	zanger-es
-esse	-aris	secret-aris 'secretary'	secretar-esse
-euse	-eur	mass-eur 'masseur'	mass-euse
-ica	-icus	historic-us 'historian'	historic-a
-ière	-ier	cabaret-ier 'id.'	cabaret-ière
-in	—	leeuw 'lion'	leeuw-in
-ix	-or	rect-or 'id.'	rect-rix
-rice	-eur	ambassad-eur 'ambassador'	ambassad-rice
-ster	-aar	wandel-aar 'walker'	wandelaar-ster
	-ier	winkel-ier 'shopkeeper'	winkelier-ster
	-er	VVD-er 'member of VVD'	VVD-ster

3.2. THEORETICAL PRELIMINARIES

conductrice). The choice between *-es* and *-in* is not governed by specific positive conditions, but they are unproductive anyway. That is, it is not the case that there is no competition at all between the restricted cases.

A second observation is that in most cases the choice of the female suffix is determined by the suffix of the base noun. This means, contra Anderson (1992), that the internal morphological structure of a complex word must remain accessible for further morphological operations, a conclusion that is in line with our findings in Section 2.4.3 concerning the formation of perfect participles which also requires access to the internal morphological structure of words.

Thirdly, in some cases of non-native derivation the formation of female nouns takes place by suffix substitution rather than suffix addition. As to *-ster*, this suffix is primarily deverbal, unlike the other ones; however, as shown in Section 1.3, speakers of Dutch tend to interpret this pattern as the substitution of *-er* with *-ster* after a nominal stem (cf. van Santen and de Vries 1981, van Marle 1985).

The claim that the suffix *-e* is the default female suffix is, however, too strong. Examples of the use of this suffix are the following words:

(13)   *Male personal noun*   *Female personal noun*
        doc-ent 'teacher'   docent-e
        echt-genoot 'spouse'   echtgenot-e
        gids 'guide'   gids-e
        labor-ant 'laboratory employee'   laborant-e
        predik-ant 'clergyman'   predikant-e
        typ-ist 'typist'   typist-e

This suffix can also be used for the formation of female inhabitant names; as will be discussed in Section 5.3.3, in this case the form of the base is special: not the male inhabitant name, but the corresponding geographical adjective. For instance, the female counterpart of *Amerikaan* 'American' is not *Amerikane* but *Amerikaanse*, derived from a stem that is formally identical to the adjective *Amerikaans* 'American', in its turn derived from the inhabitant name *Amerikaan* 'American'. (This has led to the emergence of a suffix *-se* for female inhabitative names, cf. Fast and van Marle 1989.)

In Table 3.4, three suffixes are listed that could also be split up: *-euse*, *-rice*, and *-ière*. They might be analysed as a suffix sequence, the suffix *-e* preceded by an allomorph of the suffixes *-eur* (*-eus*, *-ric*) and *-ier* (*-ièr*) respectively.

If this analysis is chosen, it implies that the choice for the female suffix -*e* is also determined by positive conditions on the base, the presence of a specific suffix. This is in line with a more general observation in the literature (cf. de Haas and Trommelen 1993: 232–3) that the suffix -*e* is in almost all cases attached to a suffixed noun. That is, the presence of a suffix is a precondition. Such an analysis clearly goes against the claim that the most generally usable suffix -*e* does not have positive conditions on its derivational domain. However, it might be argued that synchronically these three suffix sequences function as units, and substitute the final suffix of the corresponding male noun (van Marle 1990*b*).

The derivation of female personal nouns in Dutch is restricted anyway. There are many personal nouns for which a female counterpart does not exist, although it is perhaps not absolutely impossible to coin such nouns if the base word ends in a suffix. If there is no final suffix, as in *minister* 'id.', a female counterpart is simply impossible:

(14) aut-eur 'author'   ?auteur-e, ?auteus-e, ?autrice
      ingeni-eur 'engineer'   ?ingenieur-e, ?ingeni-eus-e
      minister 'id.'   *minister-e
      profess-or 'id.'   ?professor-e

Hence, personal nouns can be used for men and women alike, as in *Mevrouw de minister* 'Madam minister'. It is only in specific contexts that a neutral personal noun receives a specific male interpretation, for instance in the phrase *Schrijvers en schrijfsters* 'Writers and female writers' (cf. Becker (1997) for a semantic analysis of such cases in German).

On the other hand, a male suffixed noun in -*ant*, -*ent*, or -*ist* always allows for the derivation of a female counterpart in -*e* which suggest once more that this word-formation pattern is also subject to positive conditions on the morphological shape of its base words. Therefore, we have to conclude that the competition between different types of derivation does not imply that there is always one general affix whose derivational domain is only paradigmatically restricted.[9]

There are also competing affixes for which the choice between them has to be accounted for in terms of phonological output constraints instead of

---

[9] Van Marle (1986) points out that his domain hypothesis is meant primarily as a heuristic hypothesis, and acknowledges that there are problems for this hypothesis.

input constraints, similar to what we have seen for the choice between the two plural suffixes. This applies to competing suffixes like *-er* and *-aar*. This topic will be dealt with in Section 5.4.

3.2.4. Derivation and semantics

The basic hypothesis for the semantic interpretation of complex words is the principle of compositionality (Hoeksema 2000), which states that the meaning of a complex word is a compositional function of the meaning of its parts. This formulation presupposes that we can assign a specific meaning to each derivational affix, and this will indeed be the hypothesis to be defended here. It is quite obvious, however, that there is no one-to-one correspondence between form and meaning in morphology. First, there are many synonymous affixes, for instance those for female personal nouns. Synonymy is a normal phenomenon whenever we encounter meaningful morphemes. On the other hand, there are many polysemous affixes, with more than one, but related meanings. Again, polysemy is a normal situation for meaningful morphemes. Therefore, we should not separate form and meaning in morphology as being two different levels of analysis (as suggested by Beard 1995), but try to explain the polysemy involved as much as possible.

Different semantic interpretations for affixes that are polyfunctional may correlate with a difference in category of the base. This semantic role of the category of the base implies that instead of speaking about the meaning of affixes, it would be more precise to speak of the meaning contribution of a word-formation process in which that affix is used with a specific class of base words. However, for ease of exposition, I will continue to speak of the meaning of affixes except where this might cause confusion. In addition, an affix may be polysemous with respect to base words of one category, that is, within a specific word-formation process. Both kinds of semantic variation are found in words with the suffix *-achtig*: as a deadjectival suffix, it has the meaning 'somewhat', whereas it has different but related meanings when it is denominal or deverbal. In its denominal use it is clearly polysemous:

(15) A-achtig   'somewhat'   groen-achtig 'greenish'
      N-achtig   'like'   aap-achtig 'like a monkey'
                 'liking'   pasta-achtig 'liking pasta'
                 'having a lot of' rots-achtig 'rocky'
      V-achtig   'inclined to'   weiger-achtig 'unwilling'

The polysemy of a particular morphological category can be systematically extended, in the form of extension schemata. As argued in Booij (1986), we may assume a conceptual extension schema of the following kind that accounts for the polysemy of many deverbal nouns in -*er*, and for the variation in meaning between such nouns:

(16)   Agent > Impersonal Agent > Instrument

This scheme says that a noun that denotes a personal agent can also be used for denoting impersonal agents and instruments, and sometimes all three possible meanings may be established ones for such a noun. For instance, the deverbal noun *zender* 'sender' has three meanings: person who sends, impersonal agent that sends (radio or TV station), and instrument (device used for sending messages). It is not necessary that all three meanings actually occur: some of them are just possible words. For instance, the noun *wijzer* 'lit. pointer, hand of a clock' is used in the Impersonal Agent interpretation, but the Agent and Instrument interpretations are also possible.

Since this extension schema refers to concepts, not to a specific morphological category, we expect it to also apply to other classes of nouns that can be used to create agent nouns, and this is indeed the case as shown by the following examples:

(17)   *Agent interpretation*   *Instrument interpretation*
       teken-aar 'drawer'   rammel-aar 'rattle'
       reparat-eur 'repairer'   regulat-eur 'regulator'
       coup-euse 'cutter'   frit-euse 'deep fat fryer'
       organisat-or 'organizer'   condensat-or 'condenser'

For the same reason, we predict this polysemy pattern will also occur in other languages, a correct prediction (Booij 1986).

Another case of regular polysemy is the class of deverbal -*ing*-nouns: they denote primarily actions and processes, but systematically also the result of these actions/processes. In addition, they may also denote object, means, place, or collective agent, and again, this is a pattern found across different morphological classes, as illustrated by the following examples (all these morphological types have a primary action interpretation):

(18)   result   ge-dicht 'poem', schilder-ij 'painting', vertal-ing 'translation'
        object   bijsluit-er 'enclosure', stort-ing 'deposit', verzin-sel 'fiction'

means	smeer-sel 'ointment', voed-ing 'food', verzacht-er 'softener'	
collective	beweg-ing 'movement', ge-hoor 'audience'	

Diminutive formation is also a telling case of regular polysemy. The basic meaning is 'small', not necessarily in a purely objective, physical sense, but primarily in an evaluative sense. The interpretational possibilities of the diminutive suffix are illustrated in (19). Note that often a diminutive noun has more than one of these interpretations; in particular, the endearment interpretation is almost always possible.[10]

(19)
Meaning	Base word	Diminutive
small	tafel 'table'	tafel-tje 'small table'
endearment	huis 'house'	huis-je 'small house, dear house'
	kat 'cat'	kat-je 'pussy-cat'
	kind 'child'	kind-je 'sweetheart'
contempt	auto 'car'	autoo-tje 'not so good car'
	boek 'book'	boek-je 'unimportant book'
unimportant	brief 'letter'	briefje 'non-official letter'
individuation	bier 'beer'	bier-tje 'glass of beer'
	lief 'dear'	lief-je 'sweetheart'
	speel 'to play'	speel-tje 'toy'
	tien 'ten'	tien-tje 'ten-guilder note'
	onder ons 'between us'	onderons-je 'private chat'
	dit en dat 'this and that'	dit-jes en dat-jes 'odds and ends'
female	Geert 'boy's name'	Geert-je 'girl's name'
	Jan 'John'	Jan-tje 'girl's name'
intensification	hart 'heart, centre'	(in het) hart-je 'right in the centre'

---

[10] Cf. also Bauer (1990: 552 ff.) for a discussion of semantic aspects of Dutch diminutives. As Bauer points out, the individuating effect of diminutives makes them typically referring expressions, which blocks them from appearing in non-referring positions, as shown by the example *Zij zijn benoemd tot hoogleraar/*hoogleraartje* 'They have been appointed professors', where it is impossible to use the diminutive form.

As shown by Jurafsky (1996), these polysemy patterns, which are based on the interpretational mechanisms of metonymy and metaphor, can be found in many languages across the globe, as is to be expected given the conceptual semantic nature of such interpretational patterns.

A persistent source of polysemy is vagueness: the semantic contribution of an affix is often nothing else but 'related to what is denoted by the base'. This is illustrated by the set of relational adjectives. In the phrase *een muzikale aanleg* 'a musical disposition, a talent for music', the only function of the suffix *-aal* is to express that there is a relation between the head of the NP, *aanleg*, and the base word of the adjective *muzikaal*, *muziek* 'music'. In other words, this type of expression is an alternative to using the compound *muziekaanleg* 'lit. music disposition'. Dutch has fourteen such denominal relational adjectival suffixes (Heynderickx 1994) (Table 3.5).

Due to their relational nature, these adjectives cannot be modified (by a degree adverb, comparative or superlative), nor can they be preceded by the negative prefix *on-* (instead, they can be preceded by *niet-* or *non-* because these latter prefixes do not assign a specific property). Also, they cannot be followed by suffixes such as *-achtig* and *-heid* that denote qualities and hence

TABLE 3.5. *Relational adjectives*

Suffix	Example
-aal	muzik-aal talent 'musical talent'
-air	atom-aire fysica 'nuclear physics'
-eel	structur-ele analyse 'structural analysis'
-en	zilver-en ring 'silver ring'
-er	Edamm-er kaas 'Edam cheese'
-ief	educat-ief verlof 'educational sabbatical'
-iek	period-ieke controle 'regular check'
-iel	civ-iel effect 'civil effect'
-ig	toekomst-ige man 'to be husband'
-isch	filosof-ische discussie 'philosophical debate'
-lijk	vader-lijk gezag 'paternal authority'
-ling	monde-ling examen 'oral examination'
-oir	emancipat-oire activiteiten 'emancipatory activities'
-s	buitenland-se betrekkingen 'foreign relations'
	Amerikaan-se regering 'American government'

attach to qualitative adjectives only, and cannot appear in predicative position, as shown here for the relational adjective *presidentiëel* 'presidential':

(20) het presidentiële paleis 'the presidential palace'
  *erg presidentiëel 'very presidential'
  *presidentiël-er 'more presidential', *presidentiëel-st 'most presidential'
  een niet-presidentiëel paleis, *een on-presidentiëel paleis 'an unpresidential palace'
  *presidentiëel-achtig, *presidentiëel-heid
  *Dit paleis is presidentiëel 'This palace is presidential'[11]

Exceptions to the rule that relational adjectives do not appear in predicative position are their predicate use with a restrictive modifier, as in *Deze ziekte is viraal van aard* 'This illness is viral in nature', and their contrastive use (cf. fn. 11).

Individual instances of relational adjectives also function as qualitative adjectives that express a specific property. The adjective *muzikaal*, for instance, has the qualitative interpretation 'having musical talent', just like the English equivalent *musical*. The qualitative interpretation can also be obtained by type coercion. In the sentence *Zij ziet er zeer Amerikaans uit* 'She looks very American', the degree adverb imposes a qualitative interpretation on the adjective, and hence the adjective is going to mean 'typically American'. It is not the case that all adjectives allow for a relational interpretation: there is also a set of adjectival suffixes (like *-achtig*) that always create qualitative adjectives (Section 3.4).

The very vague relational meaning that we found for denominal adjectival suffixes is also a property of denominal nominal affixes. The same relational meaning is expressed by conversion (Section 3.5) and by the compound construction (Section 4.2.2). These nominal suffixes all create personal nouns, and are also used to create a specific subcategory of personal nouns, inhabitant names. Table 3.6 presents a survey of these suffixes. As we can conclude from Table 3.6, all suffixes except *-air* and *-ist* are used for coining inhabitant names.

---

[11] It is, however, possible to use relational adjectives in predicative position if used contrastively, as in *Deze onderneming is niet Europees, maar Amerikaans* 'This company is not European, but American'.

TABLE 3.6. *Denominal nominal suffixes*

Suffix	Personal noun	Inhabitant name
-(i)aan	Chomsky-aan 'Chomskyan'	Amerik-aan 'American'
-aar	molen-aar 'miller'	Leuven-aar 'inhabitant of Leuven'
-aard	stand-aard 'standard'	Spanj-aard 'Spaniard'
-aat	kandid-aat 'candidate'	Azi-aat 'Asian'
-air	diamant-air 'diamond dealer'	
-een	benz-een 'benzene'	Chil-een 'Chilean'
-ees	Bagwan-ees 'Bagwan follower'	Taiwan-ees 'Taiwanese'
-ein	republik-ein 'republican'	Rom-ein 'Roman'
-enaar	moord-enaar 'murderer'	Parijz-enaar 'Parisian'
-er	wetenschapp-er 'scientist'	Amsterdamm-er 'inhabitant of A'
-ier	herberg-ier 'inn keeper'	Arab-ier 'Arab'
-iër	agrar-iër 'farmer'	Israël-iër 'Israeli'
-iet	meteor-iet 'meteorite'	Aden-iet 'Adenite'
-ijn	rabb-ijn 'rabbi'	Alexandr-ijn 'Alexandrine'
-ist	humor-ist 'id.'	
-(e)ling	dorp-eling 'villager'	Brugge-ling 'inhabitant of Bruges'
-oot	psych-oot 'psychotic'	Cypri-oot 'Cypriot'

This means that we do not have to recognize a special class of inhabitant suffixes. For instance, the suffix *-er* used in *Amsterdammer* is the same as that used in *wetenschapper* 'scientist'. However, it is probably the case that the specific and frequent use of this denominal suffix for coining native inhabitant names is observed as such by the native speaker. In other words, we should try to model morphological competence in such a way that it can be expressed in terms of certain uses of a suffix being more productive than others'. A possible formal interpretation is that the quantitative productivity of a suffix is formalized as correlating with the kind of base word involved: geographical nouns and names of organizations as bases, for instance, will boost the degree of productivity of denominal *-er* (cf. Booij 1988*a* and van Santen 1992*b* for discussion).

3.3. PREFIXATION

As we saw above, a lot of prefixation is category-neutral. This applies to the non-native prefixes discussed in the previous section, and also to the native prefixes in Table 3.7.

3.3. PREFIXATION

TABLE 3.7. *Category-neutral native prefixes*

Prefix	Meaning	Base category	Example
aarts-	intense	A	aarts-lui 'very lazy'
		N	aarts-schurk 'enormous crook'
	hierarchy	N	aarts-bisschop 'arch-bishop'
her-	re-	V	her-schrijf 'to rewrite'
niet-	non-	N	niet-roker 'non-smoker'
		A	niet-Christelijk 'non-Christian'
oer-	intense	A	oer-gezond 'very healthy'
	original	N	oer-mens 'primitive man'
on-	negative	A	on-gezond 'unhealthy'
		N	on-zin 'nonsense'
opper-	upper	N	opper-hoofd 'chief'
oud-	ex-	N	oud-student 'former student'

The prefix *oud-* is a nice example of grammaticalization. This morpheme also exists as an adjective with the meaning 'old, former', whereas it means 'former' only when used as a prefix, and hence it is an affixoid. Similarly, the negative prefix *niet-* is the grammaticalized counterpart of the negative adverb *niet* 'not'. More examples of this kind of grammaticalization will be discussed in Section 4.3.1.

The prefix *her-* that attaches to verbs, also occurs in a number of nouns (Schultink 1964):

(21) herbegin 'new start', herbouw 'rebuilding', herdruk 'reprint'

This does not prove, however, that this prefix also attaches to nouns since such nouns may be interpreted as nominalizations of complex verbs prefixed with *her-*: *herbeginnen* 'to begin again', *herbouwen* 'to rebuild', and *herdrukken* 'to reprint'.

A special property of the prefix *her-* is that it can replace an unstressed verbal prefix when it is attached to verbs with these prefixes:

(22) be-straat 'to pave'   her-straat 'to repave'
     ge-bruik 'to use'   her-bruik 'to reuse'
     ver-over 'to conquer'   her-over 'to reconquer'

Note that the simplex verbs *straten*, *bruiken*, and *overen* do not exist, and hence could not have functioned as the bases for *her-*prefixation. It is not the case that *her-* has to replace the prefix: *her-ge-bruiken* 'to reuse' and *her-be-bouwen* 'to rebuild' are well-formed verbs.

The basic division of labour between the negative prefixes *on-* and *niet-* is clear: the prefix *on-* denies the property expressed by the base, and assigns a contrary property, whereas *niet-* only denies the property or relation expressed by the base word. For instance, there is a clear difference between *onchristelijk* 'unchristian', an adjective that assigns a specific property, and *niet-christelijk* 'non-Christian' that only states the absence of the property *christelijk*. Therefore, *niet-* can be used with more adjectives than *on-*. However, there are also negative adjectives where there is no clear meaning difference between the two adjectives; for instance, *onproductief* 'unproductive' and *niet-produktief* 'unproductive' are synonymous, as the glosses show.

A characteristic property of *on*-adjectives is that there are many for which the stem is an adjective that does not exist as such, but is nevertheless a well-formed deverbal adjective:

(23)

	Verb	on-*adjective*
-baar	navolg 'to imitate'	on-navolg-baar 'inimitable'
	ontkoom 'to escape'	on-ontkoom-baar 'inescapable'
-elijk	afscheid 'to separate'	on-afscheid-elijk 'inseparable'
	doorgrond 'to fathom'	on-doorgrond-elijk 'unfathomable'
	noem 'to mention'	on-noem-elijk 'untold'
	ontbeer 'to miss'	on-ontbeer-lijk 'indispensible'
-end	deug 'to be virtuous'	on-deug-end 'naughty'
-zaam	acht 'to take care'	on-acht-zaam 'careless'
	herberg 'to lodge'	on-herberg-zaam 'inhospitable'

It is not possible to explain these cases as derivation from a possible instead of from an existing word since some of the adjectives involved, in particular *-elijk* and *-zaam* are no longer productive. This is in line with the observation that if the positive counterpart adjective is used, this is felt by speakers of Dutch as a back formation. What we observe here is that one derivational process, *on-*prefixation, triggers (or presupposes the result of) another derivational process, deverbal adjectivalization. This is a phenomenon that we will also come across in Section 4.3.2, where synthetic compounds are discussed. That is, we have to assume templates of the following type for these adjectives:

3.3. PREFIXATION

(24) [on[[V]suffix]_A]_A

This template expresses the correlation of two independently established word-formation processes, *on*-prefixation, and deverbal adjectivalization. Note that these are not instances of synaffixes, because here, each affix has its own regular meaning contribution.

3.3.1. Verbal prefixes

There are three productive category-changing verbalizing native prefixes in Dutch that attach to all three lexical categories (N, V, A): *be-*, *ver-*, and *ont-* (the prefixes *er-* and *ge-* are unproductive) (Table 3.8).

The three productive verbalizing prefixes exhibit a uniform valency effect, that is, whatever the syntactic category of the input, the output is always a verb of a specific semantic class. This applies in particular to recent coinings of this type; there is quite some semantic variation within the set of long established verbs of this type (cf. de Vries 1975). The meaning contribution of *be-* can be described as 'to direct an action towards an object such that the object is affected'.[12] The entity denoted by the base noun, the property denoted by the base adjective, and the action denoted by the base verb play a role in that action. The specific role, however, varies from verb to verb, and

TABLE 3.8. *Verbal category-changing prefixes*

Prefix	Class of base	Base word	Prefixed verb
be-	N	dijk 'dike'	be-dijk 'to provide with a dike'
	A	zat 'drunken'	be-zat 'to hit the bottle'
	V	kijk 'to look'	be-kijk 'to watch'
ver-	N	film 'id.'	ver-film 'to film'
	A	bleek 'pale'	ver-bleek 'to bleach'
	V	koop 'to buy'	ver-koop 'to sell'
ont-	N	kurk 'cork'	ont-kurk 'to uncork'
	A	eigen 'own'	ont-eigen 'to expropriate'
	V	bind 'to bind'	ont-bind 'to dissolve'
ge-	V	leid 'to guide'	ge-leid 'to guide'
er-	V	ken 'to know'	er-ken 'to recognize'

---

[12] An exception is the inchoative verb *bekoelen* 'to cool down'. This use of *be-* appears to be unproductive (de Vries 1975: 179).

also depends on extra-linguistic knowledge, as is illustrated by the following examples of denominal *be*-verbs:

(25)
Base noun	be-*verb*
bos 'wood'	be-bos 'to afforest'
lichaam 'body'	be-lichaam 'to embody'
man 'man'	be-man 'to man'
nadeel 'disadvantage'	be-nadeel 'to harm'
volk 'people'	be-volk 'to populate'

The consequence of this systematic meaning of *be*-verbs as circumscribed above is that they are always obligatorily transitive (cf. Section 6.2), except for some idiosyncratic verbs such as *beginnen* 'to begin'.

The verbalizing prefix *ver-* is different in that it creates both inchoative (intransitive) and causative (transitive) verbs that express a change. That is, the uniform valency effect is obscured here by the optionality of the causer role of the process expressed by *ver*-verbs (cf. Section 6.2). There is, however, uniformity in that words with all three categories of bases (N, A, V) have both possibilities:

(26)
Base	Base category	ver-*verb*
jaar 'year'	N	ver-jaar (intr.) 'to be precluded by the lapse of time'
pand 'pawn'	N	ver-pand (tr.) 'to pawn'
arm 'poor'	A	ver-arm (intr.) 'to become poor'
rijk 'rich'	A	ver-rijk (tr.) 'to enrich'
koop 'to buy'	V	ver-koop (tr.) 'to sell'
loop 'to walk'	V	ver-loop (intr.) 'to expire'

The prefix *ont-* has a number of meanings: the inchoative and reversative meanings are the most common ones. The inchoative *ont*-verbs are intransitive, the reversative ones are mostly transitive. Examples are:

(27)
bijt 'to bite'	ont-bijt 'to breakfast'
bind 'to bind'	ont-bind 'to dissolve'
bloot 'nude'	ont-bloot 'to uncover'
bos 'forest'	ont-bos 'to deforest'
brand 'to burn'	ont-brand 'to ignite'

A characteristic of these prefixed verbs is that there is a subset of verbs

3.3. PREFIXATION

that are formally complex only, i.e. for which there is no corresponding base word:

(28)   be-gin 'to begin', ge-schied 'to happen', ont-gin 'to develop', ver-dwijn 'to disappear'

Such verbs still behave as complex words in that they have perfect participles without the prefix *ge-*.

A special class of *be*-verbs is formed by verbs with the structure *be-V-ig* such as:

(29)   *Base*   *Complex verb*
       eed 'oath'   be-ed-ig 'to swear in'
       kost 'cost'   be-kost-ig 'to bear the cost of'
       schade 'damage'   be-schad-ig 'to damage'

Here it looks as if a discontinuous affix *be . . . ig* has been at work, because there are no base words *edig, kostig,* or *schadig* available. What is at stake here is paradigmatic word formation. Consider the following *be*-verbs in which the base is a denominal adjective in *-ig*:

(30)   kracht 'power'   kracht-ig 'powerful'   be-kracht-ig 'to confirm'
       moed 'courage'   moed-ig 'brave'   be-moed-ig 'to encourage'
       vocht 'moisture'   vocht-ig 'moist'   be-vocht-ig 'to moisten'

In these cases, a direct relation between noun and *be*-verb can be established, with the effect that, for instance, the verb *bevochtigen* is interpreted as being directly related to the noun *vocht*. Consequently, the synaffix *be-* . . . *-ig* could arise, which then leads to verbs such as *beëdigen*, derived directly from the noun *eed* 'oath', since the adjective *edig* does not exist.

The prefix *ver-* in its deadjectival use sometimes takes the comparative form of the adjective as its base. This is the case for the following verbs:

(31)   ver-erg-er 'to worsen', ver-mind-er 'to reduce', ver-oud-er 'to get older', ver-slecht-er 'to worsen', ver-wild-er 'to run wild'

These are cases of inherent inflection feeding word formation (cf. Section 2.5). For most deadjectival *ver*-verbs, the degree component in its meaning is not expressed separately. For instance, *vergelen* means 'to become yellow', with a degree component in its meaning, but without this being expressed by a comparative morpheme. What is at stake here is the tendency to express a certain meaning component in a systematic way (isomorphy between form and meaning, also referred to as Von Humboldt's principle), in this case the concept of 'degree' by means of the comparative suffix. In Section 3.4 we will see more cases of this phenomenon of 'overcharacterization'.

A second formal peculiarity of *ver*-verbs concerns verbs with an adjectival base prefixed with *on*- 'un-':

(32) on-achtzaam 'careless'   ver-ont-achtzaam 'to neglect'
     on-menselijk 'inhuman'   ver-ont-menselijk 'to dehumanize'
     on-schuldig 'innocent'   ver-ont-schuldig 'to apologize'

What we observe here is that the expected sequence *ver-on-* is replaced with the prefix sequence *ver-ont-*. This can be seen as the effect of the isomorphy tendency: *ont-* is a verbalizing prefix, and hence signals the verbal nature of a word, whereas *on-* is used in complex nouns and adjectives only. Thus, by using *ont-* instead of *on-* there is a systematic formal indication of the verbal nature of these words (hence this is called 'systematization', cf. van Marle 1978).

In addition to the class-changing verbalizing prefixes discussed above there is a set of prefixes that mainly take verbs to form verbs. These prefixes

TABLE 3.9. *Verbal prefixes which correspond to a word*

Prefix	Base word	Prefixed verb
aan-	bid 'to pray'	aan-bid 'to worship'
achter-	haal 'to fetch'	achter-haal 'to find out'
door-	snijd 'to cut'	door-snijd 'to cut through'
	spek 'pork'	door-spek 'to interlard with'
mis-	vorm 'to form'	mis-vorm 'to deform'
om-	sluit 'to close'	om-sluit 'to enclose'
	cirkel 'circle'	om-cirkel 'to encircle'
onder-	breek 'to break'	onder-breek 'to interrupt'
	titel 'title'	onder-titel 'to subtitle'
over-	win 'to win'	over-win 'to defeat'
	brug 'bridge'	over-brug 'to bridge'
vol-	maak 'to make'	vol-maak 'to bring to perfection'
voor-	kom 'to come'	voor-kom 'to prevent'
weer-	schijn 'to shine'	weer-schijn 'to reflect'

have counterparts in the forms of particles and of independent lexemes (adverbs and prepositions), since they are grammaticalizations of lexemes, with particles as an intermediate stage (cf. Section 6.4). When these morphemes are used as prefixes, they have a specific, aspectual, meaning, and do not have the full range of meanings of the lexemic counterpart. This is why we subsume these patterns of word formation under derivation, and not under compounding. A systematic phonological property of these prefixes is that they do not bear the main stress of the prefixed verb. Furthermore, they have perfect participles without *ge-*, in line with the generalization that the presence of an unstressed prefix precludes the occurrence of the participial prefix *ge-*.

The explanation for the fact that they mainly attach to verbs is that they are grammaticalized reflexes of particles, i. e. preverbs, which by definition combine with a verb. A verb like *overbruggen* 'to bridge', for instance, originates from a particle verb, in which *over* is separable from the verb (Section 6.4). Some of these prefixes have become productive as verbalizing prefixes: they now also attach to nouns and adjectives to form a verb. This is the case for the prefixes *door-*, *om-*, *onder-* and *over-*:

(33) | *Base noun* | *Verb* |
|---|---|
| kelder 'cellar' | onderkelder 'to put a cellar beneath' |
| meester 'master' | overmeester 'to overpower' |
| raster 'fence' | omraster 'to fence in' |
| spek 'bacon' | doorspek 'to interlard with' |

The meaning of these prefixes is a primarily aspectual one: they assign telic aspect, and hence these verbs are obligatorily transitive (cf. Section 6.2). They express an action (with an endpoint) towards an object, whereby the specific prefix indicates the spatial orientation of the action.

3.3.2. *Nominal prefixes*

The nominalizing prefix *ge-* that is phonologically identical to the participial prefix *ge-* is used to derive nouns from verbs with the meaning 'continuous V-ing'. If the action denoted by the base verb is inherently telic, we get an iterative interpretation, as in *geblaf* 'barking'. The following examples illustrate the use of this prefix, which creates neuter nouns:

(34) Base   ge-*noun*
    bid 'to pray'   ge-bid 'continuous praying'
    klooi 'to mess around'   ge-klooi 'messing around'
    kots 'to puke'   ge-kots 'continuous/repeated puking'
    lul 'to bullshit'   ge-lul 'bullshitting'
    schrijf 'to write'   ge-schrijf 'continuous writing'
    stofzuig 'to vacuum'   ge-stofzuig 'continuous vacuuming'
    structureer 'to structure'   ge-structureer 'continuous structuring'

Many of these nouns have a pejorative connotation: the action referred to goes on too long, or is too often repeated. It is also a prefix that belongs to a rather informal register of speaking, and in this respect it contrasts with the suffix *-ing* that also nominalizes verbs, but belongs to a higher register.

As mentioned in Section 3.2.1, the base verbs for *ge-* are mostly simplex words, but it is also possible to use complex base verbs (Mackenzie 1985*a*). Thus, unlike the participial prefix *ge-*, the nominalizing *ge-* is not excluded from occurring before a verbal stem that begins with an unstressed prefix, as shown by the following examples:

(35) Base   ge-*noun*
    be-wapen 'to arm'   ge-bewapen 'arming'
    ge-loof 'to believe'   ge-geloof 'believing'
    ont-voer 'to kidnap'   ge-ontvoer 'kidnapping'
    ver-sier 'to decorate'   ge-versier 'decorating'

In addition to this productive use, the prefix *ge-* also occurs in quite a number of deverbal nouns without a systematic general meaning:

(36) *Verbal base*   ge-*noun*
    bak 'to bake'   ge-bak 'pastry'
    bouw 'to build'   ge-bouw 'building'
    hoor 'to hear'   ge-hoor 'audience'
    luk 'to succeed'   ge-luk 'happiness'

Furthermore, there are also *ge-*nouns without a corresponding base word, for instance *ge-drag* 'behaviour', *ge-laat* 'face', *ge-noegen* 'pleasure', *ge-val* 'case', *ge-zin* 'family'. These nouns are to be considered formally complex words since they fall under the generalization that *ge-*nouns are neuter (with a few exceptions such as *genoot* 'companion' and *gezant* 'envoy'): it is easy to recognize such words as complex, and thus to recognize the prefix status of the first syllable *ge-* because simplex native stems always have a full vowel in their first syllable, and never the schwa (cf. Booij 1999*b*).

The prefix *ge-* is also used in combination with the suffix *-te* for the derivation of collective nouns. Examples of the use of this unproductive synaffix are the following:

(37) *Base noun*   *Collective noun*
      berg 'mountain'   ge-berg-te 'mountain chain'
      boef 'crook'   ge-boef-te 'scum, riff-raff'
      steen 'stone'   ge-steen-te 'rock'
      vogel 'bird'   ge-vogel-te 'flock of birds'

This use of *ge-* is a reflex of the collective meaning of the prefix *ga-* in proto-Germanic that is also present in *gebroeders* 'brothers'; it is from this *ga-* that the different prefixes *ge-* derive historically.

3.4. SUFFIXATION

In contrast to prefixation, suffixation is always class-determining, and can create complex verbs, nouns, adjectives, and adverbs.

3.4.1. *Verbal suffixes*

Verbalization in Dutch is mainly done by prefixation and particle verb formation (cf. Section 6.4): there are only two verbalizing suffixes. A productive verbalizing suffix is the non-native denominal suffix *-eer*. The following examples illustrate the use of this suffix, and the kind of stem allomorphy involved:

(38) *Base noun*   *Verb in -eer*
      alarm 'id.'   alarm-eer 'to alarm'
      conditie 'condition'   condition-eer 'to condition'
      effect 'id.'   effectu-eer 'to effect'
      examen 'test'   examin-eer 'to test'
      formule 'formula'   formul-eer 'to formulate'
      privilege 'prerogative' privilegi-eer 'to give prerogatives'
      register 'register'   registr-eer 'to register'
      shock 'id.'   shock-eer 'to shock'

As will be discussed in Section 5.3, the allomorphy that is visible here is stem allomorphy because the same allomorphy occurs in other derivations. For instance, the derived adjective for *conditie* 'condition' is *conditioneel* 'conditional' with the same stem extension *on*. The productivity of *-eer* is also clear from the fact that occasionally it extends its derivational domain to native nouns, and to adjectival bases:

(39)   blond 'id.'   blond-eer 'to bleach'
       groep 'group'   groep-eer 'to group'
       kamp 'camp'   kamp-eer 'to camp'
       klein 'small'   klein-eer 'to belittle'

The second verbalizing suffix is the non-native *-iseer* that creates inchoative and causative verbs. Unlike *-eer*, it is also productively attached to adjectives:

(40)   applaus 'applause'   applaud-iseer 'to applaud'
       modern 'id.'   modern-iseer 'to modernize'
       motor 'engine'   motor-iseer 'to motorize'
       Pasteur 'id.'   pasteur-iseer 'to pasteurize'
       stabiel 'stable'   stabil-iseer 'to stabilize'
       standaard 'standard'   standaard-iseer 'to standardize'

As mentioned in Section 3.2.2, it is also used occasionally in combination with native stems.

The suffix *-iseer* is actually a bimorphemic sequence. This is clear when we look at nominalizations of these verbs. Verbs in *-eer* can be nominalized by replacing the suffix *-eer* with the suffix *-atie*; verbs in *-iseer* have a nominalization in *-atie* in which this latter suffix has replaced the part *-eer*, whereas the part *-is-* remains present in the nominalization:

(41)   *Verbal stem*   *Nominalization*
       anticip-eer 'to anticipate'   anticip-atie 'anticipation'
       reden-eer 'to reason'   reden-atie 'reasoning'
       stabil-is-eer 'to stabilize'   stabilis-atie 'stabilization'
       alfabet-is-eer 'to alphabetize' alfabetis-atie 'alphabetization'

This pattern of nominalization shows that *-iseer* has internal morphological structure and consists of the morpheme sequence *-is-eer*. Note, however, that this is not a synaffix in the strict sense, because the morpheme *is*

3.4.2. Nominal suffixes

Nominal suffixation is used for the creation of diminutives (Section 3.2), personal nouns, object denoting nouns, nomina actionis, and nouns denoting abstracta. The gender of these nouns is always determined by the nominal suffix. As mentioned above, the default gender is non-neuter; if a suffix imposes neuter gender, this is indicated by the symbol *n*.

Dutch has quite a number of suffixes for the formation of personal nouns. Above, we saw that there are a number of non-native suffixes for coining personal nouns including inhabitant names and their female counterparts. A survey of the native personal name creating suffixes is given in Table 3.10. The suffix *-e* can also be used for creating deadjectival personal names (cf. Section 2.3.3).

TABLE 3.10. *Native suffixes for personal nouns*

Suffix	Base category	Base	Example
-aar	V	wandel 'to walk'	wandel-aar 'walker'
	N	zonde 'sin'	zond-aar 'sinner'
	A	eigen 'own'	eigen-aar 'owner'
-aard	A	wreed 'cruel'	wreed-aard 'cruel person'
	N	Spanje 'Spain'	Spanj-aard 'Spaniard'
-der	V	bestuur 'to govern'	bestuur-der 'governor'
	N	Langweer 'id.'	Langweer-der 'inhabitant of L.'
-enaar	N	schuld 'debt'	schuld-enaar 'debtor'
		Utrecht 'id.'	Utrecht-enaar 'inhabitant of U.'
-er	V	werk 'to work'	werk-er 'worker'
	N	schip 'ship'	schipp-er 'skipper'
	Num	tien 'ten'	tien-er 'teenager'
	S	doe het zelf 'do it yourself'	doe-het-zelv-er 'do it yourselfer'
-erd	A	vies 'dirty'	viez-erd 'dirty person'
-erik	A	vies 'dirty'	viez-erik 'dirty person'
-ier	N	winkel 'shop'	winkel-ier 'shopkeeper'
-(e)ling	V	zuig 'to suck'	zuig-eling 'infant'
	N	stad 'city'	sted-eling 'city-dweller'
	A	stom 'stupid'	stomm-eling 'idiot'
	Num	twee 'two'	twee-ling 'twins'

The most productive suffix is *-er* which is in complementary distribution with *-aar* and *-der*: the suffix *-aar* occurs after stems ending in a coronal sonorant consonant preceded by schwa, and *-der* occurs after stems ending in /r/ (cf. Section 5.4). However, this distribution is not completely phonologically governed since there are some nouns in *-aar* and *-der* with stems of a different phonological make-up, such as *ler-aar* 'teacher' (< *leer* 'to teach') and *dien-der* 'policeman' (< *dien* 'to serve'); cf. Section 5.4.

These three suffixes have a denominal and a deverbal use. In their deverbal use, it is often said that they create agent nouns that denote the agent of the action mentioned by the verbal stem. In fact, they are also used with verbs that do not refer to an action but a process. Hence, the qualification 'subject name' is more appropriate since the subject of a verb does not always bear the Agent role (Booij 1986: 507), but sometimes the Theme role. The following examples illustrate this:

(42)   *Verb with Theme subject*   *Deverbal noun*
      begin 'to begin'   beginn-er 'beginner, freshman'
      blijf 'to stay'   blijv-er 'stayer'
      breek 'to break'   brek-er 'breaker, wave that breaks'
      daal 'to drop'   dal-er 'dropper' (said of shares in the stock market)
      groei 'to grow'   groei-er 'grower' (said of shares in the stock market)
      stijg 'to rise'   stijg-er 'riser' (said of shares in the stock market)
      uitval 'to drop out'   uitvall-er 'drop out'
      zink 'to sink'   zink-er 'sinker, underwater main'

The qualification 'subject name' correctly predicts that verbs without a lexical subject such as those in (43) cannot be affixed with *-er*:

(43)   blijk 'to appear'   *blijk-er
      lijk 'to seem'   *lijk-er
      schijn 'to seem'   *schijn-er

Obviously, most nouns of this type will be agent names since for most verbs, the subject bears the Agent role. In Section 3.2.4 we saw that deverbal nouns in *-er* are regularly polysemous because they can also receive an impersonal agent or instrumental interpretation, which derives from the subject name

3.4. SUFFIXATION

interpretation. In addition, there are some other interpretations; of these, the object name interpretation is quite productive:

(44)
Verb stem	Interpretation	Example
aanraad 'to advise'	object	aanrad-er 'thing one should buy/read/do'
bijsluit 'to enclose'	object	bijsluit-er 'enclosure'
krijg 'to get'	object	krijg-er-tje 'gift'
mis 'to miss'	event	miss-er 'failure'
tref 'to hit'	event	treff-er 'hit'
afknap 'to break down'	causer	afknapp-er 'what makes you break down'
gil 'to scream'	causer	gill-er 'what makes you scream'

Hence we have to assume polysemy for the deverbal -*er*-suffix in the sense that it does not only create subject names, but also names for object, causers, and events.[13] This polysemy also occurs in other types of deverbal nouns; for instance, *gijzel-aar* 'hostage' (< *gijzelen* 'to take hostage') and *arrest-ant* (< *arresteren* 'to arrest') are also object names.

The denominal suffix -*er* is also very productive (Booij 1988*a*, van Santen 1992*b*). It is particularly popular for coining names for persons belonging to a geographical entity, an institution, or an organization. Even phrases that function as names can be used as bases for this suffix. Sometimes the institution or organization is indicated by its acronym:

(45)
Amsterdam 'id.'	Amsterdamm-er 'inhabitant of A.'
deeltijd 'part time'	deeltijd-er 'part-timer'
jeugdkapel 'youth chapel'	jeugdkapell-er 'visitor of youth chapel'
watersport 'id.'	watersport-er 'water sportsman'
eerste graad 'first grade'	eerstegrad-er 'first grade (teacher)'
Rode Kruis 'Red Cross'	Rode Kruiser 'Red Cross employee'
VVD (political party)	VVD-er 'member of the VVD'
PTT (Postal Service)	PTT-er 'postal worker'
AOW (state pension)	AOW-er 'pensioner'

Sometimes the last letter of the acronym itself stands for a personal noun. In

---

[13] This problem is discussed in detail in Booij (1986, 1992) and de Caluwe (1992).

such cases, we observe a tendency to add the strictly speaking superfluous suffix *-er*, as in:

(46) BBT (Beroepssoldaat Bepaalde Tijd 'professional soldier for a fixed time') > BBT-er
BN (Bekende Nederlander 'famous Dutchman') > BN-er
KVV (Kort Verband Vrijwilliger 'short contract voluntary') > KVV-er
UHD (Universitair Hoofd Docent 'university head teacher')
> UHD-er
Dominic-aan 'Dominican' > Dominican-er
Francisc-aan 'Franciscan' > Franciscan-er

This is another case of the tendency to adhere to isomorphy between form and meaning, and to systematically express the concept 'person' by means of *-er*, with the effects of systematization and overcharacterization (the latter notion applies since the concept 'person' is expressed twice) (cf. van Marle 1978, 1994).

Dutch also has a specific object name suffix, the deverbal suffix *-sel*. This suffix creates object names, primarily for the affected objects of transitive verbs (Taeldeman 1990). With intransitive verbs that express a change, they function as subject names. The unifying qualification for these two uses of *-sel*-nouns is 'Theme name' since both the subjects of such intransitive verbs and the objects of transitive verbs bear the Theme role (Booij 1986). This suffix also exhibits polysemy because it can also be used for deriving instrument nouns:

(47) *Transitive verb* *Object name*
aanhang 'to append' aanhang-sel 'appendix'
bedenk 'to think' bedenk-sel 'idea'
bouw 'to build' bouw-sel 'building'

Intransitive verb *Subject name*
aanslib 'to deposit' aanslib-sel 'deposit'
schep 'to create' schep-sel 'creature'
uitvloei 'to flow out' uitvloei-sel 'consequence'

Transitive verb *Instrument name*
stijf 'to starch' stijf-sel 'starch'
voed 'to feed' voed-sel 'food'
wit 'to white-wash' wit-sel 'white-wash'

3.4. SUFFIXATION

TABLE 3.11. *Nomina actionis*

Suffix	Base word	Derived word
-atie	organis-eer 'to organize'	organis-atie 'organization'
-erij	vlieg 'to fly'	vlieg-erij 'flying business'
	heks 'witch'	heks-erij 'witchcraft'
-ing	meet 'to measure'	met-ing 'measurement'
	bewapen 'to arm'	bewapen-ing 'armament'
-nis	stoor 'to disturb'	stoor-nis 'disturbance'
(-enis)	verrijs 'to rise'	verrijz-enis 'resurrection'
(-tenis)	gebeur 'to happen'	gebeur-tenis 'happening'
-st	kom 'to come'	koms-t 'coming'
-t	teel 'to grow'	teel-t 'growing'

If the base verbs are intransitive, as is the case for *uitvloeien*, these verbs denote a process or change and are non-accusative verbs that select the auxiliary *zijn*.[14] All *sel*-nouns have neuter gender, even a noun such as *schepsel* that denotes human and other animate beings. The suffix is unproductive.

A second large class of derived nouns are the so-called nomina actionis that express an activity's result or another related meaning. They are listed in Table 3.11. Of these suffixes, the native suffix *-ing* is the most productive one. It is particularly productive for complex verbs, since many simplex verbs have another type of corresponding deverbal noun, which will either block the coinage of a deverbal noun in *-ing*, or have the effect of assigning a somewhat different meaning to the *-ing*-noun (cf. van Haeringen 1971):

(48) | *Base verb* | *Noun* | *Noun in* -ing |
| --- | --- | --- |
| be-leef 'to live to see' | belev-enis 'experience' | belev-ing 'experiencing' |
| be-strijd 'to fight' | — | bestrijd-ing 'fight against' |
| be-toog 'to argue' | betoog 'argument' | betog-ing '(public) demonstration' |
| bid 'to pray' | ge-bed 'prayer' | *bidd-ing |

---

[14] If the assumption that such non-accusative verbs are represented lexically as having no external argument is correct, *-sel* can be qualified as binding the internal argument of the verb. This is actually the proposal in Knopper (1984).

126   DERIVATION

kom 'to come'	kom-st 'coming'	*kom-ing
ont-kom 'to escape'	*ontkom-st	ontkom-ing 'escape'
roep 'to call'	roep 'call'	roep-ing 'vocation'
speel 'to play'	spel 'play'	spel-ing 'freak (of nature)'
strijd 'to fight'	strijd 'fight'	*strijd-ing

In addition, the suffix *-ing* competes with *ge-*, in particular for verbs belonging to the informal register, and with the suffix *-erij* (cf. Hüning 1992, 1999). The native suffixes *-(e)nis*, *-st*, and *-t* are unproductive.

The suffix *-ing* also competes with *-atie* in the domains of verbs in *-eer*. However, in this case both forms are often possible, without a difference in meaning, as in *redenering – redenatie* 'reasoning', both derived from the verb *redeneren* 'to reason'. Sometimes, the noun in *-atie* is only possible in southern Dutch. For instance, whereas *constatatie* 'observation', derived from the verb *constateren* 'to observe' is normal in southern Dutch, one has to use the form *constatering* in northern Dutch.

As to the suffix *-erij*, it has two basic meanings: it either mentions a particular (sometimes annoying) kind of behaviour, or it refers to a hobby, profession, or business (Hüning 1999: 213). Unlike the other suffixes listed in Table 3.11, it can also take nouns as bases, and also functions to coin synthetic deverbal compounds. This suffix has a number of allomorphs, and also attaches to nouns. It is historically related to the French suffix *-erie* that has also been borrowed as such in present-day Dutch, as shown by recent coinings such as *condomerie* 'condom shop' and *baderie* 'bathroom shop'. Here is a survey of the different allomorphs of this suffix, and of its uses:

(49)   *Base*   *Derived noun*

		Base	Derived noun
-erij	V	droom 'to dream'	drom-erij 'dreaming'
		vlieg 'to fly'	vlieg-erij 'the world of flying'
	N	bloemist 'florist'	bloemist-erij 'florist's shop'
		smeerlap 'dirty fellow'	smeerlapp-erij 'filthy behaviour'
	A+V	mooi 'beautiful', praat 'to talk'	'mooi-prat-erij 'humbug'
	N+V	pret 'fun', maak 'to make'	pret-mak-erij 'fun making'

3.4. SUFFIXATION

-derij	V	promoveer 'to graduate'	promoveer-derij 'graduation'
		sorteer 'to sort'	sorteer-derij 'sorting out'
-arij	V	smokkel 'to smuggle'	smokkel-arij 'smuggling'
		wandel 'to walk'	wandel-arij 'walking'

The choice between the three allomorphs will be discussed in Section 5.4.

Historically, the suffix *-erij* is a sequence of two suffixes *-er-ij*, like the corresponding French suffix *-erie* from which it derives. The unproductive suffix *-ij* is found in words like *voogd-ij* 'guardianship' from *voogd* 'guardian', and *ambtenar-ij* ' bureaucracy' < *ambtenaar* 'civil servant'.[15]

The question therefore arises whether it is synchronically a suffix or a suffix sequence. For a noun such as *vliegerij* one might argue that it has been derived from the deverbal noun *vlieger* through addition of the denominal suffix *-ij*, similar to the derivation of *voogdij* from *voogd*. There is, however, evidence for the unitary nature of *-erij*: it has been added directly to nouns such as *smeerlap* and *bloemist*. Therefore, I will interpret the sequence *-erij* as a synaffix. There is independent evidence for the internal morphological structuring of *-erij*: the allomorphs *-arij* and *-derij* have the same complementary distribution with respect to *-erij* as *-aar* and *-der* have with respect to *-er* (cf. Section 5.4). In order to make the relevant generalization, we have therefore to assume that *-erij* has the structure *-er-ij*.[16]

In the non-native stratum of Dutch morphology, there is only one productive nominalizing affix, *-atie*, which attaches productively to verbs in *-iseer* and *-eer*. It always replaces the stem-final verbal suffix:

(50) *Verbal stem*   *Deverbal noun*
   demonstr-eer 'to demonstrate'   demonstr-atie 'demonstration'
   install-eer 'to install'   install-atie 'installation'
   kanal-iseer 'to canalize'   kanalis-atie 'canalization'
   stabil-iseer 'to stabilize'   stabilis-atie 'stabilization'

There is a difference in behaviour here between the two classes of verbs: whereas verbs in *-iseer* always allow for a nominalization in *-atie*, this is not the case for verbs in *-eer*. For instance, the verb *alarmeren* 'to alarm' cannot

---

[15] Exceptional allomorphs of this suffix *-ij* are *-dij* (*makelaar-dij* 'estate agency'), *-ernij* (*slav-ernij* 'slavery'), *-enij* (*arts-enij* 'medicine'), and *-nij* (*lekker-nij* 'delicious food').

[16] Cf. Hüning (1999) for a detailed synchronic and diacronic study of the suffix *-erij*.

have the nominalization *alarmatie*; instead, *alarmering* has to be used.

The ending -*atie* is also to be seen as a bimorphemic sequence: adjectives in -*ief* can be derived from nouns in -*ie*, but the part -*at*- is not replaced:

(51) agress-ie 'aggression'   agress-ief 'aggressive'
     demonstr-atie 'demonstration' demonstrat-ief 'demonstrative'
     imit-atie 'imitation'   imita-tief 'imitating'
     supplet-ie 'suppletion'   supplet-ief 'suppletive'

The last class of nominalizing suffixes to be discussed here are those suffixes that create abstract nouns: -*heid*, -*te*, -*schap*, and -*dom* (the suffix -*e* can also be used for creating abstract nouns, cf. Section 2.3.3). The suffix -*heid* '-ness' is the productive suffix for creating (non-neuter) abstract nouns from adjectives:

(52) leeg 'empty'   leeg-heid 'emptiness'
     stabiel 'stable'   stabiel-heid 'stability'
     vrij 'free'   vrij-heid 'freedom'
     verantwoordelijk 'responsible' verantwoordelijk-heid
                                       'responsibility'

The competing suffix -*te* only occurs with native simplex adjectival stems (cf. Section 3.2.1), whereas -*heid* can be used with all kinds of stems. In the domain where these two suffixes compete, -*heid* is never blocked by -*te*, but in some cases there is a meaning difference between the two types of noun:

(53) groen 'green'   groente 'vegetables'   groenheid 'greenness'
     leeg 'empty'   leegte 'emptiness, blank'   leegheid 'emptiness'

As is quite common for productive affixes, -*heid* also takes stems of other categories, for instance nouns (*mens-heid* 'mankind' < *mens* 'human being') and quantifiers (*veelheid* 'large quantity' < *veel* 'much'). Furthermore, the suffix -*heid* also combines with the adjectival suffix -*ig* into a deadjectival synaffix -*igheid* with the specific meaning 'substance with the property denoted by A':

(54) gek 'foolish'   gekkig 'somewhat foolish'   gekkigheid 'foolishness'
     naar   narig 'somewhat   narigheid 'misery'
       'unpleasant'   unpleasant'
     vies 'dirty'   viezig 'dirtyish'   viezigheid 'dirt'

The adjectives *gekkig* and *narig* are non-existent (but possible) adjectives. They should not be taken as intermediate steps in the derivation of the nouns in *-igheid* because the meaning of *-ig* '-ish' does not form part of the meaning of the resulting complex noun. In other words, the suffix sequence *-igheid* has become a suffix of its own, with a specific meaning that is not computable on the basis of the meanings of *-ig* and *-heid* (cf. Section 1.5).

The suffix *-schap* '-ship' has two uses. First, it can be attached to nouns to denote a quality or institution. The nouns created are neuter. Secondly, it combines with nouns and a few adjectives to form nouns with the meaning 'being N/A', with non-neuter gender:

(55)   *Neuter nouns*
       QUALITY: hoogleraar-schap 'professorship', leider-schap 'leadership', moeder-schap 'motherhood'
       INSTITUTION: agent-schap 'agency', genoot-schap 'society', water-schap 'watership'

   Non-neuter nouns
       NOUN STEM: kameraad-schap 'comradeship', vriend-schap 'friendship'
       ADJECTIVE STEM: dronken-schap 'drunkenness', zwanger-schap 'pregnancy'

Lexicalized nouns of this form are *landschap* 'landscape' (< *land* 'land'), a word that has been borrowed into English, and *boodschap* 'message'(< *bode* 'messenger'). There are also a few words of this type with a stem that has the form of an infinitive:

(56)   nalaten-schap 'heritage'   < nalaten 'to leave behind'
       wedden-schap 'bet'   < wedden 'to bet'
       weten-schap 'science'   < weten 'to know'

Since infinitives can behave as nouns, this is what we might expect given the primarily denominal nature of the suffix *-schap*. But we also know that inflectional endings function as closing morphemes, i.e. they normally preclude further suffixation (cf. Section 2.5). The fact that *-schap* can nevertheless be attached after the ending *-en* has to do with the fact that *-schap* forms a prosodic word of its own (cf. Section 5.2). That is, the notion 'closing morpheme' should be interpreted to mean 'morpheme that must appear at the right edge of a prosodic word'. This interpretation of the closing morpheme nature of inflectional endings is supported by the behaviour of the suffix *-dom* that creates neuter collective nouns, and allows for stems that end in a plural nominal ending; this suffix also forms a prosodic word of its own:

(57) *Singular stem*
christen 'Christian'   christen-dom 'Christianity'
mens 'human being'   mens-dom 'humanity'
Plural stem
goden 'gods'   goden-dom 'the gods'
leerlingen 'pupils'   leerlingen-dom 'the pupils'

As in the case of *-schap*, there are also a few adjectives that combine with *-dom*, although is it primarily denominal, and this also correlates with a difference in gender: such deadjectival nouns are non-neuter, unlike the denominal *dom*-nouns with collective meaning, which are neuter:

(58) rijk 'rich'   rijkdom 'wealth'
ouder 'older'   ouderdom 'old age'

An exception with respect to gender is the neuter noun *eigendom* 'property' (< *eigen* 'own').

3.4.3. Adjectival suffixes

In Section 3.2 a number of adjectival suffixes have already been mentioned: the non-native suffixes in Tables 3.1 and 3.2, and the denominal relational (native and non-native) adjectival suffixes in Table 3.5. As pointed out, individual relational adjectives can also be interpreted as adjectives expressing a specific quality. Dutch also has a number of native adjectival suffixes that create only adjectives with a qualitative interpretation: the productive suffixes *-achtig, -baar, -loos,* and *-erig,* and the unproductive suffix *-zaam*. Moreover, some of the suffixes that attach to nouns to form relational adjectives are also used for the formation of qualitative adjectives in combination with adjectival or verbal stems. This applies to *-ig* and *-(e)lijk*.

The suffix *-baar* '-able' is attached productively to transitive verbs, and produces adjectives with the meaning 'able to be V-ed'. Thus, it forms a clear case of a syntactic restriction on the input of a word-formation process. In addition, there are a few inchoative verbs and non-transitive verbs that occur with this suffix:

(59) ontbrand 'to take fire' > ontbrand-baar 'inflammable'
 ontplof 'to explode' > ontplof-baar 'explosive'
 studeer 'to study' > studeer-baar 'studiable'
 werk 'to work' > werk-baar 'workable'

Verbal stems with a prepositional object are normally excluded from suffixation with -*baar*. For instance, we cannot form *vechtbaar 'fightable' from the verb *vechten* that requires a prepositional object. This implies that the syntactic restrictions on input words have to have access to the level of syntactic subcategorization of a lexical item. However, there are adjectives with -*baar* that derive from verbs with prepositional objects such as *beschikbaar* 'available' (< *beschikken over* 'to dispose of') and *onontkoombaar* 'inescapable' (< *ontkomen aan* 'to escape from').

TABLE 3.12. *Native adjectival suffixes for qualitative adjectives*

Suffix	Stem		Derived adjective
-achtig	N	rots 'rock'	rots-achtig 'rocky'
	V	weiger 'to refuse'	weiger-achtig 'refusing persistently'
	A	groen 'green'	groen-achtig 'greenish'
-baar	V	draag 'to carry'	draag-baar 'portable'
	N	vrucht 'fruit'	vrucht-baar 'fruitful'
-elijk	N	god 'god'	godd-elijk 'divine'
	V	erf 'to inherit'	erf-elijk 'hereditary'
	A	bang 'afraid'	bang-elijk 'timid'
-erig	N	hout 'wood'	hout-erig 'stiff'
	V	bijt 'to bite'	bijt-erig 'biting'
	A	groen 'green'	groen-erig 'sort of greenish'
-ig	N	bloed 'blood'	bloed-ig 'bloody'
	V	nalaat 'to neglect'	nalat-ig 'negligent'
	A	groen 'green'	groen-ig 'greenish'
-loos	N	naam 'name'	naam-loos 'nameless'
-zaam	N	deugd 'virtue'	deugd-zaam 'virtuous'
	V	werk 'to work'	werk-zaam 'active'
	A	lang 'long'	lang-zaam 'slow'

In a number of *-baar*-adjectives we find additional meaning aspects. The following interpretational categories are distinguished by Hüning and van Santen (1994): (i) incorporation of the derived implication into the meaning of the adjective; (ii) modal readings, and (iii) metaphorical interpretations. The same categories can be found for deverbal adjectives in *-(e)lijk*:

(60) (a) aantrekk-elijk 'attractive' < aantrek 'to attract', lees-baar 'readable' < lees 'to read'
 (b) betaal-baar 'affordable' < betaal 'to pay', verwerp-elijk 'objectionable' < verwerp 'to reject'
 (c) onaantastbaar 'inviolable' < aantast 'to violate', ondraaglijk 'unbearable' < draag 'to bear'

The unproductive deverbal suffix *-(e)lijk* can have the same meaning contribution as *-baar* in combination with transitive verbal stems. It also occurs with intransitive verbs such as *sterven* 'to die', and it can also denote a subject property:

(61) draag 'to bear'   draag-lijk 'bearable'
     erger 'to annoy'   erger-lijk 'annoying'
     sterf 'to die'   sterf-elijk 'mortal'
     verwerp 'to reject' verwerp-elijk 'objectionable'

As Hüning and van Santen (1994) pointed out, the formal and semantic heterogeneity of the suffix *-(e)lijk* may be the cause of its present unproductivity, because productivity requires semantic transparency of a word-formation pattern (Aronoff 1976, cf. also van Marle 1984, 1988). The use of *-baar* is clearly more systematic, also as far as the syntactic category of the base is concerned: a denominal adjective in *-baar* such as *vruchtbaar* 'fruitful' is a real exception, and its etymological meaning 'fruit bearing' nicely illustrates that this suffix derives from the ancestor of the verb *to bear*.

The adjectival suffixes *-ig* and *-erig* have similar meanings, in particular with nominal and adjectival bases. The subtle difference in meaning between these suffixes can be defined as follows: if both suffixes can be used with a particular stem, then the use of *-erig* may involve a more subjective, relativizing interpretation, as illustrated by the difference in meaning between *groenig* 'greenish' and *groenerig* 'sort of greenish' (Schultink 1962). The interesting point of this observation is that this more subjective interpretation of the *-erig*-adjective depends on a paradigmatic relation with another word derived from the same stem. The existence of such a paradigmatic relation between X-*ig* and X-*erig* adjectives is confirmed by the formation of adjectives in -*erig* from adjectives in -*ig* that have no lexematic stem (*deft* and *zuin* do not exist as words):

(62)   deft-ig 'solemn'   deft-erig 'solemnish'
       zuin-ig 'thrifty'   zuin-erig 'thriftyish'

There are other differences between these two suffixes as well. In particular, the deverbal use of -*ig* is unproductive, whereas it is very productive for -*erig* which then has the meaning 'inclined to V'. Moreover, the suffix -*ig* does not attach to already suffixed nouns (Section 3.2.1), unlike -*erig*. For instance, whereas *held-inn-ig* 'heroine-like' is ill-formed, *heldinn-erig* is fine.

The suffix -*ig* is also used in synthetic compounds, and will therefore also be discussed in Section 4.3.2.

3.4.4. Adverbial suffixes

In Dutch, adjectives can be used adverbially without any morphological marking. Nevertheless, there are a few processes for the creation of adverbs. First, the sufffix sequence -*tje-s* (and its allomorphs) can be used for creating adverbs from (mainly simplex) adjectives:

(63)   *Adjective*   *Adverb*
       fris 'fresh'   fris-jes 'rather fresh'
       gewoon 'common'   gewoon-tjes 'rather common'
       stil 'quiet'   still-etjes 'rather quiet'
       warm 'warm'   warm-pjes 'rather warm'

The reason for analysing -*tjes* as a suffix sequence is that it exhibits the same kind of allomorphy as the diminutive suffix -*tje* (cf. Section 5.3.1) which therefore should be identified as such in -*tjes* and its allomorphs.

A second, rather archaic adverbial suffix that can be used with some simplex adjectives is the suffix -*elijk*:

(64)   hoog 'high'   hog-elijk 'highly'
       laatst 'recent' laatst-elijk 'recently'
       wijs 'wise'   wijs-elijk 'wisely'

In addition, the non-native suffix -*iter* can be used with some non-native adjectives, for instance *normal-iter* 'normally' and *idealiter* 'ideally'.

Dutch also has the following adverbial suffixes:

(65) -(e)lings beurt 'turn'   beurt-elings 'alternately'
                 blind 'blind'   blind-elings 'blindly'
      -erwijs   menselijk 'human'   menselijk-erwijs 'humanly'
                 redelijk 'reasonable' redelijk-erwijs 'reasonable'
      -gewijs   groep 'group'   groeps-gewijs 'by group'
                 steekproef 'sample' steekproefs-gewijs 'by sample'
      -halve   beroep 'profession' beroeps-halve 'by virtue of one's profession'
                 fatsoen 'decency'   fatsoens-halve 'for decency's sake'
      -waarts   huis 'home'   huis-waarts 'to home'
                 zee 'sea'   zee-waarts 'to the sea'
      -weg   dom 'stupid'   dom-weg 'simply'
                 simpel 'simple'   simpel-weg 'simply'

None of these processes is very productive, however.

3.5. CONVERSION

Conversion can be defined as the derivation of a word without any phonological change of its base word. Consider the following pairs of words in Dutch:

(66) *Noun*   *Verb*
      douche 'shower'   douche 'to shower'
      fiets 'bicycle'   fiets 'to cycle'
      hamer 'hammer'   hamer 'to hammer'
      winkel 'shop'   winkel 'to shop'

We have good reasons to assume that in this case the verbs have been formed on the basis of the nouns: the meaning of the verbs can be defined as a compositional function of the meaning of the corresponding nouns. For instance, the meaning of the verb *douchen* 'to shower' is an action in which what is denoted by the noun plays a role.

This kind of word formation can be accounted for by means of a template of the following type:

3.5. CONVERSION

(67) $[[x]_N]_V$ 'to V, with N playing a role in the action denoted by V'

The use of such a template for expressing conversion avoids the problems connected to calling this kind of word formation zero-affixation. If we assume a zero-affix, we have to arbitrarily decide if it is a prefix or a suffix, since both prefixes and suffixes have category-changing power in Dutch. The idea behind the concept of zero-affixation is obviously that functionally, conversion is equivalent to category-changing affixation. For instance, it is also possible to form a new verb by prefixation or by means of suffixation, as shown above. It is also the functional equivalence that is the reason for dealing with conversion in this chapter on derivation, although strictly speaking it is another type of word formation.

The direction of conversion has been established here on the basis of the meanings of the corresponding words. The assumption of a direction 'N to V' is confirmed by the fact that this is a productive relationship: in principle, each Dutch noun can be converted into a verb, whereas the opposite is not the case: it is not possible to convert any verb whatever into a noun. For instance, we cannot convert the verbal stem *eet* 'to eat' into the noun *eet* 'food', nor the verbal stem *schrijf* 'to write' into the noun *schrijf* 'writing'.

The direction of this form of conversion is also revealed by the fact that in such cases the verb always has the default conjugation, even if there is an Ablauting verbal root related to the noun. For instance, in addition to the Ablauting verb *prijzen* 'to praise' we find the noun *prijs* 'price' with the corresponding regular verb *prijzen* 'to price'. Another indication of the direction of the conversion is phonological make-up. Simplex verbs in Dutch consist of either one syllable, or two syllables, the second of which contains a schwa. Therefore, verbs like *papegaaien* 'to parrot' and *dominoën* 'to play dominoes', which have a more complex phonological composition, betray their nominal origin, and have been converted from the nouns *papegaai* 'parrot' and *domino* 'dominoes' respectively (Don 1993).

Due to the very general meaning contribution of the conversion construction, the range of specific meanings of conversion verbs is enormous. We find, for instance, the following meaning classes:

(68) | *Meaning* | *Noun* | *Verb* |
| --- | --- | --- |
| to behave as N | ijsbeer 'polar bear' | ijsbeer 'to pace up and down' |
| | moeder 'mother' | moeder 'to play mother' |
| | tuinier 'gardener' | tuinier 'to garden' |

make into N	bundel 'bundle'	bundel 'to bundle'
	knecht 'servant'	knecht 'to subjugate'
to do something with N	huis 'house'	huis 'to live'
	schroef 'screw'	schroef 'to screw'
	zon 'sun'	zon 'to sunbathe'
produce N	big 'piglet'	big 'to pig'
	bloesem 'blossom'	bloesem 'to blossom'
	jong 'young one'	jong 'to give birth'

The semantic versatility of this word-formation process (also observed for English by Clark and Clark 1979) is certainly an important cause of its high productivity. This is also grasped very early in the process of language acquisition, and hence Dutch children appear to coin many verbs in this way that never get established. The following verbs, for example, were coined by my daughters Suzanne and Rebecca:

(69) au 'to hurt' < au 'ouch' (2 years, 10 months)
 drop 'to eat a piece of liquorice' < drop 'liquorice' (3 years, 2 months)
 telefoon 'to make a phone call' < telefoon 'telephone' (3 years, 3 months)
 viltstift 'to draw with a feltpen' < viltstift 'feltpen' (4 years, 10 months)

In many other European languages, children use this kind of conversion productively (Clark 1993: ch. 11). Most of these converted nouns are simplex ones, or compounds with a simplex head such as *voetbal* 'football' with the corresponding verb *voetballen* 'to play football': it is not easy to find derivationally complex nouns that feed conversion. An example is *tuinieren* 'to garden' from the noun *tuinier* 'gardener'.

In addition to conversion of nouns to verbs there are other patterns of conversion, but these are all marginally productive, or have a very restricted domain of application, and apply to simplex stems only, except for nominalization of verbs that also applies to prefixed verbs (but not to suffixed verbs):

(70) V to N
 aanvang 'to begin' (de) aanvang 'begin'
 behoud 'to keep' (het) behoud 'preservation'
 kook 'to boil' (de) kook 'boiling'

loop 'to walk'	(de) loop 'walk'
pak 'to fetch'	(het) pak 'pack'
zeur 'to nag'	(de) zeur 'nag'

A to N

dwaas 'silly'	(de) dwaas 'idiot'
gek 'mad'	(de) gek 'madman'
rood 'red'	(het) rood 'red colour'

A to V

wit 'white'	wit 'to whiten'
zuiver 'pure'	zuiver 'to purify'
zwart 'black'	zwart 'to blacken'

(cf. Schultink 1962: 62 ff.). From this survey we can conclude that there is no conversion of nouns or verbs into adjectives. There are quite a number of N–A pairs in the non-native lexicon, for which the direction of conversion may seem less straightforward:

(71) *Adjective* *Noun*
     collectief 'collective' (het) collectief 'the collective'
     explosief 'explosive' (het) explosief 'the explosive'
     periodiek 'periodical' (de, het) periodiek 'the periodical'
     politiek 'political' (de) politiek 'politics'

In terms of meaning, however, it appears that the meaning of the noun can be defined more easily as a compositional function of that of the adjective, than vice versa. For instance, a *periodiek* is a journal with a *periodiek* appearance. It is in particular words in *-ief* and in *-iek* that have these kind of conversion pairs. Thus, we can maintain the generalization for Dutch that there is only conversion into verbs and nouns. As noted by Heynderickx (1994), as far as complex adjectives are concerned, it is in particular non-native complex adjectives that lend themselves to conversion.

As will be shown in Section 6.4, conversion of nouns and adjectives into verbs is also triggered by the combination of a particle (preverb) with a noun or adjective, as in *uit-huwelijken* 'to marry off' from *huwelijk* 'marriage', and *ophogen* 'to heighten' from *hoog* 'high'.

As mentioned above, prefixed verbs and particle verbs often have a corresponding noun, although this is not a productive process any more. Interestingly, the gender of the corresponding noun can be predicted systematically:

nouns from prefixed verbs are neuter, and nouns from particle verbs are non-neuter:

(72)

Prefixed verbal stem	Neuter noun
be-roep 'to appeal'	beroep 'appeal, profession'
be-toog 'to argue'	betoog 'argument'
ge-bruik 'to use'	gebruik 'use'
mis-bruik 'to misuse'	misbruik 'misuse'
onder-wijs 'to teach'	onderwijs 'teaching'
over-leg 'to deliberate'	overleg 'deliberation'
ver-val 'to decay'	verval 'decay'
ver-raad 'to betray'	verraad 'betrayal'
ont-werp 'to design'	ontwerp 'design'
ont-zet 'to relieve'	ontzet 'relief'

Particle verb stems	Non-neuter noun
aan-voer 'to supply'	aanvoer 'supply'
af-trap 'to kick off'	aftrap 'kick off'
bij-val 'to approve'	bijval 'approval'
in-koop 'purchase'	inkoop 'purchase'
na-galm 'to echo'	nagalm 'echo'
op-vang 'to support'	opvang 'support'
uit-leen 'to lend'	uitleen 'lending'

These nouns have been derived from the corresponding verbs, and not from simplex nouns by means of prefixation or particle attachment: in many cases the corresponding noun either does not exist, or has a different meaning. For instance, there is no noun *werp* that could have been used as base word for the formation of the noun *ontwerp*. Moreover, the prefixes involved can only be attached to nouns to form verbs.

The predictability of the gender of these converted nouns on the basis of the morphological structure of the verbal bases has interesting theoretical implications. First, it shows that this kind of conversion should not be represented as zero-suffixation, because in that case we would expect uniform gender assignment by the zero-affix to the resulting noun. In other words, these facts form a counterargument to a zero-affix interpretation of conversion.[17] Second, it shows once more that the internal morphological structure

---

[17] In Don (1993), a dissertation devoted to the analysis of conversion in Dutch, an attempt is made to derive the neuter gender of the prefixed verb conversions by assuming the

of a complex word, once it has been coined, must remain accessible for further morphological computations, a conclusion we also reached above on the basis of other evidence (cf. Sections 2.4.3 and 3.2.1).

The notion 'conversion' might be extended to cases where there is no change in category, but in subcategory. For instance, it is often possible to use a causative verb ending in -*iseer* or beginning with *ver*- as an intransitive verb as well, and this intransitive use of such verbs is increasing in present-day Dutch:

(73) De zon vergeelt het wasgoed 'The sun turns the laundry yellow'
 Het wasgoed vergeelt 'The laundry turns yellow'
 De regering stabiliseert de situatie 'The government stabilizes the situation'
 De situatie stabiliseert 'The situation stabilizes'

Since this productive intransitive use is related to specific affixes, Baayen and Lieber (1994) proposed to account for this systematic variation in valency by making the causer role in the lexical conceptual structure attributed by these affixes optional.[18]

Another type of category-internal valency change is the formation of middle verbs on the basis of verbs that occur with an object, or a prepositional adjunct that denotes an instrument, a location, or an external circumstance (Booij 1992, Ackema and Schoorlemmer 1994, 1995, Peeters 1999):

(74) Deze aardappelen schillen gemakkelijk 'These potatoes peel easily'
 Mars hapt zo heerlijk weg '*lit*. Mars eats so nicely away'
 Dat paard rijdt lekker '*lit*. That horse rides nicely'
 Regenweer wandelt niet gezellig 'Rainy weather does not walk nicely'
 Het zingt hier gemakkelijk voor mij '*lit*. It sings here easily for me, I can sing here easily'

---

nominalizing prefix *ge*- that derives neuter nouns to be present underlyingly in such nouns, and by having a rule that deletes *ge*- before this prefix, an idea also found in de Haas (1990). The empirical problem for this analysis is that the prefix *ge*- is actually kept before prefixed verbs, as shown in Section 3.3.2. For instance, a noun such as *ge-belazer* 'cheating' from the verbal stem *be-lazer* 'to cheat' is a well-formed noun. Moreover, nominalization with *ge*- is productive whereas this is not the case for this kind of nominalization of prefixed verbs; thus, a wrong prediction is made as to the productivity of this process.

[18] Cf. Jackendoff (1990: 75) and Plag (1999: 135) for the same solution for this kind of alternation.

As argued in Booij (1992) and Ackema and Schoorlemmer (1994, 1995), this intransitive use of verbs cannot be a matter of syntax, but requires a lexical rule that applies to the lexical conceptual structure of verbs that express an action. The resulting middle verbs do not express an action, but a property. The meaning of these middle verbs can be defined as follows: the property of x (x the subject of the middle verb) of being able to be involved in the event expressed by the base verb. This definition implies that the agent of the event expressed by the base verb is always left unspecified (it can be expressed, though, by an adjunct-PP with the preposition *voor* 'for', as illustrated by the last example in (74)). These middle verbs usually require some evaluative expression to be present in the clause in which they occur that specifies how well the subject can be involved in the event. As the last example shows, the subject position can even be filled by the dummy-pronoun *het*.

Middle verbs thus differ from passive verbs in that they express a property instead of an event. Consequently, they cannot occur with an optional agent-PP with the preposition *door* 'by', unlike passive verbs. This difference is also manifest in the choice of auxiliary: middle verbs have periphrastic tenses with the auxiliary *hebben* as shown by the following minimal pair:

(75) Dit boek heeft goed verkocht 'This book has sold well'
      Dit boek is goed verkocht 'This book has been sold well'

This formal difference underscores the semantic differences between passive and middle verbs, which also manifest themselves in control phenomena (cf. Section 6.2).

For the sake of completeness, it is proper to mention that the adjectival use of participles, and the nominal use of infinitives as discussed in Chapter 2 can also be seen as cases of conversion.

4

Compounding

4.1. INTRODUCTION

Compounding is a very productive process in Dutch. The defining criterion for compounding as opposed to derivation is that in compounding two lexemes are combined into a new lexeme. For instance, the word *bureaulade* 'desk drawer' is a compound formed from the nouns *bureau* 'desk' and *lade* 'drawer'. In this definition, I refer to the notion 'lexeme', and not the notion 'free form' since the constituents of a compound are not necessarily free forms that occur as words. A lexeme in a compound may have a specific form that does not occur as a word in a concrete sentence, because the stem of the first lexeme of a Dutch compound may have a special 'combining form' in that it has an extra [s] or [ə] at the end, as in *schaapskop* 'sheep's head' and *schapewol* 'sheep's wool' (cf. Section 5.3.3).

Dutch compounds are right-headed: the right constituent is the head, and hence determines the semantic class, the syntactic category, and—in the case of nouns—the gender of the compound.[1] Compounding with nouns and adjectives is productive, whereas compounding with verbal heads is unproductive. Since word formation can only expand the fund of words of lexical categories (N, A, V, Adv), we do not find compounds with a non-lexical category in head position.

---

[1] The rightheadedness of Dutch compounds does not follow from a universal Righthand Head Rule, as suggested by Williams (1981), since there are also many languages with left-headed compounds, such as Indonesian and Vietnamese. It may be that the direction of headedness is a parameter. In that case, each language would have either right-headed or left-headed compounds. This issue is particularly relevant in relation to Romance languages which seem to have both left- and right-headed compounds. However, the parameter approach can be maintained if it can be shown that the left-headed compounds are in fact lexicalized phrases. See Scalise (1992) for discussion of this issue.

4.2. NOMINAL COMPOUNDS

Nominal compounding is the most productive type of compounding in Dutch (cf. de Caluwe 1991). The non-head position can be taken by nouns, adjectives, verbs, prepositions, adverbs, quantifiers, and phrases, as illustrated by the following examples:

(1) NN   [[bureau]$_N$[lade]$_N$]$_N$ 'desk drawer'
      AN   [[groot]$_A$[vader]$_N$]$_N$ 'grandfather'
      VN   [[kook]$_V$[pot]$_N$]$_N$ 'cooking pot'
      PN   [[voor]$_P$[gerecht]$_N$]$_N$ 'first course'
      AdvN   [[lang]$_{Adv}$[slaper]$_N$]$_N$ '*lit.* long sleeper, late riser'
      QA   [[drie]$_Q$[hoek]$_N$]$_N$ 'triangle'
      NP N   [[oude mannen]$_{NP}$ [huis]$_N$]$_N$ 'old men's house'

The productivity of nominal compounding, in particular of NN compounds, is increased by the fact that both constituents can be compounds themselves, that is, they exhibit recursivity, as illustrated in (2):

(2)   [[[[woon]$_V$[ruimte]$_N$]$_N$[verdelings]$_N$]$_N$[[advies]$_N$[commissie]$_N$]$_N$]$_N$
        'housing accommodation distribution advice committee'
    [[[[milieu]$_N$[effect]$_N$]$_N$[rapportage]$_N$]$_N$[[bijeen]$_{Adv}$[komst]$_N$]$_N$]$_N$
        'environment effect reporting meeting'

There is no structural constraint on the degree of recursivity allowed, but it is obvious that a compound with too much recursivity will cause processing problems. The head status of the right constituent of a nominal compound is not only clear from its semantic interpretation (an XY is a kind of Y with some relation to X, not vice versa), and from the fact that the right constituent determines the syntactic category, but also from its gender, and in some cases the choice of the plural suffix. Since the gender of compounds is that of the right constituent, we find pairs such as the following (cf. Trommelen and Zonneveld 1986):

(3)   de soep 'the soup'   het vlees 'the meat'
        de vleessoep 'the meat soup'   het soepvlees 'the soup meat'

        het geld 'the money'   de zak 'the pocket/bag'
        het zakgeld 'the pocket money'   de geldzak 'the money bag'

de bal 'the ball'   het bal 'the ball, dancing'
de voetbal 'the football'   het avondbal 'the night ball'

That the choice of the plural suffix is determined by the right noun, is shown nicely by cases of lexically determined choice of the plural suffix, and if there is stem allomorphy. For instance, there are two words *portier*, each with its own gender, meaning, and plural suffix; the plural-suffix choice is transferred to compounds with these words as right constituents:

(4) portier 'doorkeeper' (non-neuter)   portier-s 'pl.'
     nachtportier 'night doorkeeper'   nachtportier-s 'pl.'
     portier 'car door' (neuter)   portier-en 'pl.'
     autoportier 'car door'   autoportier-en 'pl.'
     kind 'child'   kinder-en 'pl.'
     kleinkind 'grandchild'   kleinkinder-en 'pl.'

This rightheadedness of Dutch compounds can be expressed by assuming a general template for Dutch compounds of the following type: $[XY]_Y$ where Y = N or A (note that verbal compounding is not productive). By having the Y variable both as right constituent and dominating node is expressed the fact that all properties of the constituent Y are identical to those of the dominating Y. This template is therefore a template for endocentric compounds.

Does Dutch also have exocentric compounds? The answer is negative as far as morphological structure is concerned: what have been called exocentric compounds or bahuvrihi compounds are a specific semantic category of endocentric compounds based on metonymy: a part of an entity is used to refer to the whole entity. This is what is at stake with the classical English example of a bahuvrihi compound *redskin*. Generally, lexical or phrasal referring expressions can be used in this way, in particular to refer to persons by mentioning a characteristic of that person:

(5) Die regenjas is een detective 'lit. That raincoat is a detective, the person with the raincoat is a detective'
     Die rode trui moet zijn mond houden 'lit. That red sweater should shut up, the person with the red sweater should shut up'

So the fact that a *bleekneus* 'lit. pale nose, pale person' is not a *neus* does not indicate that this is an exocentric compound, but only reveals the special semantic interpretation of this word. There is, however, a number of such bahuvrihi compounds in which the gender of the compound is non-neuter, whereas that of the formal head is neuter. This is the effect of the semantic generalization that nouns referring to human beings are non-neuter (cf. Section 2.2):

(6) het oog 'the eye'   (de) spleetoog 'slit-eye'
     het oor 'the ear'   (de) domoor '*lit.* stupid ear, idiot'
     het been 'the leg'   (de) brekebeen '*lit.* break leg, dead loss'

The following compounds are examples of lexicalized bahuvrihi-compounds:

(7) blauwkous 'blue-stocking', bleekgezicht 'paleface', duizendpoot '*lit.* thousand-pede, centipede, jack-of-all-trades', roodborstje '*lit.* redbreast, robin', stijfkop 'hardhead'

A second category of nominal compounds with a special status are compounds such as

(8) minister-president 'prime minister', prins-gemaal 'prince consort', stadhouder-koning 'stadtholder-king', tuinman-chauffeur 'gardener-chauffeur'

Such compounds have been called copulative compounds because both parts of such compounds mention properties of the same person: a *tuinman-chauffeur* is someone who is both a gardener and a chauffeur. Note, however, that such compounds are not conjunctions of words since the compounds behave as singular nouns with respect to verbal agreement. In other words, what is special about such compounds is the nature of the relation between the head and the non-head: a *tuinman-chauffeur* is a chauffeur who is also a gardener. This is supported by the fact that the expected plural form of this compound is *tuinman-chauffeurs*. The claim that such compounds are in fact endocentric compounds is supported by cases in which the gender of the two constituents differ. For instance, in the compound *kindster* 'child star, star who is still a child' (with the plural form *kindsterren*), the word *star* is non-neuter, whereas the word *kind* is a neuter noun. The compound is a non-neuter noun, thus clearly exhibiting the effect of rightheadedness.[2]

---

[2] An exceptional formation in this respect is *minister-president* '*lit.* minister president, prime minister' with the double plural form *ministers-presidenten*. Although this is the official norm, most native speakers spontaneously coin the plural form *minister-presidenten*,

4.2. NOMINAL COMPOUNDS

A third class of expressions that one might be inclined to interpret as left-headed compounds are word combinations such as the following:

(9) de commissie Staal '*lit.* the committee Staal, the Staal-committee'
     de regering Kok '*lit.* the government Kok, the Kok-government'
     de zaak Oltmans '*lit.* the case Oltmans, the Oltmans-case'

However, such word combinations can be considered syntactic constructs, parallel to *station Amsterdam* 'Amsterdam station' in which the second noun functions as an apposition to the first noun, which is the head, and may be pluralized, as in *de heren Booij* 'the sirs Booij'.

4.2.1. *The left constituent of nominal compounds*

The most frequent kind of left constituent is the nominal stem. It is important to realize that it is indeed the nominal stem, not the singular noun that occurs in this position because the nominal stem does not necessarily have a singular interpretation. For instance, in the compound *boekverkoper* 'bookseller' it is clear that this word does not refer to a singular book, but to the category 'book'.[3]

A special property of the left constituent is that it may have an extended stem form in -*s*, -*e*, -*en*, or -*er*. The regularities in the occurrence of these long stem allomorphs and their historical background will be discussed in Section 5.3.3. Although these extensions occur mainly after nominal stems, there are also verbal stems that exhibit this kind of extension, with -*e* or -*s*:[4]

(10) breke-been '*lit.* break leg, dead loss'
     drinke-broer '*lit.* drink brother, heavy drinker'
     hebbe-dingetje '*lit.* have thing, gadget'

---

with only the right constituent in the plural form. Other isolated cases are *secretaris-generaal* 'secretary general' and *gouverneur-generaal* 'governor general', with the plural forms *secretarissen-generaal* and *gouverneurs-generaal* respectively. These compounds are clearly left-headed, but are historical relics and loan translations of French left-headed NPs that function as terms.

[3] This is why Mattens (1970) introduced the notion 'indifferentialis' as a third category for nouns, besides the singular and plural category. However, we do not need a third category of this kind to express this insight if we make the distinction between stem and word.

[4] The -*e* in *wittebrood* 'white bread' may also be interpreted as an extension of the adjectival stem *wit* 'white'. However, this compound could also be interpreted as a lexicalized phrase.

huile-balk *'lit.* cry beam, cry baby'
scheids-rechter *'lit.* separate judge, referee'
voorbehoeds-middel *'lit.* prevent means, preservative'

This shows once more that synchronically, these extensions do not have a morphological status, but only function to create stem allomorphs in specific morphological contexts: obviously, a verb cannot have case endings.

A characteristic feature of nominal compounds is that the non-head can also be phrasal (Hoeksema 1988). The following data illustrate this generalization:

(11) [AN]$_{NP}$ [blote-vrouwen]$_{NP}$ blad 'nude women magazine'
   [hete-lucht]$_{NP}$ ballon 'hot air balloon'
[QN]$_{NP}$ [drie-landen]$_{NP}$ punt 'three countries point, where three countries meet'
   [vier-kleuren]$_{NP}$ druk *'lit.* four colours printing'

The phrasal status of the AN sequences in the non-head position is shown by the facts of inflection: the adjectives end in schwa and are therefore inflected, which is only possible within phrases. In addition, these word sequences have the stress patterns of phrases (main stress on the last word), not of compounds, which have main stress on the first constituent. For instance, in *heteluchtballon* the main stress of the constituent *hete lucht* is on *lucht*, as is expected if this is a phrase.

Note that it is obvious that a compound-internal phrasal constituent can only occur in non-head position: if a phrase occurred in the head position, the whole expression would be a phrase, and hence no compound. It should also be stressed that the kind of NPs that occur within compounds are not just lexicalized NPs: this is a productive pattern, and an NP need not be lexicalized in order to be used as constituent of a compound.

The theoretical implication of these facts is that the word-formation component of a grammar cannot be qualified as presyntactic, since syntactic rules such as adjective–noun agreement must be allowed to apply within these compounds. Therefore, our conception of the grammar has to be a modular one, with the modules unordered: the morphological module defines the set of well-formed words, and the syntactic module defines the set of well-formed phrases and sentences (cf. also Pinker 1999: 183 ff.). It is the morpho-

4.2. NOMINAL COMPOUNDS

logical module that states that the left constituent of nominal compounds can consist of an NP, for which the rules of the syntactic module hold.

It is not the case that all kinds of NPs can function as compound constituents. It is only the combination of a bare adjective or quantifier with a bare noun that is allowed. For instance, the following kinds of compounds in which one of the constituents of the NP is modified, are impossible:

(12) *een [heel blote vrouwen]blad 'a very nude women magazine'
 *[vier donkere kleuren]druk 'four dark colours print'
 *een [de oude mannen]huis 'a the old men's home'

This means that it is the morphological module that defines which kind of NPs can occur within compounds. The reasons for this restriction are at least partially semantic. For instance, the embedded NP cannot be a referring expression, because parts of words cannot have independent reference. Hence, we do not find determiners in compound-internal NPs.

A consequence of the possibility of NPs occurring within words is that we find plural nouns within compounds. Examples are the following:

(13) [daken]zee 'sea of roofs'
 [huizen]rij 'row of houses'
 [vakken]pakket '*lit.* packet of subjects, subjects chosen for graduation'

In these examples the head nouns refer to a kind of container or a mass, and thus the use of plural nouns in the non-head position is quite natural. Note, however, as also pointed out in Section 2.5, it is only plural nouns in *-en* that occur in compound-internal phrases: compounds such as *appelsoogst* '*lit.* apples harvest' or *groene-appelsoogst* '*lit.* green apples harvest' are impossible.

The compounds in (13) have been interpreted as counterexamples to the claim that inflection is always peripheral to word formation. However, once we realize that NPs can occur within compounds, it appears that they do not form such counterevidence since plural nouns can function as heads of NP (Booij 1994: 37).[5]

---

[5] This problem is also discussed in Pinker (1999: 183) for English, with the same conclusion that such plural nouns are heads of phrases.

In this connection it is relevant to observe that verbal infinitives also appear as left constituent of compounds, sometimes followed by a 'linking phoneme':

(14) [eten-s]tijd 'eating time'
      [varen-s]man 'seafarer'
      [uitgaan-s]verbod '*lit.* outgoing prohibition, curfew'
      [zien-s]wijze '*lit.* seeing way, view'

However, this requires no special provision since infinitives can function as nouns, and hence occur within NN-compounds in the left position.

It is not only NPs that occur within compounds: we also find sentences, sometimes in the form of imperative sentences, PPs, and APs (bare adjectives followed by a complement) within compounds:

(15) [ban-de-bom]$_S$-demonstratie 'ban the bomb demonstration'
      [blijf-van-mijn-lijf]$_S$-huis '*lit.* stay away from my body home, women's shelter'
      [doe-het-zelf]$_S$-winkel 'do it yourself shop'
      [God-is-dood]$_S$-theologie 'God is dead theology'
      de [wie-heeft-het-gedaan]$_S$-vraag 'the whodunit question'
      [onder water]$_{PP}$-camera 'underwater camera'
      [buiten boord]$_{PP}$-motor 'outboard engine'
      [ver-van-mijn-bed]$_{AP}$-show 'far away from my bed show'
      [blij-dat-ik-rij]$_{AP}$-campagne 'glad that I ride campaign'

A second kind of syntax within compounds is that of coordination: Ns, Vs, and As can be conjoined, with or without a conjunction:

(16) [N (en) N]   [peper en zout]stel '*lit.* pepper and salt set, salt and pepper set'
                   [huis-tuin-en-keuken]voorbeeld '*lit.* house, garden, and kitchen example, household, common or garden example'
      [V en V]   [luister-en-kijk]geld '*lit.* listening and watching money, radio/TV licence fee'
                   [gooi- en smijt]film '*lit.* throw and smash film, slapstick film'

There is evidence, however, that the coordination involved here is not a

4.2. NOMINAL COMPOUNDS

case of real syntax: in the case of V-coordination it is not words, but verbal stems that are coordinated, without an inflectional ending whereas syntactic coordination can only pertain to concrete, inflected words.[6] This kind of morphological coordination also occurs without compounding: there are coordinated nouns and adjectives which behave as word-like units in that it is only the second word that is inflected:

(17) kop-en-schotel 'cup and saucer' kop-en-schotel-s (plural)
    kant-en-klaar 'ready made' kant-en-klar-e (inflected form)

In other words, it is the rightmost constituent that functions as head, although coordination is involved. The special status of this kind of coordination is confirmed by the locus of the main stress, which is on the last word of the sequence, whereas in cases of syntactic coordination there is equal stress on both words; compare:

(18) een kóp en een schótel 'a cup and a saucer' *versus* een kop-en-schótel
    péper en zóut 'pepper and salt' *versus* een peper-en-zóut-stel
    kíjken en lúisteren 'to listen and to watch' *versus* kijk-en-lúister-geld

Therefore, I will assign no phrasal status to these coordinations, and assume that they are dominated by an X^0-node.

Word-internal asyndetic coordination, that is coordination without an overt conjunction, is also found in compounds. Examples are the following:

(19) *Coordination of nouns*
   [Holland-Amérika]lijn 'Holland–America line'
   [maag-dárm]kanaal 'gastro-intestinal tract'
   [moeder-kínd]relatie '*lit.* mother–child relation, relation between mother and child'

   Coordination of verbs
   [slaap-wáak]ritme 'sleep–wake rhythm'
   [woon-wérk]verkeer '*lit.* live–work traffic, commuter traffic'
   [zit-sláap]kamer '*lit.* sit–sleep room, bedsitting room'

   Coordination of adjectives
   [los-vást]relatie '*lit.* loose–fast relationship, informal relationship'

---

[6] As pointed out in Chapter 2, verbal stems are phonologically identical to first person singular present forms; however, these morphosyntactic features are not present in compound-internal coordination of verbs.

Finally, there is also a number of nominal compounds of which the left constituent consists of the sequence NPN, for example:

(20) [huis-aan-huis]$_{NP}$ blad '*lit.* house-to-house magazine, door-to-door magazine'
[mond-op-mond]$_{NP}$ beademing 'mouth-to-mouth resuscitation'
[nek-aan-nek]$_{NP}$ race 'neck-and-neck race'

In these words, the nouns involved in such constructions are usually identical. The embedded NPs function as adverbial modifiers.

There is a third kind of word sequence that occurs in the left position of nominal compounds but is not a syntactic phrase. These are AN, QN, and NV sequences:

(21) AN   [blauw][buik]salamander 'blue belly salamander'
            [breed][band]antenne 'broadband aerial'
            [groot][hoek]lens 'wide angle lens'
       QN   [twee][persoons]bed '*lit.* two person bed, double bed'
            [twee][richtings]verkeer 'two way traffic'
            [vier][kamer]flat 'four room flat'
       NV   [aardappel][schrap]machine '*lit.* potato scrape machine, potato scraper'
            [brand][blus]installatie '*lit.* fire extinguish installation, fire extinguisher'
            [koffie][zet]apparaat '*lit.* coffee make machine, coffee machine'

In the case of AN sequences, we know they are not NPs because there is no inflection of the adjective. For instance, the non-neuter noun *buik* 'belly' would require the inflected form *blauwe* if the noun were head of an NP. In the case of QN sequences, the quantifiers *twee* 'two' and higher require a plural head noun in an NP. As to the NV sequences, the verbs have the stem form, and hence are not inflected words, as would be the case if they were heads of a verbal phrase. Note also that we find the stem-extension *s* that is characteristic of nominal stems: NPs do not have stem extensions. Therefore, the structures of these compounds are the following respectively:

(22) [[AN]$_N$ N]$_N$, [[QN]$_N$ N]$_N$, [[NV]$_V$N]$_N$

By grouping the first two words into a constituent, we maintain the binary structure of compounds. Semantically, the first two words do form a unit: they function together as a modifier of the head.

In the case of AN as left constituent, we might want to say that there is nothing special about such compounds except that they are possible, not (yet) existing compounds. As to QN compounds, they are rather rare in isolation, although they do exist, for example *duizendpoot* 'lit. thousand leg, centipede, jack-of-all-trades' and *vierhoek* 'lit. four corner, quadrangle', but only with the semantic interpretation of bahuvrihi-compounds. It is clear, therefore, that they are only productive as left constituents of a compound. This also applies to the NV sequences: this kind of compounding is unproductive except as left constituent of nominal compounds. The theoretical implication of this observation is that the morphological module has to contain templates of the kind given in (22), i.e. compound templates with embedded compound templates, in order to express the fact that certain kinds of compounding (the embedded types) are only productive within these larger morphological configurations.

In sum, the left constituent of nominal compounds can consist of word sequences which do not occur as free phrases, and therefore, these configurations have to be defined as well-formed by the morphological module of the grammar, in the non-head position of nominal compounds. In addition, there are types of compounds that are only productive if embedded as the left constituent of nominal compounds.

4.2.2. *The semantic interpretation of nominal compounds*

Traditionally, the semantic relation between the two constituents of a nominal compound is seen as vague: an XY is a Y with some relation to X (Downing 1977). The nature of this relation is not a matter of linguistic knowledge, but rather of conceptual and factual knowledge. Consider, for instance, the following cases of compounding with the noun *molen* 'mill' as their head:

(22) betonmolen 'concrete mixer', houtmolen 'saw mill', korenmolen 'corn mill', mosterdmolen 'mustard mill', verfmolen 'paint mill', watermolen 'water mill', windmolen 'wind mill'

It will be clear that the exact interpretational relationship between *molen* and the modifier noun depends on knowledge of the world. In some cases, there is more than one interpretation. A *watermolen*, for instance, can be a mill powered by water, or a mill powered by wind with the function to transport water. This flexibility in the interpretational relationship between the constituents of a compound obviously enhances the productivity of nominal compounding.

If the head noun is a deverbal noun, the noun in left position may receive a specific interpretation as semantic (object) argument of the verbal base of that head noun, as in *telefoonbeantwoorder* '*lit*. telephone answerer, answering machine'. The interpretational mechanism involved here will be discussed in detail in Section 6.2.1.

The usefulness of compounding as a word-formation pattern is also strengthened by the fact that the left constituent may evoke new meanings for the head constituent. For instance, the noun *bank* has the meaning of 'financial institution' in *spaarbank* 'savings bank', but this meaning is extended to 'depository' in a number of compounds, whereas the word *bank* does not have this second meaning in isolation:

(23) bloedbank 'blood bank', databank 'data base', spermabank 'sperm bank'

The formation and interpretation is not always a syntagmatic operation, the concatenation of two lexemes: they may also be formed paradigmatically (cf. Moerdijk 1987). For example, when the compound *kerstvrouw* 'Mother Christmas' was formed, this was clearly done on the basis of the existing compound *Kerstman* 'Father Christmas'. And the formation of the compound *grondoorlog* 'ground war' has certainly to do with the existence of the compound *luchtoorlog* 'air war' to which it stands in opposition. Other examples of such compounds are:

(24) muisvaardigheid '(computer) mouse skill' *compare:* handvaardigheid 'manual skill'
vadertaal 'father language' *compare:* moedertaal 'mother language'

The head noun of a compound may develop into a suffix. An example is the compound *groenteboer* '*lit*. vegetable farmer, greengrocer'. In this compound, the word *boer* has been reinterpreted as meaning 'trader'. Hence, we find a number of compounds in -*boer* where the original meaning 'farmer' has become completely irrelevant:

(25)   kolenboer 'coal trader', lesboer '*lit.* lesson-farmer, teacher',
       patatboer 'chip seller', sigarenboer 'cigar seller'

It will be clear that such a semantic development will be furthered by paradigmatic compound formation: very probably, *kolenboer* has been coined on the basis of the relation: *groente – groenteboer / kolen – kolenboer*. The development of *boer* into a suffix is also an example of grammaticalization: a lexical morpheme becomes a derivational suffix through reinterpretation (cf. Hopper and Traugott 1993).

It is also possible for the first part of an NN compound to develop into a prefix. For instance, there is a number of compounds that begin with the noun *marathon* 'marathon'. This noun developed into a prefix with the meaning 'taking a long time, as in *marathonzitting* 'very long session' and *marathonvergadering* 'very long meeting'. Examples of nouns that have become pejorative prefixes are *kanker* 'cancer', *klote(n)* 'balls', *kut* 'cunt', *pest* 'plague', and *rot* 'to rot' which are used as pejorative modifiers, as in:

(26)   kankerschool 'bloody school', klotehouding 'bad attitude', kutding
       'worthless thing', pesthumeur 'very bad mood', rotmeid 'bitch'

This pejorative use of *kut* is so widespread that this modifier has also been reinterpreted as an adjective with the meaning 'bad', as in *Ik vind dit kut* 'I find this awful'. This also applies to *klote(n)* and *rot*. A positive and presently fashionable prefix of this kind is *wereld-* 'world-, fantastic', as in the phrase *twee wereldmeiden* 'two fantastic girls'. The difference between such nouns and real prefixes is that the former also occur as independent words, with the original, literal meaning.

4.3. ADJECTIVAL COMPOUNDS

Adjectival compounds form a productive category of Dutch compounds. The left constituent can be N, A, Adv, or V:

(27)   NA $[[auto]_N[vrij]_A]_A$ 'car free'
              $[[peper]_N[duur]_A]_A$ '*lit.* pepper expensive, very expensive'
       AA $[[jong]_A[getrouwd]_A]_A$ '*lit.* young married, married young'
              $[[licht]_A[grijs]_A]_A$ 'light grey'

AdvA [[niet]$_{Adv}$[productief]$_A$]$_A$ 'non-productive'
      [[wel]$_{Adv}$[bekend]$_A$]$_A$ 'well known'
VA   [[kots]$_V$[misselijk]$_A$]$_A$ '*lit.* vomit sick, very sick'
      [[spil]$_V$[ziek]$_A$]$_A$ '*lit.* waste sick, wasteful'

The adjectival head can be either simplex or complex (including present and perfect participles), examples with complex heads are the following:

(28) [[adem]$_N$[benem-end]$_A$]$_A$ 'breathtaking'
      [[computer]$_N$[ge-stuur-d]$_A$]$_A$ 'computer-controlled'
      [[milieu]$_N$[vriend-elijk]$_A$]$_A$ 'environment friendly'
      [[vrouw]$_N$[vijand-ig]$_A$]$_A$ '*lit.* woman hostile, hostile toward women'

The non-head position can also be occupied by quantifiers, and adverbs:

(29) *quantifiers:* drie-dimensioneel 'three-dimensional', drie-dubbel '*lit.* three-double, triple'
      adverbs: door-nat 'very wet', in-triest 'very sad', over-gelukkig 'very happy', boven-natuurlijk 'supernatural'

In such compounds, the words *door*, *in*, and *over* have the specific meaning 'very' that they do not have as adverbs. In other words, these words have grammaticalized into intensifying prefixes.

A remarkable property of the intensifiers *in* and *door* is that they can be coordinated, thus expressing the highest intensity possible, a form of repetition with iconic value:

(30) in-en-in-triest 'very, very sad'
      door-en-door-koud 'very, very cold'

The same kind of repetition is found for nominal left constituents that function as intensifiers (cf. Section 4.3.1).

Nouns that are used in adjectival compounds may have special stem allomorphs with *-e* or *-s*, just like NN compounds:

(31) ape-trots 'very proud' < aap 'monkey'
      bere-sterk 'very strong' < beer 'bear'
      doods-bang 'very frightened' < dood 'death'
      honds-brutaal 'very impertinent' < hond 'dog'

The regularities in this kind of stem allomorphy will be discussed in Section 5.3.3.

4.3. ADJECTIVAL COMPOUNDS

There are also copulative adjectival compounds such as *rood-wit-blauw* 'red–white–blue' and *Duits-Frans* 'German–French'. Only the adjectival head will bear an inflectional ending when used attributively, and hence these compounds are not copulative from a formal point of view: the rightmost adjective is the head, as illustrated by the following examples with inflected adjectives:

(32)   de rood-wit-blauwe vlag 'the red–white–blue flag'
       Duits-Franse betrekkingen 'German–French relationships'

Just as was the case for nominal compounds, there are also adjectival compounds with cranberry morphs, that is constituents that do not occur as words by themselves such as *lendig, rucht,* and *tjok*:

(33)   lam-lendig 'wretched'   < lam 'lame'
       roem-rucht 'illustrious'   < roem 'fame'
       tjok-vol 'chock-full'   < vol 'full'

A special intensifier is the productive prefix *aller-* that requires the adjectival head to appear in superlative form:

(34)   aller-aardigst 'very nice', aller-laatst 'very late', aller-hoogst 'very high', aller-liefst 'very sweet'

This special form *aller* can also be repeated, in an asyndetic conjunction: *de aller-aller-liefste schat* 'the most beloved sweatheart'.

4.3.1. *The semantic interpretation of adjectival compounds*

The semantic interpretation of AA-compounds does not require much discussion: the first adjective usually functions as a modifier with respect to the adjectival head. If the first constituent is a verb, it will either function as an intensifier as in *kotsmisselijk* 'very sick' (cf. *kotsen* 'to vomit'), or it will bear a thematic role of the adjective, as in *spilziek* 'wasteful' (cf. *spillen* 'to waste').

There are two main semantic classes of NA-compounds. First, in many cases the noun functions as the point of comparison with respect to the property expressed by the adjectival head. This is the case for the following compounds:

(35)   boter-zacht '*lit.* butter-soft, as soft as butter, very soft'
       ijzer-sterk '*lit.* iron strong, as strong as iron, very strong'
       lijk-bleek '*lit.* corpse-pale, as pale as a corpse, very pale'

steen-koud '*lit.* stone-cold, cold as stone, very cold'
vuur-rood '*lit.* fire-red, red as fire, very red'

In most cases, the noun that functions as the point of comparison has developed into an intensifier with the general meaning 'very'. In addition, there is quite a number of NA compounds in which the noun also functions as an intensifier without the original interpretation (point of comparison) being possible. This applies for instance to the following compounds:

(36) brood-nuchter '*lit.* bread-sober, stone-sober'
 dood-eerlijk '*lit.* dead-honest, deadly honest'
 olie-dom '*lit.* oil-stupid, very stupid'
 stok-doof '*lit.* stick-deaf, very deaf'
 straat-arm '*lit.* street-poor, very poor'

Interestingly, there is a correlation between the intensifier interpretation of the noun and the stress pattern of such adjectival compounds. Generally, the two constituents of an adjectival compound have either equal stress, or the location of the main stress is variable, depending on rhythmic factors and syntactic position (cf. Booij 1995). However, if the noun is interpreted as an intensifier, the main stress of the word is on the first, intensifying constituent. In other words, the stress pattern of an adjectival compound is codetermined by its semantic interpretation, and not only by its structural properties.

Due to this intensifier meaning of the first constituent, it is rather odd to form comparatives and superlatives of such adjectives: forms such as *ijzersterkst* and *vuurroder* are semantically odd, although not completely impossible. For instance, a sentence such as *De ouders waren nog vuurroder dan hun kinderen* 'The parents were even more extremely red than their children' is certainly possible.

As pointed out, the intensifying meaning originates from comparison. In some cases, the original comparison meaning completely disappeared, and thus the noun lost its original meaning, and acquired a purely intensifying meaning, thus acquiring the function of a prefix. The prefixal use of some of these nouns has become productive, and they are attached to all kinds of adjectives (Fletcher 1980):

(37) bere- '*lit.* bear' beregoed 'very good', bereleuk 'very nice'
 bloed- '*lit.* blood' bloedmooi 'very beautiful', bloednerveus 'very nervous'

4.3. ADJECTIVAL COMPOUNDS

    dood- '*lit.* dead'   doodgewoon 'very common', doodziek 'very ill'
    kei- '*lit.* boulder'   keigaaf 'very nice', keigoed 'very good',
                         keileuk 'very funny'

In these cases, we may conclude that the nouns have really developed into prefixes.

The second semantic class of NA compounds is that in which the noun plays a particular semantic role with respect to the adjectival head that can be explicated by means of a PP with that noun (van den Toorn 1997: 506):

(38)   energie-zuinig   zuinig met energie 'economical with energy'
          hitte-bestendig   bestand tegen hitte 'resistant against heat'
          lood-vrij   vrij van lood 'free from lead'
          milieu-vriendelijk   vriendelijk voor het milieu 'friendly to the environment'
          sneeuw-zeker   zeker van sneeuw 'with guaranteed snow'
          vet-arm   arm aan vet 'poor in fat'

If an adjective allows for two semantic roles, then the noun will fulfil one of the roles. That the left constituent fulfils a semantic role of the head, is confirmed by the impossibility of adding a PP-complement to such adjectival compounds: a phrase such as *energiezuinig met gas* 'energy-economical with gas' is ill-formed.

If the adjectival head has the form of a present participle, the nominal non-head has the Theme role, whereas with past participles as heads, the noun has a variety of roles. The latter kind of adjectival compound has become very popular (van den Toorn 1997), probably under the influence of English:

(39)   *Present participles*
       energie-besparend 'energy saving', grens-overschrijdend '*lit.* border crossing, breaking new ground', hart-verscheurend '*lit.* heart tearing, heart breaking', nood-lijdend '*lit.* need suffering, needy'

     Past participles
     inbraak-beveiligd '*lit.* burglary-protected, safeguarded against burglary', lucht-gekoeld 'air cooled', nood-gedwongen '*lit.* need-forced, out of necessity', tijd-gebonden 'time-bound', toekomst-gericht 'future-oriented'

4.3.2. *Synthetic compounds*

Synthetic compounds are complex words that seem to be formed by the simultaneous application of compounding and derivation. A clear example is the adjective *blauwogig* 'blue-eyed'. There is no compound *blauwoog* from which this word could have been derived, nor a derived word *ogig* that could function as the head of the compound *blauwogig*. Other examples are given in (40):

(40)   kort-adem-ig 'short of breath'
       lang-ben-ig 'long-legged'
       twee-lettergrep-ig 'disyllabic'

The analysis of this kind of adjectival compounds has been the subject of an interesting debate among students of Dutch morphology (cf. Botha 1984, Hoeksema 1984, van Santen 1986; 1992*a*) since a number of theoretical issues are involved.

One analysis that is clearly incorrect is the derivation of *blauwogig* from an NP *blauw oog* 'blue eye'. This option has been discussed with respect to similar compounds in English, and is meant to express the fact that the adjective *blauw* does not modify *ogig* but *oog* 'eye'. However, this solution is impossible because the adjective in such complex words is never inflected: a non-neuter noun like *voet* 'foot' always requires an adjective ending in -*e*; nevertheless, we do not find inflection in *snelvoetig* 'swift-footed'. Consequently, this kind of compounding cannot be used as evidence for syntax feeding morphology. What remains open as an analytical option is the interpretation of such adjectives as being derived from a possible, but non-existent compound. Such an analysis is similar to the one defended in Section 4.2.1 for compounds such as *groothoeklens* 'wide-angle lens'. In other words, we then claim that one word-formation process, the addition of the suffix -*ig* to a noun, triggers the application of another word-formation pattern, that of nominal compounding. That is, there is a template $[[AN]_N ig]_A$.

An alternative analysis also proposed in the literature mentioned above is that *blauwogig* is an adjectival compound of which the head is a possible, but non-existent derived adjective. The reason why *ogig* does not exist by itself is semantic: there is no use for such a compound because all human beings have eyes, and hence such an adjective cannot be used to refer to a distinctive property. It is only in combination with *blauw* that a distinguishing property is mentioned.

As to the special semantic property that in this analysis the adjective has to be interpreted as a modifier of the base of the complex adjectival head, there is independent evidence that we have to allow for modifiers to have this kind of restricted scope. Dutch has a productive class of adjectives of which the head has the form of a past participle:

(41) breed-ge[schouder]d   'broad-shouldered'
      kort-ge[rok]t   'short-skirted'
      wit-ge[jas]t   'white-coated'

In these words, the adjective does not modify the whole head, but only the nominal base. That is, we have independent evidence for the claim that the adjectival non-head may have this kind of restricted semantic scope with respect to the head, and hence such a restricted semantic scope can also be assumed for *blauw* in *blauwogig*. As Beard (1991) pointed out, this is a very general phenomenon.

The same reasoning can be applied to compounds such as *tweejaarlijks* 'biennial' and *driewekelijks* 'three-weekly'. The suffix *-lijks* is unproductive, and only occurs with nouns like *week* 'week', *maand* 'month', and *jaar* 'year'. Hence, *tweejaarlijks* must be analysed as *twee* + *jaarlijks*, and cannot be analysed as *tweejaar* + *-lijks*. Yet, it is clear that the scope of *twee* is over the nominal base of *jaarlijks*, *jaar*. Similarly, in the compound adjective *driedimensioneel* 'three-dimensional', the quantifier *drie* pertains to the base noun of *dimensioneel*, *dimensie* 'dimension'.

Therefore, if we want to assign the same structure to all adjectival synthetic compounds, we have to interpret complex adjectives such as *blauwogig* as adjectival compounds, with the special property that their heads are possible but non-existent adjectives in *-ig*. However, uniformity of analysis is not a compelling argument.

This latter analysis implies that synthetic compounds do not form a formal category of their own, but are normal compounds with two special properties: the restricted semantic scope of the adjectival modifier, and a head that does not necessarily exist as an independent word. It is possible to express the fact that, for instance, *ogig* only occurs within a compound, by assuming a specific template for such words of the following kind:

(42) $[A [N-ig]_A]_A$

in which two slots, for an adjective and for a noun, are open. This template does not introduce a new formal type of complex words, but expresses the fact that it is the combination of two independently motivated word-formation processes that systematically and productively co-occur.[7] In Section 4.2 we encountered the same phenomenon with respect to nominal compounds with simultaneous verbal compounding, as in *koffiezetmachine* 'lit. coffee make machine, coffee maker': these verbal compounds only occur in a specific morphological context.

Present participles in *-end* also appear as constituents of adjectival synthetic compounds. The following examples all contain present participles used as adjectives that are not established words, although they are well-formed words of Dutch:

(43) [haat]$_N$[drag-end]$_A$ 'lit. hate bearing, resentful'
      [ijzer]$_N$[houd-end]$_A$ 'iron containing'
      [niets]$_N$[zegg-end]$_A$ 'lit. nothing saying, meaningless'
      [tijd]$_N$[rov-end]$_A$ 'time consuming'

As was the case for *-ig*, there are two analytical options: they are either derived through suffixation with *-end* from possible but non-existent verbal compounds like *haatdragen*, or they are adjectival compounds with a possible, but non-existent adjective in *-ig* as head. Both analyses imply that possible, non-existent words can feed word formation. But this general claim is not enough: we have to express that it is word formation of specific types, such as those of words in *-ig* and *-end*, that triggers the formation of possible words. This is why templates such as (42) are called for, which express the co-occurrence of certain word-formation patterns.

Adjectival compounds of the type *breedgeschouderd* can only be analysed as adjectival compounds with a possible word as head: *geschouderd* does not exist by itself, nor its base, the verb *schouderen*. So it appears that the conversion of the noun *schouder* 'shoulder' to a verb which is the formal basis of the participial adjective is dependent on this specific morphological context. This can be expressed by the following template that indicates the implied conversion of a noun to a verb:

---

[7] This is also the basic idea behind the categorial morphology approach in Hoeksema (1984) in which a categorial notation is used to express the fact that, for instance, the suffix *-ig* not only takes a noun to form an adjective, but also belongs to a second category, which takes a noun to form an adjective of the category A\A, that is an adjective that in its turn takes an adjective to form an adjective (i.e. an adjectival compound).

(44) $[_A [[ge [[N]_V]d]_V]_A]_A$

Such an analysis avoids the otherwise necessary complication that the discontinuous participial affix *ge . . . t/d* is not only attached to verbal but also to nominal bases to form adjectives. What we do need to express is that certain independently established word-formation patterns co-occur: the use of one pattern implies use of the other.

The possibility of such an interpretation of synthetic compounds is not restricted to adjectival compounds, but may also be relevant for compounds with a deverbal nominal head in *-er* such as *houthakker* 'wood chopper'. As will be shown in Section 6.2.1, the interpretation of *hout* as the Theme of the verbal base of *hakker* can be accounted for on the basis of the semantic properties of the head noun, without additional formal machinery. Nevertheless, it remains true that the nominalizing suffix *-er* behaves similarly to *-ig* in that it creates a class of deverbal nouns that are only used in a compounding context. Unlike the noun *hakker*, the noun *zegger* 'sayer', for instance, does not occur as an independent word, only in the head position of compounds, as in *oomzegger* 'lit. uncle sayer, nephew or niece'. This can be expressed in the same way, by a template that expresses the co-occurrence of independently established morphological patterns: $[N [V-er]_N]_N$.

A similar class of nominal synthetic compounds is formed by words of the form [QN -er] such as *dubbeldekker* 'double-decker', *tientonner* 'ten-tonner' and *tweewieler* 'two-wheeler'. Formally they can be interpreted as compounds of a numeral and a possible denominal noun, with the quantifier having scope over the base of the head noun in *-er*. However, words such as *tonner* and *wieler* are not used as independent words (*wieler* does occur, though, in the compound *wielerwedstrijd* 'cycling contest'). Hence, there is a template $[Q [N-er]_N]_N$. Again, the alternative is to consider these nouns as derived from possible compounds, that is, as formed according to the template $[[QN]_N er]_N$, parallel to compounds such as *vierkamerflat* 'four-room apartment' discussed in Section 4.2.1.

4.4. VERBAL COMPOUNDS

As mentioned in Section 4.1, verbal compounding is unproductive in Dutch. That does not mean, however, that there are no verbal compounds at all. In the first place, it is possible to convert nominal compounds into verbs. Such a process implies that there is no verbal head for such compounds. Examples are:

(45) | Compound noun | Verb |
|---|---|
| blinddoek 'blindfold' | blinddoek 'to blindfold' |
| blokfluit '*lit.* block flute, recorder' | blokfluit 'to play the recorder' |
| glimlach 'smile' | glimlach 'to smile' |
| ijsbeer 'polar bear' | ijsbeer 'to pace up and down' |
| sjoelbak 'shovelboard' | sjoelbak 'to play shovelboard' |
| voetbal 'football' | voetbal 'to play football' |

Two of the examples are of particular interest since Dutch has the strong verb *fluiten* 'to whistle' and the partially strong verb *lachen* 'to laugh' with the strong perfect participle *gelachen*. Since these verbs do not form the heads of the compounds *blokfluiten* and *glimlachen*, the converted verbs are inflected according to the regular pattern, the default conjugation:

(46) blokfluit – blokfluitte – geblokfluit *versus* fluit – floot – gefloten
glimlach – glimlachte – geglimlacht *versus* lach – lachte – gelachen

In this respect they are similar to English verbs like *to grandstand* with the past tense form *grandstanded* and *to joy-ride* with the past tense form *joy-rided*. Kiparsky (1982) proposed accounting for the regular inflection of such compound verbs by assuming a morphological module with three levels: irregular inflection takes place at the first level, whereas regular inflection takes place at the third level, and is ordered after the second level at which conversion takes place. A similar account of the Dutch facts has been proposed by Paulissen and Zonneveld (1988). However, as argued in Booij (1989), the representation of such verbs as conversions of compound nouns will suffice to trigger regular inflection since they are not verbs with an irregular verb as their head. Hence, we can avoid the additional formal machinery of level ordering within the morphological module of Dutch (and English).

A second source of verbal compounds are compounds in which the head position is normally occupied by an infinitive. Since the infinitive is partially nominal in nature, this is in effect a case of nominal compounding, and hence to be expected. Examples of such compounds are (cf. Ackema 1999*a*: 232 for a survey):

(47) mast-klimmen 'pole-climbing'
      school-zwemmen 'schoolswimming'
      touw-trekken 'rope-pulling'

These compounds are used in particular for all kinds of sports. If the head is indeed seen as an infinitive, this implies that there are no finite forms available, and the only way of using finite forms is by means of periphrastic constructions such as *aan het* + infinitive, as in *Mijn zusje is aan het schoolzwemmen* 'My sister is school-swimming' or *gaan* + infinitive (*Mijn zusje gaat schoolzwemmen* 'My sister is going to school-swim'). Alternatively, Dutch speakers may reinterpret such infinitival compounds as separable complex verbs (cf. Section 6.4), or as verbal compounds; in both interpretations, finite forms are possible (cf. van Marle 2000*b*).

A third category of verbal compounds has arisen through back formation. For instance, the nominal compound *stofzuiger* '*lit*. dust-sucker, vacuum cleaner' gave rise to the verb *stofzuigen* 'to vacuum-clean' through reinterpretation of this compound as a deverbal -*er* derivative. Other examples of this kind of back formation are:

(48) *Back-formed verb*   *Nominal compound source*
      beeldhouw 'to sculpture' $[[beeld]_N[[houw]_V er]_N]_N$
                                      'sculptor'
      bloemlees 'to make an anthology' $[[bloem]_N[[lez]_V ing]_N]_N$
                                      'anthology'
      hongerstaak 'to hunger-strike' $[[honger]_N[[stak]_V ing]_N]N$
                                      'hunger strike'
      paardrijd 'to horse-ride' $[[paard]_N[[rijd]_V en]_N]_N$
                                      'horse riding'
      tekstverwerk 'to word-process' $[[tekst]_N[[verwerk]_V er]_N]_N$
                                      'word processor'

This kind of back formation from compounds headed by deverbal nouns in -*en*, -*er*, and -*ing* is similar to the formation of English *to sculpt* from *sculptor* and *to babysit* from *babysitter*.[8] The consequence of this origin of such verbal compounds is that they receive the regular inflection, even if the corresponding simplex verb is an ablauting verb:

[8] Other examples of this kind of back formation are provided by van den Toorn (1997).

(49)	Verb	Past tense singular	Perfect participle
	beeldhouw	beeldhouwde	gebeeldhouwd
		(*beeldhieuw)	(*gebeeldhouwen)
	bloemlees	bloemleesde	gebloemleesd (*gebloemlezen)
		(*bloemlas)
	paardrijd	paardrijdde	gepaardrijd (*gepaardreden)[9]
	stofzuig	stofzuigde	gestofzuigd (*gestofzogen)

In the case of *stofzuigen* we do find the ablauting forms since this verb has been reinterpreted by some speakers of Dutch as a separable complex verb. Hence, we do get the participle *stofgezogen*, but never the participle **gestofzogen*. Furthermore, if the tensed form *stofzoog* is used, the two parts will be separated in a main clause: *Jan zoog stof* 'John vacuumed' is grammatical, but *Jan stofzoog* is not. The same applies to *paardrijden*.

Paradigmatic word formation applied to English loans may also lead to such infinitival compounds (Posthumus 1991): the English suffix *-ing* is replaced with the Dutch suffix *-en*:

(50)	English *-ing-form*	Dutch *-en-form*
	aquaplaning	aquaplanen
	body-building	bodybuilden
	car-pooling	carpoolen
	brainstorming	brainstormen

Two other unproductive categories of verbal compound deserve mention here. First, there are verbal compounds with a verbal non-head, as in:

(51) spelevaar 'to go boating'
      hoesteproest 'to cough and sneeze'
      zweefvlieg 'to glide'

Secondly, we find about twenty-five verbal compounds with a verbal left constituent and a noun on the right; yet these words are verbs, not nouns. These nouns typically refer to body parts, and the function of the noun is instrumental (Weggelaar 1986). A possible origin of this kind of verbal compound is the reanalysis of verbs such as *knipogen* 'to wink'. This verb is perhaps a conversion of the nominal compound *knipoog* 'wink, *lit.* cut eye', with the

---

[9] These regular forms of *paardrijden* were used by my daughters Suzanne and Rebecca.

structure [[[knip]_V[oog]_N]_N]_V. Through reanalysis this verb may then have been assigned the structure [[knip]_V[oog]_N]_V, and subsequently other words of that structure may have been coined. It remains, however, an unproductive pattern, with only an occasional extension in literary language (Weggelaar 1986: 301):

(52)
Verb	Verbal stem	Noun
klappertand 'to have chattering teeth'	klapper 'to rattle'	tand 'tooth'
kortwiek 'to clip the wings'	kort 'to clip'	wiek 'wing'
likkebaard 'to lick one's lips'	lik 'to lick'	baard 'beard'
schuimbek 'to have foam at the mouth'	schuim 'to foam'	bek '(animal's) mouth'
stampvoet 'to stamp one's feet'	stamp 'to stamp'	voet 'foot'
trekkebek 'to pull a face'	trek 'to pull'	bek '(animal's) mouth'

It is clear that the left, verbal constituent is not the head of these compounds since verbal inflection appears at the right periphery. For instance, the past tense singular form of *trekkebekken* is *trekkebekte*.

We are then left with a few verbal compounds such as *raadplegen* 'lit. to advice commit, to consult', *grasduinen* 'lit. to grass-dune, to browse', and *zinspelen* 'lit. to sense-play, to allude' to which none of the analyses above apply (they have finite forms). But this class of words is a closed one, and the meaning of these verbs is not a compositional function of that of their constituents, unlike what is the case for productive categories of compounding.

In sum, we have seen that Dutch has a number of verbal compounds of different types, each of them with a special source, and not created directly by means of straightforward verbal compounding.

4.5. NUMERAL COMPOUNDS

Complex numerals form a special class of complex words. The pattern for their formation is as follows:

(53) 1–12 *simplex words*: een, twee, drie, vier, vijf, zes, zeven, acht, negen, tien, elf, twaalf
13–19 *number* + tien 'ten': dertien, veertien, vijftien, zestien, zeventien, achttien, negentien
20 *simplex word*: twintig
21–99 een-en-twintig, twee-en-twintig, etc.
100 honderd
101 honderd(en)een, honderd(en)twee, etc.
200 tweehonderd, driehonderd, etc.
2000 tweeduizend, drieduizend, etc.

The feature that distinguishes Dutch (and German) from English, French, and many other European languages is that for numbers between 21 and 99, the ones come before the tens. The two numbers are obligatorily connected by *en* 'and' which is not pronounced as [ɛn], the phonetic form when used as a conjunction, but as [ən]. In numbers above 100, the connective *en* is optional, and is always pronounced as [ɛn]. What we see then in the pattern for the numbers 21–99 is a morphologization of an original syntactic pattern of coordination, with a concomitant phonetic weakening of the full vowel of the conjunction *en* into schwa, the typical vowel of grammatical morphemes (cf. Section 5.2.1). In numbers above 100, the pattern is formally (including phonetically) still identical to that of syntactic coordination, but such numeral expressions are felt and written as one word. Hence, we consider this pattern also as a morphological construction that originated through the morphologization of a syntactic construction. This is confirmed by the fact that the main stress of such numerals is located on the last constituent (for example, *honderd(en)éen*), whereas there are equal stresses on the parts of a syntactic coordination.

5

The Interface of Morphology and Phonology

5.1. INTRODUCTION

Morphology and phonology interact in Dutch in a number of interesting ways. The main generalizations and theoretical assumptions about the phonology of Dutch that form the background of this chapter can be found in Booij (1995). The following domains of interaction can be distinguished:

a. the morphological structure of a word codetermines its prosodic structure, and thus its phonetic realization;
b. in Dutch, both stems and affixes exhibit allomorphy. The question therefore arises to what extent these allomorphy patterns follow from principles of phonology, and how the relevant generalizations can be expressed;
c. there are phonological constraints on the attachment of affixes to bases. For example, the choice between the two nominal plural suffixes is governed by phonological constraints (Chapter 2).

These phenomena and their analysis will be dealt with in the next sections of this chapter. An exception will be made, however, for the stress patterns of complex words. They clearly illustrate that morphological structure codetermines the prosodic structure of words. Since they have been dealt with extensively in Booij (1995), they are not discussed systematically in this book.[1]

---

[1] For a general discussion of the interaction between phonology and morphology in the framework of Lexical Phonology, see Booij (2000c).

5.2. MORPHOLOGICAL AND PROSODIC DOMAINS

Morphological structure influences the phonetic realization of complex words primarily because it determines the prosodic structure of complex words, and it is to the constituents of prosodic structure that phonological generalizations apply. Therefore, we have to specify how exactly the mapping between morphological and prosodic structure takes place. The basic hierarchy of prosodic categories that we need for a proper understanding of the phonological behaviour of Dutch complex words is the following:

(1) syllable (σ), foot (F), prosodic word (ω)

Segments form syllables, syllables form feet, and feet form prosodic words. This hierarchy is the lexical part of the well-known hierarchy proposed in the theory of Prosodic Phonology (cf. Nespor and Vogel 1986). An important insight of this theory is that, although morphology codetermines the prosodic structuring of complex words, there is no complete isomorphy between morphological and prosodic domains. Grammatical words may be either smaller or larger than one prosodic word.[2] The basic generalizations for Dutch are the following:

First, each constituent of a compound corresponds to a prosodic word. Prosodic words form the domain of syllabification, and hence, the boundaries between the constituents of a compound coincide with syllable boundaries. This is illustrated by the following example:

(2) [[land]$_N$[adel]$_N$]$_N$ 'landed gentry', phonetic form [lɑnt.a:.dəl]

(the dots indicate the word-internal syllable boundaries). The morphological constituents of this compound, *land* and *adel*, form prosodic words of their own. If *landadel* were treated as one prosodic word, the final /d/ of the constituent *land* would form a syllable with the next vowel /a:/, and be pronounced as [d], in conformity with the principle that empty onsets should be avoided. However, since the compound-internal morphological boundary coincides with a prosodic word boundary, we get another syllable pattern, in which the first /d/ occurs in coda position, and is therefore

---

[2] See Hall (1999) for a good survey of the literature on the phonological word and its relation to morphology.

5.2. MORPHOLOGICAL AND PROSODIC DOMAINS

devoiced, due to the constraint that obstruents in coda position are voiceless in Dutch. A second role of the prosodic word is that it forms a domain of stress assignment, for both main stress and secondary stress.

For Dutch suffixes, two classes have to be distinguished, cohering suffixes and non-cohering ones. Cohering suffixes form a prosodic word with their stem, and thus the suffix boundary does not necessarily coincide with a prosodic boundary. All non-native suffixes, and most native suffixes are cohering. A number of native suffixes, however, are non-cohering: they form a prosodic word of their own. These are the following suffixes, which all derive historically from lexemes:

(3) -achtig, - baar, -dom, -heid, -ling, -loos, -schap, -zaam

Thus, we find the following contrast in syllabification between the words *roodachtig* and *rodig*, with the same meaning 'reddish':

(4) rood-achtig [roːt.ɑx.təx]; rod-ig [roː.dəx]

If a cohering suffix is attached to a compound, it will form a prosodic word with the last prosodic word of that compound. For instance, the morphological and prosodic structure of the word *godsdienstig* 'religious', derived from the compound *godsdienst* 'religion', are as follows:

(5) *morphological structure*:   [[[gods]$_N$[dienst]$_N$]$_N$ig]$_A$
     prosodic structure: (ɣɔts)$_\omega$(din.stəx)$_\omega$

This underscores the non-isomorphy of morphological and prosodic structure mentioned above.

5.2.1. *The phonological make-up of affixes*

As far as the native suffixes of Dutch are concerned, there is a correlation between the classification of a suffix as cohering or non-cohering and its phonological make-up. A Dutch prosodic word has to contain at least one full vowel (i.e. no schwa), and therefore non-cohering suffixes all contain a full vowel, whereas many cohering suffixes have the schwa (spelled as *e*, *i*, or *ij*) as their only vowel:

(6) *Cohering native suffixes of Dutch with schwa*: -der, -e, -el, -(e)lijk, -en, -end, -er, -erd, - erig, -ig, -sel, -ster, -te/de, -tje/etje/pje/kje/je, -tig

Some cohering native suffixes do have a full vowel, however. Some of them behave phonologically as non-native suffixes in that they bear the main stress of the word. These are suffixes that are originally non-native. The others can bear secondary stress for rhythmic reasons, that is, when following an unstressed syllable:

(7)   *Cohering native suffixes with full vowels*
      WITH MAIN STRESS: -erij, -es, -in, -ij
      WITH RHYTHMIC STRESS: -aar, -enaar, -erik, -ing, -nis

If a cohering suffix consists of consonants only, the only possible consonants are /d/, /s/, and /t/. This follows from the fact that these are the only consonants that can be stacked up at the end of a phonological word, since the phonological word in Dutch has a so-called final appendix, in which one or more coronal obstruents can be placed. Therefore, consonantal suffixes always have the form -*s*, -*t*, -*d*, or -*st*.

Furthermore, we can observe that many cohering suffixes begin with a schwa, whereas words of lexical categories never begin with a schwa. This follows from the constraint that Dutch prosodic words can never begin with a schwa (Booij 1995: 47). Cohering suffixes do not have to comply with this constraint exactly because being cohering they will never form the beginning of a prosodic word.

The phonological classification of Dutch prefixes is slightly different. If they have a full vowel, they form prosodic words of their own, just like the constituents of compounds and non-cohering suffixes (for instance, *door-*, *her-*, *on-*) . But when they have a schwa as their vowel, as is the case for prefixes such as *be-* and *ge-*, they do not fully integrate prosodically into their stem: a prefix boundary coincides with a syllable boundary, although such prefixes cannot form a prosodic word of their own due to the absence of a

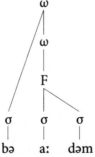

FIGURE 5.1. *The prosodic structure of* beadem

5.2. MORPHOLOGICAL AND PROSODIC DOMAINS

full vowel. That is, they form syllables of their own which are adjoined to the prosodic word of the stem. For instance, a verbal stem like *beadem* 'to breathe' will have the prosodic structure in Figure 5.1. This prosodic structure also explains why the schwa of the prefix does not disappear before a vowel, unlike prevocalic schwas within a prosodic word which always delete.

There are no consonantal prefixes, which is to be expected, since Dutch prosodic words do not have an initial appendix, which guarantees that such prefixes do not lead to problems for the phonotactic make-up of prefixed words.

5.2.2. *Prosodic gapping*

Words with non-cohering suffixes share a number of properties with compounds, and prosodically, they cannot be distinguished. For instance, there is no phonetic difference whatsoever between the compound *draagbaar* 'stretcher' and the deverbal adjective *draagbaar* 'portable'. In both words, the part *baar* functions as an independent prosodic word. The special property that I will focus on here is the identical behaviour of compound parts and non-cohering suffixes under prosodic gapping. As shown in Booij (1985), parts of compounds and non-cohering suffixes can be omitted under identity:

(8)   *Backward gapping in compounds*
        land- en tuinbouw 'agriculture and horticulture'
        wespe- en bijesteken 'wasp stings and bee stings'
        hoofd- of nevenaccent 'main stress or secondary stress'

   Forward gapping in compounds
        regelordening en -toepassing 'rule-ordering and rule application'
        herenschoenen en -jassen 'men's shoes and men's coats'

   Backward gapping in derived words
        storm- en regenachtig 'stormy and rainy'
        zicht- en tastbaar 'visible and tangible'
        christen- en heidendom 'Christianity and heathendom'
        eenzijdig- of partijdigheid 'onesidedness or partiality'
        twee- en drielingen 'twins and triplets'
        oever- en zouteloos '*lit.* bankless and saltless, endless and insipid'
        zwanger- en moederschap 'pregnancy and motherhood'
        eer- en deugdzaam 'respectable and virtuous'

The relevant generalization is that it is prosodic words, not grammatical, words that can be omitted under identity. This explains why it is not possible to apply gapping to derived words with cohering suffixes; a gapping such as

(9)   *rod- of groenig 'reddish or greenish'

is ungrammatical. Moreover, this prosodic conditioning also explains why the constituents of which one is gapped need not have identical syntactic or morphological status. For instance, in the gapped phrase *ijs- en bruine beren* 'polar bears and brown bears' the part *beren* that is omitted is part of the compound *ijsberen* whereas it is the head of the phrase *bruine beren*.

The prosodic analysis also explains why gapping is possible in the phrase *wis- en natuurkunde* 'mathematics and physics'. This phrase is a coordination of the compounds *wiskunde*, with the adjective *wis* 'certain' as its first constituent, and the compound *natuurkunde* 'physics' with the noun *natuur* 'nature'. The formation of *wis- en natuurkunde* cannot be a matter of word-internal coordination in the non-head position of the compound, because it is normally impossible to coordinate constituents of unlike categories. It is the gapping analysis that explains why such phrases are nevertheless possible. Moreover, the gapping analysis predicts correctly, unlike the word-internal coordination analysis, that the phrase *wis- en natuurkunde* is a plural NP that requires a plural finite verbal form:

(10) Wis- en natuurkunde zijn moeilijke vakken 'Mathematics and physics are difficult subjects'

If the two constituents *wis* and *natuur* had been conjoined in the non-head position of the compound, the phrase *wis- en natuurkunde* would have a singular head that requires a singular verbal form.

Finally, the prosodic gapping analysis also explains why a gapping like the following is possible:

(11) wis- en natuurkundige overwegingen 'mathematical and physical considerations'

In this example, it is the part *kundige* that has been omitted. Note that this is only a constituent in the prosodic structure of the relevant words, not in the morphological structure:

(12)   [[[[wis]$_A$[kunde]$_N$]$_N$ig]$_A$e]$_A$ (wis)$_\omega$(kun.di.ge)$_\omega$
       [[[[natuur]$_N$[kunde]$_N$]$_N$ig]$_A$e]$_A$ (na.tuur)$_\omega$(kun.di.ge)$_\omega$

5.2. MORPHOLOGICAL AND PROSODIC DOMAINS

This once more illustrates that it is one of two identical prosodic words that is omitted.

There are a number of words that are not compounds in the morphological sense of the word (although they may have been compounds in the past), but that nevertheless have the same stress pattern as compounds: main stress on the most prominent syllable of the first constituent, and secondary stress on the most prominent syllable of the second constituent. Examples are the following words, which have main stress on the first syllable, and secondary stress on the second, just like bisyllabic compounds:

(13) áalmòes 'alms', máarschàlk 'marshall', óordèel 'verdict'

Such words have been qualified in the literature as 'formal compounds' on the basis of their stress patterns. However, as argued in Booij (1999b), we do not have to assign them morphological structure in order to derive the correct stress pattern: on the basis of their segmental composition it can be predicted that they form two prosodic words each, although they are morphologically simplex. It is only the last syllable of a prosodic word that can be superheavy (that is a syllable with a long vowel followed by a consonant, or a short vowel followed by two consonants), and therefore, a word like *oordeel* with a superheavy first syllable must consist of two prosodic words. Thus, this is another example of asymmetry between morphological and prosodic structure, with the additional advantage that we do not have to assign unmotivated morphological structure to such morphologically simplex words.

The relation between morphological and prosodic structure also plays a role in the explanation of certain patterns of morphological change. A first observation is that, when compounds lose their semantic transparency, this may affect their phonetic form because they will then be prosodified as simplex words. This is illustrated by the word *aardappel* 'potato'. This word is historically a compound, $[[aard]_N[appel]_N]_N$ 'lit. earth apple'. Since it is no longer perceived as a compound, its prosodic structure is now that of a simplex word, and hence, the phonetic form has changed as well:

(14) *Compound interpretation*: $(aard)_\omega(appel)_\omega$
               phonetic form [aːrt.ɑ.pəl]
      Simplex interpretation: $(aardappel)_\omega$
               phonetic form [aːr.dɑ.pəl]

The change in prosodic structure is reflected directly by the voiced realization of the underlying /d/, which no longer stands in coda position, and hence is not devoiced.

The condition on prosodic words that they must contain at least one full vowel also explains why some affixes could be reinterpreted as words, namely those that have at least one full vowel. This pertains to the following affixes:

(15) her- > her 'reexamination'
ex- > ex 'ex-husband/wife'
-schap > schap 'society'

Moreover, the suffix -tig /təɣ/ that occurs in number names such as *twintig* 'twenty' and *dertig* 'thirty' has been reinterpreted as a word with the meaning 'undetermined number of', but with a concomitant change of the vowel, from schwa to [ɪ], because a word cannot have schwa as its only vowel. Hence, used as a word it will be pronounced as [tɪx].

5.3. ALLOMORPHY

Allomorphy is the phenomenon that a morpheme has more than one phonetic form. In the previous chapters, we have already encountered some cases of allomorphy. Here, I will give a more systematic exposition on the different patterns found in Dutch. The preliminary question is to what extent allomorphy is a phonological phenomenon, and where morphology comes in. If allomorphy is the consequence of phonological constraints, there is no role for morphology. This is the case for the allomorphy effects of Final Devoicing, the constraint that requires obstruents in coda position to be voiceless. This constraint explains the difference in phonetic form between the singular noun *hoed* [hut] and the plural form *hoeden* [hudən]. There are, however, many cases of allomorphy, both of stems and of affixes, where there is no straightforward phonological account (cf. Rubach and Booij 2001). It is this kind of allomorphy that will be discussed in this section. Below, I will use the term 'allomorphy' exclusively to refer to variation in phonetic form that cannot be fully accounted for in terms of general phonological constraints.

5.3.1. *Affix allomorphy*

A number of Dutch affixes exhibit allomorphy. The most famous case is the allomorphy of the diminutive suffix that has five allomorphs: *-tje*, *-je*, *-etje*, *-kje*, and *-pje*. The distribution of these five allomorphs is governed by the phonological properties of the stem to which they attach (cf. Booij 1995: 69–72 for the relevant generalizations). Classical generative phonology attempted to reduce allomorphy as much as possible to phonology, by assigning the allomorphs a common underlying form, and deriving the different phonetic forms by means of phonological rules. The problem for such analyses is that these rules have to be made dependent on specific morphemes, and therefore do not express real phonological generalizations. For example, there is no phonological constraint for Dutch that requires the /t/ of *-tje* to change into [p] after an /m/, as we would need for deriving *riempje* 'belt', dim. from underlying /rim-tjə/. Moreover, such analyses cannot explain why such rules allow for exceptions. For instance, Dutch has two diminutive nouns for the word *bloem* 'flower', the regular form *bloempje* and the irregular form *bloemetje* with the idiosyncratic meaning 'bunch of flowers'. Consequently, the five allomorphs of the diminutive suffix have to be listed, and we will then have to specify for each allomorph the phonological conditions that they impose on the stem to which they are attached. That is, for each of these five allomorphs there will be phonological constraints on their bases. In Section 5.4 I will show that the selection of allomorphs can sometimes be performed by general phonological output constraints.

The following kinds of affix allomorphy are found in Dutch (Booij 1995: 69–92):

(16)   *Native suffixes*
-er/-der (nominal suffix): schrijv-er 'writer', bestuur-der 'governor'
-er/-der (comparative suffix): grot-er 'bigger', raar-der 'stranger'
-erig/-derig: vret-erig 'inclined to eat a lot', zeur-derig 'nagging'
-erij/-derij: stom-erij 'dry-cleaning shop', boer-derij 'farmhouse'
-tje/-je/-pje/-kje/-etje (diminutive suffix): traan-tje 'tear', dim., huis-je 'house', dim., riem-pje 'belt', dim., konin-kje 'king', dim., ring-etje 'ring', dim.
-tjes/-jes/-pjes/-etjes (adverbial suffix): gewoontjes 'ordinarily', stilletjes 'quietly', warmpjes 'warmly', zachtjes 'softly'

Non-native suffixes
-eel/aal: fundament-eel 'fundamental', fundament-al-ist 'fundamentalist'

-air/-aar: milit-air 'military', milit-ar-ist 'militarist'
-eur/-oor: direct-eur 'director', direct-or-aat 'directorate'
-eus/-oos: nerv-eus 'nervous', nerv-os-iteit 'nervousness'
-iek/-ic [is]: kathol-iek 'catholic', kathol-ic-isme 'catholicism'
-eur/-eus/-ric: mont-eur 'technician', mont-eus-e 'technician', fem., ambassad-eur 'ambassador', ambassad-ric-e 'ambassador', fem.

Non-native prefixes

in-/im-/iŋ-/il -/ir-: in-tolerant 'intolerant', im-populair 'unpopular', in-consistent 'inconsistent', il-legaal 'illegal', ir-rationeel 'irrational'

con-/com-/coŋ-/col-/cor-: con-sistent 'consistent', com-plex 'com plex', con-claaf 'conclave', col-laboratie 'collaboration', cor-relatie 'correlation'

a-/an-: a-moreel 'immoral', an-organisch 'inorganic'

de-/des-: de-valuatie 'devaluation', des-interesse 'disinterest'

In the case of non-native affixes, the allomorphy patterns have been borrowed from the source languages, Greek, French, and Latin. The assimilation pattern for *in-* and *con-* is also found for non-native prefixes that mainly co-occur with roots (that is, in borrowed words) such as:

(17)   ad-jungeren 'adjoin', af-fix 'affix', ag-glutineren 'to agglutinate', ar-rangeren 'to arrange', as-simileren 'to assimilate'; sub-script 'subscript', suf-fix 'suffix', sup-poneren 'to suppose', sur-rogaat 'surrogate'; syn-these 'synthesis', sym-metrie 'symmetry', sy-steem 'system'

Therefore, it comes as no surprise that these allomorphy patterns do not follow from the phonology of Dutch, and thus the different allomorphs have to be listed.

5.3.2. *Stem allomorphy*

Stem allomorphy is a pervasive phenomenon in Dutch. In the native lexicon, it is primarily a residue of phonological processes that were once active, but disappeared from Dutch as productive rules. This applies to schwa apocope, *de*-deletion and *d*-deletion. This allomorphy is lexically governed: one has to learn which allomorph is used in which complex word, and therefore it has at first sight no particular morphological interest. Below, I give an example of each of these types of allomorphy:

5.3. ALLOMORPHY

(18) *schwa apocope*: einde/eind 'end' – eind-oordeel/*einde-oordeel 'final conclusion'
 de-*deletion*: broeder/broer 'brother' – broederschap 'brotherhood', zijde/zij 'silk' – zijderups/*zij-rups 'silkworm'
 d-*deletion*: glijden/glijen 'to glide' – glijbaan/*glijd-baan 'slide'

Note that the base words have two forms, each of them listed in the lexicon, and both usable as independent words. In the complex words, however, there is normally no choice: one of the forms has to be used. For instance, *zijderups* is the conventional compound for 'silk worm', and hence *zijrups*, although a possible compound, is not used, a case of token-blocking.

In the case of plural nouns with stem allomorphy (cf. Section 2.2.1) we have to conclude that these inflected forms have been lexically stored with the effects of the now lost processes encoded. This also applies to some of the allomorphy in the paradigms of the strong verbs. For instance, the [r] in the past tense forms of *verliezen* 'to lose', *verloor/verloren* is the reflex of rhoticization of an intervocalic /z/. This effect could be kept because these past tense forms are lexically stored.

Another reflex of diachronic phonology is the alternation between words ending in the velar nasal and corresponding stems with a velar nasal followed by /k/, as in:

(19) | *Stem in* -ŋ | *Stem in* -ŋk |
| --- | --- |
| jong 'young' | jonk-vrouw 'lady', jonk-heer 'esquire', jonk-ie 'young person' |
| koning 'king' | konink-lijk 'royal', konink-rijk 'kingdom' |
| oorsprong 'origin' | oorspronk-elijk 'original' |
| spring 'to jump' | sprink-haan 'grasshopper' |
| toegang 'access' | toegank-elijk 'accessible' |

Historically, the letter sequence *ng* stands for a velar nasal plus voiced velar stop. This stop was devoiced in compounds and before certain suffixes, but disappeared word-finally. The long stem with final /k/ (the velar stop devoiced by Final Devoicing) was only kept in a number of compounds and derived words; the plural forms and new derivatives and compounds of these nouns surface without [k] (as in *springmatras* [sprɪŋmaːtrɑs] 'jumping mattress').

In the non-native stratum of the lexicon we encounter a lot of stem allomorphy. For instance, the word *Plato* 'id.' has the form *platon-* in all derived words with non-native suffixes, such as *platon-isch* 'platonic' and *platon-ist* 'platonist'. For all other affixation, the form *plato* is the only possible form. The extra /n/ is clearly a property of the stem, and not of the suffixes, since it recurs systematically before each non-native suffix with which the word *Plato* is combined, e.g. *platonisme* 'platonism'. Since the long stem allomorph *platon-* does not occur as an independent word, it need not be listed as such: this stem allomorph only exists in the existing words with non-native suffixes. In other words, it is only available for new coinings with non-native suffixes on the basis of the existing set of coderivatives with the stem *platon-*. This implies that this kind of stem allomorphy is regulated on the basis of paradigmatic relations between words. Here are some other examples of non-native stem allomorphy:

(20) cursus 'course'   curs-ist 'course taker'
      filter 'filter'   filtr-eer 'to filter'
      orkest 'orchestra'   orkestr-eer 'to orchestrate'
      perfect 'perfect'   perfection-eer 'to bring to perfection'
      regel 'rule'   regl-ement 'regulations', regul-eer 'to regulate'

For all these cases of non-native stem allomorphy, the generalization is that the stem form that occurs as an independent word is chosen as the base for the native morphology.[3] It is only in the case of non-native suffixation that the other stem form will be used. This once more suggests that the stock of non-native words is expanded mainly by means of paradigmatic word formation, that is, on the basis of existing non-native complex words.

5.3.3. *Allomorphy and paradigmatic relations*

Allomorphy occurs on a wide scale in the non-head position of compounds, in particular but not exclusively (cf. below) in NN-compounds: the nouns often have an extended form with an additional schwa or *-s*. Moreover, the nouns that have a lengthened allomorph in *-er* in plural forms also show up with this long allomorph in derivations and compounds:

(21) kind 'child'   kind-er-wagen 'pram', kind-er-lijk 'childish'
      schaap 'sheep' schaap-herder 'shepherd', schaap-s-kop 'sheep's
                      head', schap-e-vlees 'mutton'

---

[3] The only exception to this generalization is that the long allomorphs of non-native nouns in *-or, -on, -ol* (with long [o:]) do occur in plural forms, with the plural suffix *-en* (cf. Section 2.2.1).

The schwa and the /s/ are sometimes called link phonemes (Botha 1968) or linking phonemes since they do not contribute to the meaning of the compounds, and only function as a linking element between the two parts of the compound. Historically, the /s/ is a genitive suffix, and the schwa has essentially two potential sources: it is either a former case suffix, or it is the form of the noun before schwa apocope applied. The latter explanation applies to compounds such as *pannekoek* 'pancake' with the Middle Dutch word *panne*, and *zielerust* 'peace of mind' with the Middle Dutch word *ziele* 'soul'. Instead of *-e* we may also find the old genitive suffix *-en*, as in *her-en-huis* 'mansion'.

There are two additional complications in the data concerning these 'linking elements'. First, as we have seen in Chapter 4, plural nouns in *-en* may also occur in the non-head position of compounds. We can conclude that *-en* functions as a plural suffix in these cases because there is a semantic opposition with similar compounds with *-s*:

(22) bedrijf-s-terrein 'company's area'   bedrijv-en-terrein 'companies' area'
school-gemeenschap 'school community'   schol-en-gemeenschap 'schools' community, comprehensive school'
stad-s-raad 'city council'   sted-en-raad 'cities' council'

The second complication is that many speakers of Dutch do not pronounce /n/ after a schwa; hence, *-en* is then realized as [ə], and cannot be distinguished from *-e*. This problem, in combination with the fact that the choice between *e* and *en* cannot be predicted, has led to a recent spelling reform in the Netherlands and Belgium: the linking element with schwa is always spelled as *-en*, that is, as a plural form, if it has *-en* as its only plural suffix. Thus, the official spelling of a compound like *pannekoek* [panəkuk] 'pan cake' is now *pannenkoek* although the schwa that one pronounces has nothing to do with plurality. This has evoked a lot of discussion because Dutch speakers clearly associate the written sequence *-en* with the plural morpheme (Schreuder et al. 1998).

There are two reasons why we should interpret these linking elements as stem extensions of the first constituent of the compound, and not as linking elements that belong to neither the first nor the second part of a compound. First, the linking element is prosodically part of the first constituent. This is clear from the syllabification pattern (for instance, *scha.pe.vlees*) and the behaviour of such compounds under gapping: if the second prosodic word is deleted, the linking elements are not deleted:

(23) runder- of varkenspest 'cattle or swine fever'
      schapen- of varkensvlees 'mutton or pork'
      varkens- of schapenvlees 'pork or mutton'
      varkens- of runderpest 'swine or cattle fever'

Secondly, it is always the first part of the compound that determines whether the 'linking element' can occur, and which one. Finally, the /s/ does not only occur in compounds but also in derived words with non-cohering suffixes such as *-achtig* and *-loos*, where it exhibits the same prosodic properties, although it does not link two lexical constituents:

(24) voorjaar-s-achtig 'spring-like', arbeid-s-loos 'without work', werk-e-loos 'jobless'

The generalizations concerning the occurrence of these stem extensions can be summarized as follows:

(25) (a) *-e(n)* can only occur after nouns that have a plural form in *-en*;
      (b) *-s* can occur after nouns with a plural in *-en* (*regering-s-deelname* 'government participation', *dorp-s-café* 'lit. village café, pub'), and after nouns without a plural (*eeuwigheid-s-waarde* 'eternity value');
      (c) *-s* is obligatory if the left constituent of the compound is a diminutive noun (*meisje-s-jurk* 'girl's dress'), and after nouns that denote persons and take the plural suffix *-s* (*dame-s-hoed* 'lady's hat', *dokter-s-voorschrift* 'doctor's prescription').

These are the basic rules, but they are not fully exceptionless. For instance, the compound *moederliefde* 'maternal love' is an exception since the first constituent denotes a person, and has a plural in *-s*. What these rules exclude is a noun with the plural suffix *-s* having the linking phoneme [ə] in a compound: compounds such as **varkene-vlees* 'pork' are ill-formed. In addition, compounds with a noun in non-head position that does not denote a human being, and takes *-s* as plural suffix, will not take *s* as a stem extension, as illustrated by **rotorsblad* 'rotor blade'.

In addition, there are various tendencies concerning the choice between the different stem allomorphs (van den Toorn 1981*a*,*b*, 1982). For instance,

5.3. ALLOMORPHY

if the left constituent functions as a semantic object of the deverbal nominal head, it is usually the allomorph without extension that is used:

(26) boekverbranding 'book burning', contractbreuk 'breach of contract', misdaadbestrijding 'crime fight'

The generalization in (25a) is of particular theoretical importance because it implies that the choice of a particular allomorph is governed by a paradigmatic relation, that with the plural form of the noun in question (Booij 1997). For instance, since the plural form of *luisteraar* 'listener' is *luisteraars*, it is impossible to coin a compound such as **luisterarengedrag* 'listeners' behaviour'. It is not possible to build the conditions for the selection of the plural suffixes into the conditions for allomorph selection at stake here, because it really depends on the actual plural form of the noun. For instance, unlike *luisteraar*, the noun *handelaar* 'dealer' has two plural forms, *handelaren* and *handelaars*, and hence the compound *handelarengedrag* 'dealer's behaviour' is possible.

It should be stressed that the correlation between stem allomorphy and plural forms does not imply that the stem allomorph has necessarily plural connotations. This is particularly clear from compounds such as *rijtje-s-huis* 'terraced house' where the house clearly belongs to only one *rijtje* 'terrace'. Another example is the compound *dag-je-s-mensen* 'day trippers' specifically used to denote people who go out for the day only, which means that *dagjes* cannot receive a plural interpretation. This implies that there is only a correspondence in form between the plural form and the compounding stem allomorph of such nouns, without semantic plurality being involved.

A perhaps even more dramatic case of paradigmatically determined allomorphy is the case of geographical adjectives in *-s* or *-isch*. The formal basis for the coining of such adjectives is not the corresponding name of the country, but the inhabitant name, although semantically the adjectives express the notion 'relating to the country', and not 'relating to the inhabitant'. The crucial observation is that the inhabitant name is not productively and regularly derived from the country name, and yet it is exactly the inhabitant name that functions as the stem allomorph of the country name:

(27) | *Country* | *Inhabitative* | *Adjective* |
|---|---|---|
| Amerika 'America' | Amerikaan | Amerikaan-s |
| Denemarken 'Denmark' | Deen | Deen-s |

Griekenland 'Greece'	Griek	Griek-s
Zweden 'Sweden'	Zweed	Zweed-s
Israël 'Israel'	Israëliet	Israëlit-isch
Rusland 'Russia'	Rus	Russ-isch

This pattern also holds for other uses of the denominal suffixes *-s* and *-isch*. For instance, the adjective for *Chomsky* is *Chomskyaans*, as in *de Chomskyaanse benadering* 'the Chomskyan approach', which is formally derived from the noun *Chomskyaan* 'Chomskyan'.

This pattern illustrates that allomorphy might be governed by purely morphological considerations, in which phonology does not play a role.[4]

5.4. PHONOLOGICAL CONSTRAINTS ON WORD FORMATION

In Chapter 2, we saw how the choice between competing nominal plural suffixes and that between the allomorphs of the comparative suffix, *-er* and *-der*, are governed by phonological output constraints. In this section, we will see that phonological constraints also play a role in the selection of competing affixes and affix allomorphs in the realm of derivational morphology.

As pointed out in Chapter 2, the choice of *-der* instead of *-er* is governed by the phonological constraint that forbids the sequence /rər/. This constraint is an instantiation of a more general constraint that forbids identical consonants on both sides of a schwa. In Dutch, we never find such sequences, either in complex words or in simplex words, except for the sequence /nən/. This constraint can be seen as an OCP-constraint which forbids sequences of identical segments or segments that are identical on a particular tier, e.g. the Place tier (McCarthy 1986). OCP stands for Obligatory Contour Principle, a principle originally proposed by Will Leben as a constraint on tone sequences in the lexical items of tone languages. It forbids, for instance, a sequence of two High tones in a lexical item. McCarthy (1986) suggested extending the relevance of this principle to segmental and featural configurations. If we assume that the schwa, as the default vowel, has no place features of its own, two identical consonants on both sides of a schwa are in fact

---

[4] See Booij (1997) for more cases of paradigmatically determined allomorphy in Dutch, German, and French.

5.4. PHONOLOGICAL CONSTRAINTS ON WORD FORMATION

adjacent on the tier of place features, and thus such a sequence would violate the OCP.

In the case at hand, complex words in *-er* or *-der*, the choice of the second allomorph for words of which the base ends in /r/ is a way of avoiding violation of this OCP-constraint. For the nominalizing suffix *-er* there is a second alternative, the suffix *-aar*, that occurs after stems that end in a syllable headed by schwa and with a final coronal sonorant consonant:

(28) | *Base word* | *Derived noun with -er* |
|---|---|
| eet 'to eat' | et-er 'eater' |
| judo 'to do judo' | judo-er 'judoist' |
| Amsterdam 'id.' | Amsterdamm-er 'inhabitant of Amsterdam' |
| wetenschap 'science' | wetenschapp-er 'scientist' |
| | *Derived noun with -der* |
| vereer 'to worship' | vereer-der 'worshipper' |
| vier 'to celebrate' | vier-der 'celebrator' |
| Bijlmermeer 'id.' | Bijlmermeer-der |
| Zuidlaren 'id.' | Zuidlaar-der 'inhabitant of Zuidlaren'[5] |
| | *Derived noun with -aar* |
| loochen 'to deny' | loochen-aar |
| luister 'to listen' | luister-aar |
| knutsel 'to tinker' | knutsel-aar |
| Diemen 'id.' | Diemen-aar |
| Uddel 'id.' | Uddel-aar |

The choice between *-der* and *-aar* after a base that ends in /r/ is governed by prosodic wellformedness conditions (Booij 1998a): if the /r/ is preceded by a full vowel, it is *-der* that is selected because this will lead to an optimal foot, a disyllabic trochee. If the last syllable of the stem is headed by schwa, *-aar* is chosen because a monosyllabic foot consisting of a superheavy syllable (long vowel plus consonant) is more optimal than a sequence of two schwa-headed syllables of which the second cannot be parsed into a foot:

(29) zuur-der 'more sour'; prosodic structure $((zuur)_\sigma (dər)_\sigma)_F$

luister-aar 'listener'; prosodic structure $((luis)_\sigma (tə)_\sigma)_F ((raar)_\sigma)_F$

---

[5] Note that in this example, the base word has been truncated; the part *-en* has been deleted.

In the case of both -*der* and -*aar* the question arises of whether we should speak of competing suffixes for -*er* or of allomorphs of this suffix. The difference between allomorph and competing affix does not make any difference in term of phonological analysis since both allomorphs and competing affixes have to have their own underlying representation: -*der* also has to be represented besides -*er* because there is no general rule of /d/-insertion that could derive -*der* from -*er*. Moreover, it appears that both -*der* and -*aar* also occur exceptionally in phonological contexts other than those given above, which proves that they both have an existence of their own, and are not fully predictable surface realizations of the suffix -*er*:

(30) dien-der 'policeman', vil-der 'skinner', maal-der 'miller'
dien-aar 'servant', ler-aar 'teacher', zond-aar 'sinner'

Therefore, although it is convenient to speak of affix allomorphs in case they are phonologically similar, mostly because of a common historical origin (for instance, -*aar* derives historically from the Latin suffix -*arius*, and -*er* is a weakened form of -*aar*), this is no issue as far as their selection in terms of phonological output conditions is concerned. Synchronically, they have become competing suffixes: -*aar* and -*der* have a specific phonological environment, -*er* is the 'elsewhere' suffix.

It should also be noted that the use of phonological output constraints in the choice between competing affixes does not preclude the necessity of phonological constraints on the bases as well. A clear case is -*aar*: although it would be prosodically more optimal to use this allomorph after stems ending in /əm/ such as the verb *bezemen* 'to sweep', it is not allowed after a non-coronal sonorant consonant, and hence the derived agent noun for this verb is *bezemer* 'sweeper', with a sequence of two schwa-headed syllables.[6]

The OCP-constraint discussed here not only affects the suffixes discussed so far, but also a number of other suffixes that can give rise to the sequence C_i-ə-C_i, as is shown by the following examples of words with derivational suffixes. In some cases, the derivation is blocked, but there is an alternative because there are other suffixes with the same meaning:

(31) -erd viez-erd 'dirty person' *naar-erd /naːrərd/ 'unpleasant person'
naar-ling 'id.'

---

[6] This point is also made in Lapointe (2000).

5.4. PHONOLOGICAL CONSTRAINTS ON WORD FORMATION

-erik	viez-erik 'dirty person'	*naar-erik /naːrərɪk/ 'unpleasant person' naar-ling 'id.'
-ig	grond-ig 'thorough'	*berg-ig /bɛrɣəɣ/ 'mountainous' berg-achtig 'id.'
-eling	vreemd-eling 'stranger'	*valleling /vɑləlɪŋ/ 'fallen person' gevallene 'id.'

The suffix -ig is used, however, after a stem ending in the velar fricative if there is no alternative. For instance, in *eenogig* 'one-eyed' we find the sequence [ɣəɣ] that violates the OCP-condition, but here the suffix -achtig is not available as an alternative since it cannot be used for this kind of complex adjective. That is, this is a violable condition, that will be violated if there is no better alternative, in line with the general hypothesis of Optimality Theory that conditions are violable. This also applies to comparative forms of adjectives such as *barrer* [bɑrər] 'more severe' (cf. Chapter 2, fn. 3).

Another strategy is used in connection with the unproductive suffix -*elaar* that is used to create names for trees. In the case of stems that end in /l/, we see haplology: the word is shortened in order to comply with the constraint, as illustrated by the last two examples:[7]

(32)   appel 'apple'   appelaar 'apple tree'
        kers 'cherry'   kerselaar 'cherry tree'
        mispel 'medlar'   mispelaar 'medlar tree'
        pruim 'plum'   pruimelaar 'plum tree'

Alternatively, we may assume that there is no stem truncation, and that the general denominal suffix -*aar* competes here with the suffix -*elaar*.

The OCP-constraint obviously forbids identical consonants that are linearly adjacent, that is, not separated by schwa. This does not lead, however, to the blocking of the derivation of complex words with identical consonants at the boundary between stem and suffix; instead a process of degemination applies, with the effect that there are no geminate consonants in the phonetic forms of such words. Degemination is obligatory within the domain of the prosodic word, and optional at the boundary between pro-

---

[7] It is not clear if it is the stem that is truncated, or the suffix. This is of no importance since it is the phonetic form that complies with the constraint. Moreover, it is also possible to give a different interpretation to these facts: instead of the suffix -*elaar* it is the denominal suffix -*aar* that is attached to stems ending in -*el*.

sodic words (Booij 1995: 68). The effect of degemination is illustrated by the following examples of complex words with cohering suffixes where degemination is obligatory because these suffixes do not form prosodic words of their own:

(33) adel 'nobility'   adel-lijk /adəl-lək/ 'noble'   [aːdələk]
     Fries 'Frisian' (N) Fries /fris-s/ 'Frisian' (A)   [fris]
     pluis 'to give off fluff' pluis-sel /plœys-səl/ 'fluff'   [plœysəl]
     fiets 'to cycle'   fiets-ster /fits-stər/ 'female cyclist' [fitstər]
     breed 'wide'   breed-te /breːd-tə/ 'width'   [breːtə]
     groot 'big'   groot-te /ɣroːt-tə/ 'size'   [ɣroːtə]

These data show that the OCP-constraint is an output constraint: if it were an input constraint, these complex words could not have been formed. Since it is an output constraint, they are well-formed because degemination has removed the sequences of identical consonants.

There are also some prefix allomorphs that can be selected on the basis of phonological output constraints. This applies to the non-native prefixes *a-/an-* and *de-/des-*: the consonant-final allomorphs will be selected before a vowel-initial stem: the prefix-final consonant will then form the onset of the syllable headed by the initial vowel of the stem, and thus a violation is avoided of No Empty Onset, the universal phonological output constraint that says that empty onsets should be avoided if possible:

(34) a-theoretisch 'atheoretical' *but* an-organisch 'inorganic'
     de-motivatie 'demotivation' *but* des-informatie 'disinformation'

In conclusion, phonological output constraints play an essential role in the selection of the allomorphs of affixes, and in the selection of competing affixes.

6

The Morphology–Syntax Interface

6.1. INTRODUCTION

The relation between morphology and syntax can be studied from a number of different angles. The two main issues are: (*a*) how do these modules of the grammar interact? and (*b*) how can they be demarcated?

As to the interaction of morphology and syntax, a clear and uncontroversial example can be found in the realm of inflection: inflected forms are created by morphology, but their occurrence in sentences is sometimes regulated by the syntax. This applies in particular to contextual inflection (for instance, structural case assignment and agreement phenomena).

A second domain of interaction is that of valency-changing morphological operations. Most languages, Dutch included, have morphological processes that affect the syntactic valency of verbs. The relation between morphological operations and syntactic valency will be discussed in Section 6.2.

A third case of interaction between morphology and syntax is formed by the cases in which syntax can feed word formation. For instance, it is possible for certain kinds of phrases to occur in compounds and derived words, as we already saw in Chapters 3 and 4.

The second main issue concerning the relation of morphology and syntax is that of the demarcation of these two: we have to decide whether a particular combination of morphemes is a word or a phrase. As we will see below, there are many expressions that clearly consist of more than one word, but nevertheless function as lexical units. If a particular type of multi-word expression is productive, I will call such a pattern a constructional idiom or construction for short (Section 6.3). Telling examples of such constructions are the separable complex verbs (Section 6.4).

6.2. SYNTACTIC VALENCY EFFECTS

Morphology not only has to deal with the internal structure of complex words (that is, its internal syntax), but also with the effects of morphological processes on the syntactic valency of the words they create, the so-called external syntax of words. For example, the Dutch prefix *be-* that is used to derive verbs, creates verbs with a specific syntactic property: newly created *be*-verbs are always obligatorily transitive. This has to be accounted for in a proper morphological description of Dutch.

There is a wealth of literature on this topic (cf. Booij 1992, Baayen and Lieber 1994, Levin and Rappoport Hovav 1998, Sadler and Spencer 1998, and the literature mentioned there). The following two basic hypotheses which are also defended in these papers will form the starting point of my analysis of the Dutch facts:[1]

a. the lexical representation of words contains at least the following two related levels: Lexical-Conceptual Structure (LCS) and Predicate-Argument Structure (PAS), where PAS is a projection of LCS;
b. morphological rules may either apply at the level of LCS (and hence indirectly also affect PAS), or at the level of PAS.

The difference between these two levels of lexical representation can be illustrated by the Dutch verb with inherent telic aspect *verorberen* 'to eat completely'. This verb can be represented as follows:

(1) *verorber*, V
     LCS: EAT, x_{AGENT}, $y_{PATIENT}$ Event structure: Accomplishment
     PAS: V, x, y

LCS specifies the meaning of the verb; it refers to an event of eating with two participants, an agent and a patient (the thematic roles or theta-roles). PAS is the level that contains those aspects of lexical meaning that are grammatically relevant; it is the syntactic projection of the lexical-semantic structure.

---

[1] This approach stands in contrast to earlier work in which morphology is assumed to operate on the level of argument structure only. An example of such an approach for Dutch is Neeleman and Schipper (1993), an article that deals with *ver*-prefixation. Criticism of this approach can be found in Zubizarreta (1987), and, as far as Dutch is concerned, in Booij and van Haaften (1988), Booij (1992), and Baayen and Lieber (1994).

Thus, PAS mediates the mapping between lexical semantics and syntactic structure. In this example, PAS indicates that the verb is obligatorily transitive. Furthermore, PAS indicates that the Agent argument is to be expressed as the external argument (that is, in subject position); this is indicated by italicizing the first argument x. The other arguments in PAS are called internal arguments: a direct object is a direct internal argument, and arguments that require to be preceded by a preposition are called indirect internal arguments. Furthermore, PAS is often predictable from LCS by means of so-called linking rules. For instance, it is a well-established universal that 'in all languages, agent theta roles are external, and patient/theme theta roles are internal when a verb has both' (Baker 1988: 37). This universal is an example of a linking rule, a rule that links LCS and PAS systematically.

As proposed by Pustejovsky (1995) and others, the semantic structure of a word consists of more than one layer. One layer is that of argument structure (LCS and PAS), another is that of event structure. Traditionally, four types of events are distinguished: states, activities, accomplishments, and achievements. The kind of event expressed by the verb *verorberen* is an accomplishment: it is an activity with an implied endpoint. Hence its inherent aspect is telic. This is relevant for the relation between LCS and PAS and hence for the linking rules: a verb with inherent telic aspect requires its object argument to be always expressed syntactically. Therefore, the verb *verorberen* is obligatorily transitive.

Dutch also has the verb *eten* 'to eat'. Like its English equivalent, this verb is optionally transitive: the Patient argument need not be expressed syntactically. This means that at the level of LCS, the argument y can receive an arbitrary interpretation. Formally, this means that this variable is bound, and hence does not receive syntactic expression. A corollary of this property is that, unlike the verb *verorberen*, the verb *eten* has no inherent telic aspect, and can be used with durative aspect. It is only if it occurs with a syntactically realized Theme-argument that mentions a specified quantity that telic aspect is induced:

(2) *Jan verorbert
     Jan eet 'John is eating' (durative)
     Jan eet een boterham 'John eats a sandwich' (telic)

As stated above, most word-formation processes that affect syntactic valency are to be interpreted as operations on LCS. An example is the creation of deverbal adjectives in *-baar* '-able'. Such adjectives express the possibility of the Theme-argument of the base verb undergoing the action expressed by the verb. Hence, they require transitive base verbs. The Agent-argument of the verb can no longer be expressed, which is to be expected since the *-baar* adjectives do not express an event, but a property:

(3) Dit verschijnsel is verklaarbaar (*door mij) 'This phenomenon is explainable (*by me)'
Dit boek is goed leesbaar (*door mij) 'This book is well readable (*by me)'

The LCS of *-baar* adjectives can therefore be defined as follows:

(4) The property of *y* such that, for some x_{arb}, it is possible that x PREDICATE y

(where 'x PREDICATE y' is the LCS of the base verb). X_{arb} is the expression of the generic (arbitrary) interpretation of the variable; formally, it is an operator that binds that variable, and therefore, the *x*-variable cannot receive syntactic expression any more. The only remaining free variable is *y* which then predictably becomes the subject argument of the adjective in *-baar* since it is the only argument left. This suffix can also be attached to the verbs *verorberen* and *eten* discussed above: *verorberbaar, eetbaar*. The latter adjective illustrates again the phenomenon of type coercion that we came across in Chapter 2: *-baar* will select the transitive variant of the verb *eten* because this is the type of verb that *-baar* requires.

This kind of passive adjectives can now be compared with the formation of passive participles. The formation of the latter is a case of operation at PAS: there is no change of meaning involved in passivization, but only a change in syntactic expression. That is, it is PAS that changes: the expression of the external argument of the base verb is suppressed, but at LCS, the logical subject, if present, is still available for semantic interpretation. This is confirmed by two tests: the possibility of an agent phrase (with the preposition *door*), and the use of control clauses that require an agent to be semantically available:

(5) Dit boek werd gelezen (door mij) 'This book was read (by me)'
Dit boek werd gelezen om het geheim te ontdekken 'This book was read to discover the secret'

6.2. SYNTACTIC VALENCY EFFECTS

*Dit boek is leesbaar door mij 'This book is readable by me'

*Dit boek is leesbaar om het geheim te ontdekken 'This book is readable to discover the secret'

There is a third category of words with passive flavour, the middle verbs, already discussed in Section 3.5. Middle verbs, unlike passive verbs, do not express an event but a property. The following sentences illustrate this use of verbs (Peeters 1999):

(6) Dit boek leest fijn 'This book reads pleasantly'
Die bank zit heerlijk 'That couch sits very comfortably'
Een condoom vrijt niet zo lekker 'A condom does not make love pleasantly'

As was the case for -*baar* adjectives, middle verbs do not allow for agentive phrases or control clauses, again unlike passives:

(7) *Dit boek leest fijn door mij 'This book reads pleasantly by me'
*Die bank zit heerlijk om een boek te lezen 'That couch sits pleasantly to read a book'

Therefore, the creation of middle verbs is to be analysed as the conversion of transitive verbs into intransitive verbs with a specific semantic effect at the level of LCS; their intransitivity follows from this LCS.[2]

Most morphological operations in Dutch appear to be operations at the level of LCS: they affect the meaning of their base words. The concomitant changes in syntactic valency are therefore to be seen as the effects of changes at the level of LCS. I will first illustrate this with the prefix *be-*. This prefix nicely illustrates that in many cases morphological operations cannot be defined as operations with respect to the argument structure (PAS) of words because the attachment of *be-* exhibits a uniform valency effect: whatever the input of *be-*prefixation, its output is always an obligatorily transitive verb. This follows from an analysis in which it is the semantic effects of *be-*prefixation on LCS that are seen as its defining characteristics, and the effects on PAS are predictable from LCS by means of linking rules. The LCS of *be-* can be circumscribed as 'to direct an action towards an object such that that object is affected'. That is, it creates causative (and hence obligatorily

---

[2] See Ackema and Schoorlemmer (1994, 1995) for similar conclusions with respect to English and Dutch middle verbs.

transitive) verbs that mention an event through which the object is affected:

(8) *Type of input verb* *Output verb*
 WITH EXTERNAL ARGUMENT ONLY
 loop 'to walk' iets beloop 'to walk on s.'
 klim 'to climb' iets beklim 'to climb on s.'
 WITH INDIRECT INTERNAL ARGUMENT
 twijfel aan iets 'to doubt about s.' iets betwijfel 'to doubt s.'
 vecht met iemand 'to fight with s.' iemand bevecht 'to fight s.'
 WITH DIRECT INTERNAL ARGUMENT
 iets schilder 'to paint something' iets beschilder
   'to cover s. with paint'
 iets plak 'to glue something' iets beplak (met iets)
   'to cover s. (with s.)'
 WITH DIRECT AND INDIRECT INTERNAL ARGUMENT
 iets roof van iemand 'to rob s. from s.' iemand beroof (van iets)
   'to rob s. (from s.)'
 iets plant in iets 'to plant s. in s.' iets beplant (met iets)
   'to plant s. (with s.)'

The LCS of deverbal *be*-verbs can therefore be circumscribed as follows: x completely affects y by executing the action expressed by the input verb. That is, the resulting verbs are always telic verbs. If a telic verb has a Patient-argument, this argument must always be expressed syntactically; hence, the fact that these verbs are obligatorily transitive is fully predictable.

This analysis implies that there is no inheritance of argument structure of the base verb in the corresponding derived verb. This is corroborated by the fact that the derived verb may impose different selection restrictions on its arguments from the base verb. The verb *schilderen* 'to paint', for instance, can occur with an affected object, as in *een landschap schilderen* 'to paint a landscape', whereas the object of the verb *beschilderen* is always an affected object that already exists before the action takes place. Hence, it is impossible or at least odd to speak of *een landschap beschilderen* 'to cover a landscape with paint'.

The uniform valency effect is also found for *be*-verbs with non-verbal bases:

6.2. SYNTACTIC VALENCY EFFECTS

(9) *Nominal base*   *Obligatorily transitive verb*
bos 'wood'   bebos 'to completely cover with woods'
dijk 'dike'   bedijk 'to completely provide with dikes'

Adjectival base
veilig 'safe'   beveilig 'to safe-guard'
zat 'drunk'   bezat 'to make oneself drunk'

Thus, we can conclude that the meaning contribution of the polycategorial *be-* always has a component 'to completely affect *y*'.

The uniform valency effect also holds for the prefixes *om-*, *door-*, and *over-* which all create obligatorily transitive verbs:

(10) denk 'to think'   doordenk 'to grasp completely', overdenk 'to think about'
schijn 'to shine'   omschijn 'to shine around', doorschijn 'to shine through'
zie 'to see'   doorzie 'to see through', overzie 'to survey'

The verbalizing prefix *ver-* is different in that it creates both inchoative and causative verbs, as illustrated by the following examples; sometimes, the *ver-* verb can be used both ways. This prefix can be added to verbs, nouns, and adjectives.

(11) *Base*   *Derived verb*
arm 'poor'   verarm 'to become/make poor'
huis 'house'   verhuis 'to move house' (intr.)/'to move' (tr.)
jaag 'to chase'   verjaag 'to chase away' (tr.)
waai 'to blow'   verwaai 'to blow away' (intr.)

This shows that the meaning contribution of *ver-* has an optional part 'x CAUSE'; if that part is added, we create transitive verbs, and otherwise inchoative verbs that express a change of location or property (cf. Baayen and Lieber (1994) for detailed discussion of the semantic properties of these verbs).

The verbalizing prefix *ont-* is similar to *ver-* in that it also creates inchoative verbs and causative verbs with a reversative meaning: the property related to the base word is undone. It also atttaches to verbs, nouns, and adjectives:

(12) Base   Derived verb
brand 'to burn'   ontbrand 'to start burning' (intr.)
groen 'green'   ontgroen 'to initiate' (tr.)
haar 'hair'   onthaar 'to remove hair' (tr.)
heilig 'holy'   ontheilig 'to desecrate' (tr.)
hoofd 'head'   onthoofd 'to behead' (tr.)
keten 'to chain'   ontketen 'to unchain' (tr.)
loop 'to walk'   ontloop 'to evade' (tr.)

It is clear from these examples that there is quite some variation in the meanings of the prefixed verbs, due to the following two factors. On the one hand, the meaning contribution of the prefix itself may show variation. This is obviously the case for *ver-* and *ont-* which, as we saw, have an optional 'x CAUSE' part. Moreover, a prefix like *ont-* has a range of meanings such as inchoative and reversative meaning. That is, these prefixes are polysemous. On the other hand, the exact interpretation of the relation between the action expressed by the derived verb and the meaning expressed by the base word will also vary, and depends on non-linguistic knowledge, just as was the case for relational adjectives and conversion (Chapter 3) and compounding (Chapter 4). What these examples clearly show is that the syntactic valency of a complex verb must be determined on the basis of its meaning.

6.2.1. Deverbal nouns and inheritance

Above we saw that the syntactic valency of newly created verbs is determined by the semantics of the word-formation processes involved, and is not inherited from that of their base words. In other cases, in particular in deverbal nominalization, it seems that inheritance does take place. For instance, consider the following NPs with as their nominal head the deverbal noun *weigering* 'refusal', derived from the verb *weigeren* 'to refuse' by means of suffixation with *-ing*:

(13) (a) Jans weigering van het aanbod 'John's refusal of the offer'
      (b) De weigering van het aanbod door Jan 'the refusal of the offer by John'
      (c) De weigering van het aanbod 'the refusal of the offer'
      (d) Jans weigering 'John's refusal'
      (e) De weigering 'the refusal'

6.2. SYNTACTIC VALENCY EFFECTS

The meaning contribution of the deverbal suffix -*ing* can be defined as 'the event such that [LCS of the base verb]'. Therefore, we may say here that the LCS of the verb is inherited by the corresponding deverbal noun. For instance, the verb *weigeren* is a predicate with two semantic roles, an Agent-role and a Patient-role. The Patient-role need not be expressed syntactically: *weigeren* is optionally transitive, and a sentence such as *Jan weigerde* 'John refused', in which it is not specified what is refused, is also grammatical. In the first nominalization we see that both the Agent and the Theme are expressed, by the specifier *Jan* and the PP *van het aanbod* respectively. In (13*b*), the Agent role is expressed by the agentive *door* PP. In the next examples (13*c*–*e*) only one of the thematic roles is expressed, or none at all. This suggests that the syntactic expression of the LCS-roles of the verbal base of a deverbal noun is possible, but not required for its corresponding deverbal noun. If they are expressed, they acquire the syntactic form that is the correct one for that thematic role. For instance, an Agent-role is expressed as a specifier (only for proper names) or a *door* PP, and the Patient-role by a PP with the semantically empty preposition *van*. Note, furthermore, that the notion 'inheritance' as used here is not an additional formal mechanism; it is a term that describes the effect of the fact that the semantic structure of a deverbal noun encompasses that of its base verb, and is therefore nothing else but a consequence of the principle of compositionality in morphology: the meaning of a complex word is a compositional function of the meaning of the base word and that of the affix.

If a thematic role is not expressed, the relevant entity that bears this role will be reconstructed on the basis of knowledge of the context and situation, and knowledge of the world. In this respect nouns differ systematically from verbs because normally the thematic roles of a verb must be expressed as indicated in their Predicate-Argument Structure. For instance, since the verb *verwoesten* 'to destroy' is obligatorily transitive, both roles must be expressed, and a sentence like **De vijand verwoest* 'The enemy destroys' is ungrammatical, whereas NPs with the deverbal noun *verwoesting* as their head do not need to express the Patient-role if it is clear which entity has that role:

(14)   De verwoesting door de vijand duurde weken 'The destruction by the enemy went on for weeks'

These observations suggest that the LCS-roles of a verb are semantically still active in the corresponding deverbal noun, as expressed in the semantic characterization of *-ing* given above, but can also be identified in other ways than by means of overt syntactic expression. Both Hoeksema (1984) and Mackenzie (1985b) express this generalization in terms of a rule of optional argument reduction for deverbal nouns. The deverbal nouns then still differ from simplex ones in that the latter do not have specific semantic roles associated with them. For instance, the use of a *door* PP requires the presence at LCS of an Agent-role, and hence there is difference in wellformedness between the ungrammatical **het boek door Jelle* 'the book by Jelle' and the grammatical *de publicatie door Jelle* 'the publication by Jelle': the latter allows for an event interpretation with an Agent. Note, however, that event nouns can also acquire a result meaning; in the latter case, the event reading and the associated thematic roles are no longer available, as shown by the contrast between

(15) De publicatie door Jelle was een moedige stap 'The publication by Jelle was a courageous step'
*Die gele publicatie door Jelle was belangrijk 'That yellow publication by Jelle was important'

In the second example, the use of the colour adjective *geel* implies a result interpretation of *publicatie*. Hence, the Agent role that comes with the event interpretation is not available for linking to the *door* PP.

Similar effects of the principle of compositionality can be seen in the coinage of deverbal subject nouns in *-er*. The semantic characterization of *-er* is that it binds the x-variable of the LCS of a verb (the 'logical subject'), whatever the thematic role of x, and thus this suffix forms subject names (Booij 1979). In many cases this is the Agent-role, but in other cases, in particular for intransitive verbs, it is the Theme-role, as shown by the following examples:

(16) *Agent-role*: dod-er 'killer', jag-er 'hunter', vlieg-er 'flyer, pilot', zend-er 'sender'
Theme-role: dal-er 'dropper', groei-er 'grower', stijg-er 'riser', uitvaller 'drop-out'

If the LCS of the verbal base contains a second argument y, this variable will remain variable and is not bound by the suffix *-er*. Therefore, we also encounter inheritance effects for deverbal nouns that have transitive verbs as their bases:

(17) bedrijf 'to do'   de bedrijvers van het kwaad 'the doers of
                           harm'
      bereid 'to prepare' bereiders van maaltijden 'preparers of meals'
      veracht 'to despise' de verachters van godsdienst 'the despisers of
                           religion'

Note that the three base verbs involved are all obligatorily transitive verbs. Thus, the *van* PPs of the deverbal nouns are interpreted as expressing the *y*-variable of the LCS of their base verbs. In other words, these nouns need some complementation in order to make them semantically felicitous: it is hard to give some reasonable semantic interpretation to such -*er* nouns without a complement that expresses the Patient-role. Once the Patient has been introduced, it can however be omitted in a second use of the -*er* noun, as illustrated by the following example:[3]

(18) ... ten overstaan van enkele verachters van de religie. En dat waren niet eens ontwikkelde verachters. 'in the presence of some despisers of religion. And those people were not even well-educated despisers'

There is another way in which the Theme argument of the verbal base of an -*er* noun can be expressed: as the non-head constituent of a compound with the deverbal -*er* noun as its head (cf. Selkirk 1982 and Lieber 1983 for English, and Booij 1988*b* for Dutch). For instance, in the following compounds the left constituent is interpreted as a Theme:

(19) aardappeleter 'potato eater', ijsverkoper 'ice seller',
      jeneverdrinker 'gin drinker', schoenmaker 'shoe maker'

These compounds cannot be interpreted as deverbal derivations from verbal compounds since verbal compounding is not productive in Dutch. Hence, they are nominal compounds with a deverbal head. The Theme-role of the deverbal noun can also be expressed as a *van* PP or as a specifier:

(20) een drinker van jenever 'a drinker of gin', een verkoper van ijs 'a seller of ice'
      hun beschermer 'their protector', zijn bestrijder 'his opponent',
      zijn Maker 'his Creator'

---

[3] Source: Willem Jan Otten, *Het wonder van de losse olifanten*. Amsterdam: G. A. van Oorschot, 1999: 27.

We find many cases of compounds in which the deverbal noun does not occur by itself because it is derived from an obligatorily transitive verb. As we saw above, the corresponding deverbal noun can only be used if the Thematic roles of the base verb are either overtly expressed (syntactically or morphologically) or can be reconstructed on the basis of situation, context, or knowledge of the world. Therefore, *-er* nouns derived from obligatorily transitive verbs rarely occur without a syntactic or morphological complement, as is also illustrated by the following examples:

(21) beoefenaar 'practiser'   sportbeoefenaar/beoefenaar van sport 'sports practiser'
      bereider 'producer'   ijsbereider/bereider van ijs 'ice producer'
      nemer 'taker'   initiatiefnemer/nemer van initatieven 'initiative taker'
      verlener 'provider'   hulpverlener/verlener van hulp '*lit.* help provider, social worker'
      verspreider 'distributor' energieverspreider/verspreider van energie 'energy distributor'

Words like *nemer* require the Theme-role of the base verb to be identifiable, and hence such nouns rarely occur in isolation. For verbs like *eten* 'to eat' and *tekenen* 'to draw', on the other hand, the Theme-role can be identified conventionally as food and a drawing respectively, and hence both these verbs and the corresponding deverbal nouns *eter* 'eater' and *tekenaar* 'drawer' do occur in isolation, without explicit Theme-complement. Consequently, compounds with such deverbal nouns are ambiguous in that the non-head constituent can be interpreted as a Theme or differently, as an adjunct. This applies, for instance, to the English compound *tree eater*: *tree* can be interpreted as either the Theme or the Location of the eating.

Lexicalization also plays a role for nouns derived from obligatorily transitive verbs: for the deverbal noun, unlike its base verb, the Theme-role may be fixed, as shown by the following examples:

(22) *Obligatorily transitive verb*   *Deverbal noun without complement*
      begunstig 'to patronize'   begunstiger 'financial supporter of societies'
      bezet 'to occupy'   bezetter 'foreign occupier of one's country'

6.2. SYNTACTIC VALENCY EFFECTS

draag 'to bear' draager 'bearer of dead bodies at funerals'
hervorm 'to reform' hervormer 'reformer of the Roman Catholic church'

The deverbal noun *hebber* 'haver', derived from the obligatorily transitive verb *hebben* 'to have' occurs in compounds such as *bevelhebber* 'lit. command-haver, commander'. We do not find the 'periphrastic' counterpart *hebber van bevel* 'haver of command', probably because we have to do here with a lexicalized compound, which blocks the syntactic alternative. The deverbal noun *hebber* does occur in isolation, however, but only with a very specific meaning 'greedy person'. This blocking effect can also be seen in the use of the compound *grasmaaier* 'lawn mower'. Here, the agent noun *maaier* 'mower' is given an instrumental interpretation. In a phrase like *de maaier van het gras* 'the mower of the lawn' the only possible interpretation for *maaier* is the Agent interpretation if we want to interpret *het gras* as a Theme. That is, the word *maaier* in its instrumental interpretation has lost the thematic roles of the base verb. The semantic relation between *gras* and *maaier* in the compound *grasmaaier* will then be determined in the standard way discussed in Chapter 4, analogously to other compounds with this nominal head such as *motormaaier* 'motor mower'.

The correspondence in syntactic valency between a verb and its deverbal noun is a correspondence in terms of LCS-roles, not a correspondence at the more concrete level of syntactic subcategorization. This is clear from compounds such as *levensgenieter* 'lit. life-enjoyer, bon vivant' and *gomhandelaar* 'gum dealer'. In these compounds headed by a deverbal noun, the non-head constituents *leven* 'life' and *gom* 'gum' are interpreted as Theme-arguments, although the base verbs *genieten* and *handelen* require a prepositional object with a specific preposition: *genieten van NP, handelen in NP*. Another observation that supports this view of inheritance as an effect of the semantics of a word, is that in the following NP the complement *(van) dit huis* fulfils the role of Theme although there is no base verb for the noun *eigenaar* from which this valency could have been inherited (*eigen* 'own' is an adjective):

(23) de eigenaar van dit huis 'the owner of this house'

As observed by Selkirk (1982: 37), there is a locality condition (the First Order Projection Condition) on the interpretation of the non-head constituent of this type of compound: a phrase like *a tree eater of pasta* cannot be interpreted as 'someone who eats pasta in a tree'. In other words, if we want to link a constituent to the LCS-role of the verbal base, this must be done as locally as possible. This means that the possible theme *pasta* has to be part of the compound: the phrase *a pasta eater in a tree* is fine. The same observation holds for Dutch, as shown by the following examples:

(24)   *een pentekenaar van rivierlandschappen 'a pen drawer of river landscapes'
   *een fabrieksbereider van ijs 'an industrial maker of ice'

As pointed out by Hoeksema (1984), the non-head position of such compounds can also be interpreted as the logical subject (Theme) in case the verb is intransitive: *prijsstijging* 'price increase', *temperatuurschommeling* 'temperature fluctuation'. That is, it is the closest argument of the verb that is linked to the left constituent. If the closest argument is a predicate, as in *bekend maken* 'to make known', the Patient-argument has to appear as a PP: *de bekendmaking van de overwinning* 'the public announcement of the victory' (Hoeksema 1991b: 705).

The position taken so far is that we do not need a specific formal mechanism of inheritance in order to account for the correspondences in syntactic valency between verbs and their derived nouns. It has been observed in the literature, however, that there are sometimes correspondences at a very concrete level, that of syntactic subcategorization. This is the level below PAS that we need in those cases in which the syntactic form of a thematic role is not fully predictable. This is the case for verbs with prepositional objects that require a specific preposition to be present, such as the Dutch verbs *lijden aan* 'to suffer from' and *zoeken naar* 'to look for, to search for'. This choice of a specific preposition has to be specified lexically, at the level of syntactic subcategorization. What we see is that the deverbal noun may have the same PP-complement:

(25)   lijder aan pleinvrees 'sufferer from agoraphobia'
   zoeker naar waarheid 'searcher for truth'

Another illustration of inheritance is the verb *afhangen van* 'to depend on': the choice of *van* recurs in its derivatives:

(26) afhankelijk van iets 'dependent on something'
onafhankelijk van iets 'independent of something'
onafhankelijkheid van iets 'independence of something'

As observed in Moortgat (1981), a number of affixes exhibit this correspondence. If the word-formation process is category-neutral, the inheritance follows from the fact that the head of a complex word determines its syntactic (sub)category. However, we also find inheritance in cases of category-changing word formation, and we therefore have to explicitly characterize these suffixes as inheriting affixes. Of course, this presupposes that the correspondence in choice of preposition does not follow from semantic considerations, i.e. because the choice of a particular preposition is governed by semantics. If this were the case, there is no inheritance involved. In the following cases of category-changing word formation, the choice of preposition seems to be lexically governed, and hence they are real cases of inheritance:

(27) afkerig van NP 'averse to'   afkerigheid van NP
                                         'aversion to'
     benieuwd naar NP 'curious about'   benieuwdheid naar NP
                                         'curiosity about'
     vatbaar voor NP 'susceptible to'   vatbaarheid voor NP
                                         'susceptibility to'
     hunker naar NP 'to long for'   gehunker naar NP 'longing for'
     knoei met NP 'to tamper with'   geknoei met NP 'tampering
                                         with'
     deel door NP 'divide by'   deelbaar door NP 'divisible by'
     vergelijk met NP 'to compare to'   vergelijkbaar met NP
                                         'comparable to'
     zoek naar NP 'to look for'   gezoek naar NP 'looking for'
     hoop op NP 'to hope for'   hoop op NP 'hope for'
     vertrouw op NP 'to trust in'   vertrouwen op NP 'trust in'

As shown above, not all category-changing word-formation processes exibit inheritance. In particular, the creation of complex verbs by means of the prefixes *be-* and *ver-* excludes inheritance of subcategorizational properties of the base verb. Therefore, we have to specify which category-determining affixes have the property of inheritance.

6.3. CONSTRUCTIONS

In Chapter 2 we encountered some examples of constructions in Dutch, such as the periphrastic constructions for perfect and passive, combinations of an auxiliary and a participle. These combinations are non-morphological units because the auxiliary is the finite form that can be separated from the participle in main clauses by Verb Second. In order to express their separability, I assume that these periphrastic constructions are dominated by V', the first level of projection above V. For instance, the perfect construction can be represented as a lexical construction of one of the following forms:

(28)   [[hebben, zijn]$_V$ [perfect participle]]$_{V'}$

The perfect participle position is an open slot, unlike the auxiliary position. Thus, we express the productive nature of this periphrastic construction: it is not a lexical idiom, but a constructional idiom. The listing of such constructions in the lexicon implies that there is no sharp boundary between lexicon and syntax. The traditional demarcation of lexicon and syntax has recently been challenged in the framework of Construction Grammar (cf. Goldberg 1995), and in recent work by Jackendoff (1995, 1997a,b). The basic idea is that the lexicon does not only contain words and idioms (word combinations with unpredictable meaning), but also constructional idioms, that is, syntactic constructions with a specific meaning contributed by the construction itself, in which only a subset of the terminal elements is fixed. In Chapter 2 we have already encountered examples of such constructions, the possessor construction and the partitive construction. Goldberg (1995) therefore concluded that we should not speak any more of the lexicon, but of the 'constructicon' of a language.[4]

Another example of a constructional idiom is the combination of the verb *laten* 'to let' with another verb. As pointed out by Coopmans and Everaert (1988: 88), *laten* behaves as other verbs in that it can undergo Verb Second, and is inflected regularly, but has the properties of a bound morpheme in that it can affect the argument structure of its complement verb. It can also

---

[4] The non-isomorphy between syntactic and morphological words is also focused upon in Zwicky (1990), Ackerman and LeSourd (1997), and Ackerman and Webelhuth (1998). Classical examples of such constructions are the reflexive and the causative constructions in Romance languages, the serial verbs in African languages, and the *go and V*-construction in English.

act as a substitute for passive, inchoative, or causative morphology. This is why they speak of 'the *laten*-construction' (Coopmans and Everaert 1988: 89). The effect of *laten* on the syntactic valency of its complement verb is illustrated by the following examples:

(29)   *Passive effect*
Indriaas laat het huiswerk (door zijn moeder) controleren '*lit*. Indriaas lets the homework (by his mother) check, Indriaas has his homework checked by his mother'
Causative effect
Suzanne laat de fiets aan Rebecca zien '*lit*. Suzanne lets the bike to Rebecca see, Suzanne shows Rebecca the bike'

Many combinations of *laten* and a verb are idioms that have to be stored in the lexicon anyway because they have an unpredictable meaning. For instance, *laten varen* 'let sail' means 'no longer have', as in:

(30)   Hij heeft zijn bezwaren laten varen '*lit*. He has his objections let sail, He no longer has objections'

But the crucial point is that combinations of the verb *laten* and another verb can also be coined productively; therefore, we have to assume a constructional idiom '*laten* + V' with passive and causative meanings.

Other verbs can be used to express specific aspectual values. For instance, the verbs *blijven* 'to stay', *gaan* 'to go', and *komen* 'to come' are used in combination with a verb to express durational (*blijven*) or inchoative aspect (*gaan*, *komen*):

(31)   We blijven in Heiloo wonen 'We carry on living in Heiloo'
We gaan in Heiloo wonen 'We are going to live in Heiloo'

The verb *zitten* 'to sit' can also be used to express duration; however, it requires the infinitive of the following verb to be preceded by the particle *te* 'to', unlike the verbs *blijven* and *gaan*:

(32)   Hij zit te zeuren 'He is nagging'

Note that in this use of *zitten* its literal meaning is completely absent, it has bleached into a purely aspectual meaning.

Another example of a construction with durational meaning is the progressive construction '*aan het* + infinitive'; the verb must be non-telic:

(33)   Jan is aan het fietsen 'John is cycling'

The formal structure of this construction is that of a PP with the preposition *aan* and the neuter determiner *het* followed by the infinitive which, as we saw in Chapter 2, can function as a neuter noun. Dutch PPs can function as predicates anyway, as illustrated by the following sentences:

(34)   Jan is in de wolken '*lit.* John is in the clouds, John is very glad'
       Ik ben achter de waarheid '*lit.* I am behind the truth, I know the truth'

The specific property of the *aan het* + verb PP is that it functions as a predicate with the meaning 'V-ing'. Therefore, we have to assume a PP-construction, in which the first two words are fixed, and an open slot for the verb:

(35)   [aan [het [V-infinitive]]$_{NP}$]$_{PP}$ 'V-ing'

A final example of a word combination with a morphological function is the combination *te* + infinitive that behaves as an *-able* adjective in combination with the verb *zijn* 'to be':

(36)   Deze taak is goed te doen '*lit.* This task is good to do, this task is doable'
       Deze soep is niet te eten '*lit.* This soup is not to eat, this soup is inedible'

In sum, what we have seen here is that Dutch has a number of constructional idioms, productive classes of word combinations with a specific meaning attributed by the construction itself, and in that respect very similar to complex words. Due to their unpredictable meaning, these constructions cannot be generated by the syntactic module, but must be specified in the lexicon, which therefore is to be seen as a construction. In the next section, we will see that the so-called separable complex verbs are also instances of such constructions.

6.4. SEPARABLE COMPLEX VERBS: SYNTAX OR MORPHOLOGY?

Separable complex verbs (SCVs)—also called *samenkoppelingen* 'combinations' in Dutch grammars—are combinations of a verb and some other word which have both word-like properties and properties of a combination of words (Booij 1990). Thus, they pose the important theoretical question of how to draw the boundaries between morphology and syntax, and hence they have received a lot of attention in the morphological literature.[5] In Section 6.4.1, I will present the evidence that shows that SCVs are not words, but combinations of words. In Section 6.4.2 I will then discuss the properties of SCVs that make them look as if they are formed by morphological processes. These paradoxical properties of SCVs will then lead in Section 6.4.3 to the conclusion that they must be analysed as constructions.

6.4.1. *The syntactic nature of SCVs*

The following sentences illustrate the use of SCVs, both with SOV word order (embedded clauses) and with SVO word order (main clauses):

(37) … Hans zijn moeder opbelde/Hans belde zijn moeder op 'Hans phoned his mother'
 … de fietser neerstortte/De fietser stortte neer 'The cyclist fell down'
 … Jan het huis schoonmaakte/Jan maakte het huis schoon 'John cleaned the house'
 … Rebecca pianospeelde/Rebecca speelde piano 'Rebecca played the piano'
 … dit resultaat ons teleurstelde/Dit resultaat stelde ons teleur 'This result disappointed us'

In the first example, the word *op* 'up' that combines with the verb is also used as an adposition. In that case, the non-verbal element is also referred to as a particle, and the SCV is then referred to as a particle verb. Particle verbs form a productive class of SCVs. In the second example, the word *neer* 'down' is also used as an adverb. The next two examples show that adjectives (*schoon*) and nouns (*piano*) can also occur in SCVs. In the last example, the word *teleur* 'sad' does not occur as an independent word. The fact that SCVs are felt as word-like units is reflected by Dutch orthography, which requires SCVs to be written as one word, without internal spacing, if the two constituents are adjacent.

---

[5] Key references to the debate on the status of SCVs in Dutch are: Booij (1990) plus the references mentioned there, Neeleman (1992), and Neeleman and Weerman (1993). Key references for German are Stiebels and Wunderlich (1994) and Lüdeling (1999).

The basic reason why SCVs have to be considered as word combinations, and not as prefixed words, is that they are separable: in main clauses, the tensed verbal form appears in second position, whereas the other part is stranded. If we assumed SCVs to be words, we would violate the principle of Lexical Integrity that says that syntactic rules cannot refer to elements of morphological structure (Lapointe 1980: 8, Bresnan and Mchombo 1995).

A second phenomenon in which we see the separability of SCVs is Verb Raising. If the verb of an embedded clause is raised to the matrix clause, the SCV can be split, but it can also be treated as a unit.

(38) (a) ... dat Hans [zijn moeder op bellen]$_S$ wilde *'lit.* that Hans his mother up phone wanted'
 (b) ... dat Hans zijn moeder wilde opbellen 'that Hans wanted to phone his mother'
 (c) ... dat Hans zijn moeder op wilde bellen

In sentence (38*b*) the whole SCV *opbellen* is raised to the matrix clause, whereas in sentence (38*c*) the particle *op* is left behind in the embedded clause. This means that either the verb *bellen* only, or the whole SCV *opbellen* can be raised to the matrix clause. This shows that there is certainly a level at which the SCV does form a unit for the syntax.[6] The conclusion from sentences like (38*b*) that SCVs can behave as syntactic units is supported by the behaviour of SCVs in the progressive construction '*aan het* + infinitive'; compare:

(39) Hans is zijn moeder aan het opbellen 'Hans is phoning his mother'
 *Hans is zijn moeder op aan het bellen 'Hans is phoning his mother'
 *Hans is aan het zijn moeder bellen 'Hans is phoning his mother'
 Hans is zijn moeder aan het bellen 'Hans is phoning his mother'

Whereas *opbellen* must appear after *aan het* without being split, this is not the case for the VP *zijn moeder bellen*, which cannot appear after *aan het*.

The separability of SCVs also manifests itself in the location of the infinitival particle *te* that occurs between the two constituents of SCVs, as in *op*

---

[6] There is more evidence that Raising can affect more than one morphological word: in Flemish dialects of Dutch it is even possible to raise whole VPs, including the direct object, cf. Haegeman and van Riemsdijk (1986: 419). The difference between Verb Raising and Verb Second with respect to the stranding of the non-verbal constituent is discussed in Koopman (1995).

te bellen, and in the form of the perfect/past participle, with the prefix *ge-* in between the particle and the verbal stem: *opgebeld*. In derivational morphology, SCVs behave similarly; for instance, the *ge-*nominalization of *opbellen* is *opgebel*.

A number of these particles also function as real prefixes, i.e. as bound morphemes that cannot be separated from the verb. These prefixed verbs carry main stress on the verbal stem, not on the prefix, whereas the SCVs carry main stress on the non-verbal constituent. Thus we get minimal pairs like the following (in this section, verbs will always be given in their citation form, the infinitive):

(40)   SCV   *Prefixed verb*
       dóorboor 'to go on drilling'   doorbóor 'to perforate'
       ómblaas 'to blow down'   ombláas 'to blow around'
       ónderga 'to go down'   ondergá 'to undergo'
       óverkom 'to come over'   overkóm 'to happen to'
       vóorkom 'to occur'   voorkóm 'to prevent'

The phenomenon of Dutch SCVs is an instantiation of a widespread phenomenon, the occurrence of verbs preceded by a so-called preverb. We find SCVs in other Germanic languages like German (Stiebels and Wunderlich 1994, Lüdeling 1999), in many Indo-European languages (Watkins 1964), and in Hungarian and Estonian (Ackerman and LeSourd 1997). They form a subset of the class of phrasal predicates discussed in Ackerman and Webelhuth (1998).

The separability of the two constituents of SCVs has brought a number of linguists to propose a syntactic account of them, at least of the subset of particle verbs (Hoekstra, Lansu, and Westerduin 1987). This syntactic account usually has the form of a so-called Small Clause analysis: the particle is considered as the predicate of a Small Clause (SC), a subject–predicate combination without a copula, which is then raised to the matrix clause, and Chomsky-adjoined to the verb of the matrix clause. In such an analysis the following surface structure is assigned to the verb phrase *het huiswerk afmaken* 'to finish one's homework' (*t* is the trace of the moved PP):

(41)   [[het huiswerk]$_{NP}$[t_i]$_{PP}$]$_{SC}$ [[af]$_{PP_i}$[maken]$_V$]$_V$

In the case of *af maken* this is a reasonable analysis, because *af* 'ready, finished' does function as a predicate of its own in Dutch as in a sentence like

Het huiswerk is af 'The homework is finished'. Moreover, the word *af* can also be topicalized, which confirms its syntactic and semantic independence:

(42)   Áf maak ik het huiswerk niet 'I will not finish the homework'

However, in most cases topicalization of the particle is impossible, for instance in

(43)   *Óp bel ik mijn moeder niet 'I will not call my mother'
       *Aán val ik hem niet 'I will not attack him'

These are the cases where the particle does not function as a predicate with an independent meaning, unlike the particle *af* 'finished' in (42). This is a problem for the Small Clause analysis of particle verbs since this analysis predicts that topicalization is always possible.

6.4.2. *Lexical properties of SCVs*

Although the facts discussed in Section 6.4.1 make it clear that particle verbs are not morphological words, this does not mean that there is a straightforward syntactic account for all of them. They clearly behave as lexical units in a number of ways which I will focus on now. It is these word-like properties that have led a number of linguists to take the opposite view that particle verbs are morphological constructions created by a presyntactic morphological component (Neeleman 1992, Neeleman and Weerman 1993, Ackema 1999a, b). The basic problem for this latter view is that it does not account for the separability of particle verbs, and therefore, this position is not satisfactory either.

Related to the observation that the particles can often not be topicalized, the meaning of an SCV is often not fully predictable: because the particle has no clear individual meaning in isolation, it cannot be focused upon. The semantic unpredictability of SCVs is nicely illustrated by the different SCVs for the verb *vallen* 'to fall' which exhibits a bewildering variety of meanings, in most cases without a meaning constituent that corresponds to the meaning of the verb *vallen*:

(44)   *aanval* 'to attack', *afval* 'to lose weight', *bijval* 'to applaud', *inval* 'to invade, to set in', *meeval* 'to turn out better than expected', *omval* 'to fall down', *opval* 'to draw attention', *tegenval* 'to disappoint', *toeval* 'to come into the possession of'

6.4. SEPARABLE COMPLEX VERBS

It is obvious that, given this variation in meaning, it does not make sense to focus on the particles of these verbs only.

Lexical storage of SCVs is also necessary for other reasons: in SCVs such as *teleurstellen* 'to disappoint' and *gadeslaan* 'to watch' the first parts *teleur* and *gade* do not occur as independent words. Moreover, there are also verbal (45a) and non-verbal (45b) constituents of SCVs that do not occur as independent verbs, for instance:

(45) (a) aan-tijg 'to accuse', na-boots 'to imitate', om-kukel 'to fall down', op-kalefater 'to restore'
 (b) gade-sla 'to watch', teleur-stel 'to disappoint'

These idiosyncrasies show that many SCVs must be lexically stored; however, since syntactic units can be stored lexically as idioms, this fact does not necessarily point into a non-syntactic direction as to the formal analysis of SCVs.

A second important observation is that SCVs freely feed deverbal word formation. Normally, derivation is only fed by words, not by phrases, and this is taken by those linguists who advocate a morphological analysis of SCVs as evidence for the word-status of SCVs:

(46) *Deverbal suffixation*
 aanbied 'to offer' aanbieder 'offerer', aanbieding 'offer'
 aankom 'to arrive' aankomst 'arrival'
 aantoon 'to prove' aantoonbaar 'provable'
 aantrek 'to attract' aantrekkelijk 'attractive'

 Deverbal prefixation
 invoer 'to introduce' herinvoer 'to reintroduce'
 uitgeef 'to publish' heruitgeef 'to republish'
 uitzend 'to transmit' heruitzend 'to retransmit'

 Compounding with verbal left constituent
 doorkies 'to dial through' doorkiesnummer 'direct number'
 doorkijk 'to see through' doorkijkbloes '*lit.* see-through blouse, transparent blouse'
 opberg 'to store' opbergdoos 'store box'

On the other hand, it is not the case that syntactic constructs can never feed word formation: both compounding and affixation may be fed by units that are larger than one word. Moreover, the fact that SCVs do not feed verbal prefixation except with *her-* can be taken as support for their non-word status because the other Dutch prefixes take only words as their bases. For instance, the prefix *ver-* attaches to complex verbs, but not to SCVs:

(47) *Prefixed verbs*
 onder-stél 'to suppose' ver-onderstel 'to presuppose'
 vol-máak 'to perfect' ver-volmaak 'to make fully perfect'
 SCVs
 vól-maak 'to fill' *vervolmaak
 óver-maak 'to transfer' *verovermaak

In the case of SCVs with a nominal constituent it is also clear that SCVs are not straightforward syntactic units: an SCV with a noun in preverbal position such as *huishouden* takes *niet* as a negative element, just like all verbs, whereas syntactically independent NPs take *geen*:

(48) Jan kan niet/*geen huishouden 'John cannot run the household'
 Jan kan *niet/geen vriendin houden 'John cannot keep a girlfriend'

A nice example is the word combination *adem halen* 'to breathe' that can be interpreted as a normal VP with a free object *adem*, and as an SCV, whereas the combination *adem krijgen* 'to get breath' is not an SCV, and therefore takes only *geen* as negative element:

(49) Jan kan niet ademhalen/geen adem halen 'John cannot breathe'
 Jan kan *niet/geen adem krijgen 'John cannot get breath'

As mentioned above, these observations on the unitary nature of SCVs have been used as evidence in favour of a morphological analysis of SCVs: in that view, particle verbs are prefixed verbs with a special property, the separability of the prefix, and SCVs with a nominal or adjectival first constituent are verbal compounds, again with the special property of separability.

There are two other important observations on SCVs that seem to speak in favour of a morphological analysis. First, the addition of a particle may have the effect of category change since particle verbs can also be formed productively on the bases of adjectives and nouns. The power to change category is generally assumed to be a prerogative of morphological operations, in accordance with the Projection Principle which says that syntactic structure is a projection of lexical properties. The following examples illustrate the category-determining power of particle attachment:

(50) *Adjectival base*   *Particle verb*
helder 'clear'   ophelder 'to clarify'
hoog 'high'   ophoog 'to heighten'
knap 'tidy'   opknap 'to tidy up'
leuk 'nice'   opleuk 'to make nicer'

Nominal base   *Particle verb*
hoop 'pile'   ophoop 'to pile up'
luister 'lustre'   opluister 'to add lustre to'
som 'sum'   opsom 'to sum up'

In all these examples, the corresponding particle-less verb does not exist independently, and hence it is the combination with the particle that makes these adjectives and nouns function as verbs. Note, however, that these formations differ from verbalizing prefixation in that the adjectives and nouns themselves are turned into verbs. This is clear from the fact that they occupy the verb second position in main clauses, without the particle, as is shown by the following examples:

(51) De fabrikant hoogde de prijzen op 'The manufacturer raised the prices'
De problemen hopen zich op 'The problems pile up'

In other words, we have to assign the structure $[[hoog]_A]_V$ to the second part of the verb *ophogen*, and the structure $[[hoop]_N]_V$ to the second part of *ophopen*.

In a syntactic account of this observation we would have to assume that nouns and adjectives are turned into verbs by means of verbal conversion (a process that is normally only productive for nouns, not for adjectives, cf. de Vries 1975: 165), and that these conversion verbs are then lexically subcategorized for appearing with specific particles.

A second, related argument for a morphological view of particle verbs is that the addition of a particle may change the syntactic valency of the verb. In many cases, the SCV is transitive, whereas the verb itself is intransitive. Again, the Projection Principle implies that changes in syntactic valency must be due to lexical operations. The following examples illustrate the valency-change effect:

(52) bel (optionally transitive) 'to phone'   iemand opbel 'to phone somebody'

juich (intransitive) 'to cheer'	iemand toejuich 'to cheer somebody'
loop (intransitive) 'to walk'	de straten afloop 'to tramp the streets'
rijd (intransitive) 'to ride'	de auto inrijd 'to run in the car'
woon (intransitive) 'to live'	een vergadering bijwoon 'to attend a meeting'
zit (intransitive) 'to sit'	een straf uitzit 'to serve one's time'

As we saw in Section 6.2, it is morphological operations that typically have effects on the syntactic valency of words. In a syntactic account of these effects, the Small Clause analysis, the VP *de straten aflopen* 'to tramp the streets' would receive the following deep structure analysis:

(53) [de straten af]$_{SC}$ lopen

The verb *lopen* combines with a small clause, of which *af* forms the predicate. Hence, the superficial object *de straten* originates as subject of the small clause. Thus, it is explained why *aflopen* is a transitive verb. Semantically, however, it does not make sense to consider *af* as the predicate of *de straten* because it does not make sense to claim that *de straten* receive the property of being *af* 'finished'.

Another problem for such a syntactic analysis is that it does not relate syntactic valency to the semantics of each individual particle verb. As we argued in Section 6.2, argument structure, and hence syntactic valency, is the syntactic projection of the lexical-conceptual structure of a complex word. The crucial role of semantics can be seen in the following two sentences, in which the particle verb *aflopen* is used with two different meanings, and has corresponding syntactic valencies:

(54) De wekker loopt af (intransitive) 'The alarm clock goes off'
      Hij liep de hele tentoonstelling af (transitive) 'He did the whole exposition'

A syntactic account of valency effects does not do justice to this relation between syntactic valency and the semantics of each individual particle verb.

A final observation on particle verbs is that they form a productive category, and thus cannot simply be classified as idioms, as lexicalized syntactic constructions. For instance, the particle *af* can be used productively to form telic verbs, witness recent coinings such as *afdansen* 'to do one's dancing examination' and *afrijden* 'to do one's driving examination'. Similarly, the particle *door* can be used to create new durative verbs such as *doorvergaderen* 'to go on with a meeting' and *doordrinken* 'to go on drinking'. The point to be noted here is that the words *af* and *door* have a specific (aspectual) meaning in their use as particles.

This productive use can also be observed for the particles *aan, in, op,* and *uit*. Remarkably, the meaning contribution of the particles is very vague, and sometimes fully absent, i.e. the particle verb has about the same meaning as the verb by itself. This use of SCVs is particularly popular in the language of politicians and managers, and underscores once more the point that such particles do not function as predicates. Examples of such pairs are the following (source: van der Horst and van der Horst 1999: 351):

(55) | *Simplex verb* | *Particle verb* |
| --- | --- |
| deel 'to divide' | opdeel 'to divide' |
| huur 'to rent' | inhuur 'to rent' |
| lever 'to deliver' | aanlever 'to deliver' |
| onderhandel 'to negotiate' | uitonderhandel 'to bring the negotiations to an end' |
| schat 'to estimate' | inschat 'to estimate' |
| splits 'to split' | opsplits 'to split' |
| stuur 'to steer' | aanstuur 'to steer' |
| test 'to test' | uittest 'to test' |

The only general difference between such simplex verbs and their particle counterparts is that the particle verb is always obligatorily transitive, whereas the simplex verb may also be used without an overt direct object. That is, these particles have primarily a syntactic valency-determining function.

In conclusion, we need an analysis that can do justice to all the paradoxical properties of SCVs discussed above. The notion that we can use for such an analysis is that of the 'construction' or 'constructional idiom', discussed in the previous section.

6.4.3. *SCVs as constructional idioms*

The debate on the proper analysis of SCVs summarized in the previous section presupposes a particular and rather standard view of the lexicon: the lexicon is the fund of existing words, and this fund can be extended by morphological operations. In addition, the lexicon will also contain idioms, that is, syntactic chunks with a non-compositional semantic interpretation. Productive syntactic constructions are accounted for by the syntactic module. As we saw above, this sharp boundary between lexicon and syntax has recently been challenged.

The notion 'constructional idiom' can be used to do justice to both the syntax-like and the morphology-like properties of SCVs. The basic claim is that SCVs all have the following syntactic structure:

(56) [X [ ]$_V$]$_{V'}$ where X = P, Adv, A, or N

By assigning a V'-node to SCVs, we represent their phrasal nature, and hence their syntactic separability. The node V' indicates a first level of projection above the V-node. It cannot be equated with the VP-node in the classical sense, because we must be able to distinguish between SCVs and VPs that contain NPs: in standard Dutch, VPs of embedded clauses cannot be raised to their matrix clauses, unlike SCVs. Note, furthermore, that the left constituent is a single lexical category, and does not form a phrase. This correctly implies that they cannot be modified.

An additional argument for the non-projecting status of particles that has been used in the literature is that they are not easily topicalized. If it is only phrases that are topicalized, this would follow from their formal status. However, as argued by Hoeksema (1991a) it is not only phrases that can be topicalized. Morever, there are examples of topicalization of particles, for instance:

(57) Óp gaat de zon alleen in het oosten 'The sun only rises in the east'
      Úit voert Angola veel koffie 'Angola exports a lot of coffee'

It appears that the crucial condition for topicalization is not that of phrasal status, bur rather that of contrastive meaning: the particle *op* in *opgaan* 'to rise' can be contrasted with the SCV *ondergaan* 'to set'. Similarly, *uitvoeren* 'to export' can be contrasted to *invoeren* 'to import'. In the case of *opbellen* 'to phone' there is no semantically contrasting particle for *op* available, and hence topicalization of this *op* is impossible.

In structure (56), the verbal position is open, and can in principle be filled by any verb. The non-verbal constituent, however, is specified. That is, there are as many different constructional idioms of this kind as there are words

6.4. SEPARABLE COMPLEX VERBS

that can fill the left position. For instance, we will have the following constructional idioms:[7]

(58) [[af]$_P$[x]$_V$]$_V$, [[door]$_P$ [x]$_V$]$_V$, [[op]$_P$[x]$_V$]$_V$.

that give rise to particle verbs that begin with *af*, *door*, and *op* respectively, with a fixed terminal node for the particle constituent. This has two advantages. First, the notion 'particle' has no role outside the construction under discussion here, and therefore such words need not be specified independently as particles in the lexicon. Secondly, if a specific particle verb combination is no longer productive, we will not have the corresponding constructional idiom in the lexicon, but only a list of the individual existing cases of that type. Note that there are also cases where the verb only occurs in the SCV-construction, cases like *nabootsen* 'to imitate' and *omkukelen* 'to fall down'. In these cases, we no longer have an instantiation of a constructional idiom, but of a lexical idiom, with all terminal nodes fixed.

For each constructional idiom of this kind, its meaning will also be specified. For instance, the meaning of the constructional idiom *door-V* will be specified as 'to go on V-ing', and the constructional idiom *af-V* wil be specifed as 'to finish V-ing'.

What about those SCVs that do not take an existing verb in the open position, but an adjective or a noun? The obvious step to take is to specify constructional idioms of the type

(59) [op[[x]$_A$]$_V$]$_V$.

This means that adjectives can be converted to verbs by inserting them in the slot after the particle *op*. This makes the conversion of adjectives dependent on their occurrence in SCVs, and this is correct since, except for the particle context, conversion of adjectives to verbs is not productive in Dutch (de Vries 1975: 165). Moreover, this approach enables us to express the dependency of A to V and N to V conversion on specific particles. It is indeed the case that the particle *op* is used productively in this construction, but this does not apply to all particles. It is only the particles *op*, *uit*, and *af* that can combine with adjectives; as for nouns, they can only be used as verbs in combination with *af*, *in*, *na*, and *uit*:

---

[7] Cf. Jackendoff (1997b) for a similar analysis of the English counterpart construction with *away*.

(60)   *Adjective*   *Verb*
        diep 'deep'   uitdiep 'to deepen'
        fris 'fresh'   opfris 'to refresh'
        zwak 'weak'   afzwak 'to weaken'

        Noun
        aap 'monkey'   naäap 'to imitate'
        beeld 'image'   afbeeld 'to represent'
        huwelijk 'marriage'   uithuwelijk 'to marry off'
        polder 'id.'   inpolder 'to drain, to impolder'

As noted by Jackendoff (1995), the syntactic valency of constructional idioms can differ from that of the verbal head. This is what we observed in the preceding section for Dutch particle verbs: it is the combination of words that has a particular valency, a valency that is predictable from its semantic interpretation, as outlined in Section 6.2.

6.4.4. Grammaticalization

Although many of the words designated here as particles also occur as prepositions or postpositions, it is not the case that all adpositions can function as particles. The relevant generalization appears to be (Booij 1998c, 2000a) that only those adpositions function as particles that function as predicates in combination with the copula *zijn*. For instance, the preposition *met* 'with' cannot be used as a predicate, whereas the postposition *mee* with the same meaning 'with' can be used as such, as in the following sentences:

(61)   Jan is ook *met/mee 'John has joined'
       Ik ga met mijn moeder mee 'I will accompany my mother'

Here is a list of adpositions that can be used as predicates, and also function as particles:

(62)   *prepositions*: aan 'at', achter 'behind', bij 'at', binnen 'inside', boven 'above', buiten 'outside', na 'after', om 'around', onder 'under', tegen 'against', voor 'for'
      prepositions/postpositions: door 'through', in 'in', langs 'alongside', op 'up', rond 'round', over 'over', uit 'out', voorbij 'past'
      postpositions: af 'down', heen 'towards', mee 'with', toe 'to'

6.4. SEPARABLE COMPLEX VERBS

The following list provides examples of the use of each of these words:

(63)
Base verb	SCV
zet 'to put'	aanzet 'to stimulate'
blijf 'to stay'	achterblijf 'to stay behind'
werk 'to work'	bijwerk 'to patch up'
loop 'to walk'	binnenloop 'to enter'
kom 'to come'	bovenkom 'to surface'
sluit 'to close'	buitensluit 'to exclude'
denk 'to think'	nadenk 'to think'
breng 'to bring'	ombreng 'to kill'
duik 'to dive'	onderduik 'to hide'
kom 'to come'	tegenkom 'to meet'
kom 'to come'	voorkom 'to occur'
ga 'to go'	doorga 'to continue'
breng 'to bring'	inbreng 'to provide'
kom 'to come'	langskom 'to visit'
kom 'to come'	opkom 'to fight for'
kom 'to come'	rondkom 'to get by'
kom 'to come'	overkom 'to come over'
zet 'to put'	uitzet 'to expel'
ga 'to go'	voorbijga 'to ignore'
maak 'to make'	afmaak 'to finish'
ga 'to go'	heenga 'to die'
doe 'to do'	meedoe 'to participate'
geef 'to give'	toegeef 'to give in'

This restriction on the words that can be used as particles can be seen as a reflection of the origin of the particle verb construction: it is a grammaticalization of a syntactic configuration with secondary predication. For instance, the sentence *Jan maakte zijn huiswerk af* 'John finished his homework' can still receive a purely syntactic interpretation, with the predicate *af* functioning as a secondary predicate. That is, this sentence can receive the same structural analysis as the sentence *Jan verfde zijn fiets wit* 'John painted his bike white'. In many cases, however, the meaning of particles such as *af* has bleached, and acquired a purely aspectual value. For such cases, we have to assume that the predicate–verb combination has grammaticalized into a particle verb construction. In other words, the particle verb construction is the result of reanalysis of syntactic configurations with secondary predication. Thus, these observations illustrate two properties of grammaticalization (Hopper and Traugott 1993: 17): '(*a*) earlier forms may coexist with later ones . . .; (*b*) earlier meanings may constrain later meanings and/or structural characteristics'.

The second class of SCVs that we mentioned above are those with words that are also used as adverbs, such as:

(64)   neer 'down', samen 'together', terug 'back', thuis 'home', weg 'away'

In these cases, it is the combination of verb and adverb that is reanalysed as a unit. For instance, in the sentence *Hij legde het boek weg* 'He put the book away' it is the combination *weg leggen* that has the syntactic valency of a transitive verb, for which *het boek* functions as direct object: the sentence **Hij legde het boek* 'He put the book', without the adverb, is ungrammatical.

The phenomenon of grammaticalization can be circumscribed as: '... the process whereby lexical items and constructions come in certain linguistic contexts to serve grammatical functions, and, once grammaticalized, continue to develop new grammatical functions' (Hopper and Traugott 1993: xv). This is indeed what we observe for particle verbs: they are syntactic constructs that function as complex verbs with a number of aspectual properties, and thus have developed into constructional idioms.

From the point of view of grammaticalization particles can be seen as intermediate stages in the development of words into bound morphemes, in particular prefixes. Some particles are also used as inseparable prefixes. The following minimal pairs illustrate this:

(65)   SCV   *Inseparable Complex Verb (ICV)*
        dóorbreek 'to break through'   doorbréek 'to break'
        dóorloop 'to walk on'   doorlóop 'to pass'
        ónderga 'to go down'   ondergá 'to undergo'
        óverkom 'to come over'   overkóm 'to happen to someone'

The change from particle to prefix implies a loss of lexical meaning: the prefixes have an abstract, aspectual meaning, whereas the corresponding particles have a more concrete, spatial meaning. In sum, the following historical development can be reconstructed for Dutch:

(66)   word > part of SCV > prefix

6.4. SEPARABLE COMPLEX VERBS

Some morphemes belong to more than one of these categories, for example:

(67) word and part of SCV: af, neer 'down', op
word, part of SCV, and prefix: achter, door, mis 'wrong', om, vol 'full'

The prefixes *be-* and *ver-* derive historically from the words *bi* (modern Dutch *bij* 'at') and *voor* 'for' respectively, whereas *bij* and *voor* function as prepositions and as particles.

The idea that SCVs represent an intermediate stage in the grammaticalzation of syntactic constructs into morphological constructs is supported by the observation that many verbs which were still SCVs in Middle Dutch have developed into ICVs in modern Dutch. This applies to, for instance, the following verbs:

(68) achtervolg 'to run after', omring 'to surround', omsingel 'to suround', overbrug 'to bridge', overval 'to attack suddenly' (source: van Loey 1976)

As the glosses of these examples show, the preverbal elements, originally locational prepositions, have developed a more abstract meaning in their use as inseparable prefixes. The following examples serve to illustrate the use of the more concrete, spatial interpretation of these verbs in Middle Dutch, which correlates with separability of *overbruggen* and *omringen*:

(69) Voort gheven wy hem oorloff eene nieuwe havene te graven ende die over te brugghen 'Furthermore, we give him permisson to dig a new harbour, and to put a bridge across it'
Mettien hebben sise ommegeringhet 'Immediately have they-her surrounded'

As noted by van der Horst and van der Horst (1999: 348), there are also a number of verbs that were used as separable in eighteenth and nineteenth century Dutch, and that are now inseparable, thus instantiating the same development as took place in Middle Dutch, verbs such as *voorkomen* 'to prevent' and *doorstaan* 'to endure'. In sum, the preverb position of SCVs clearly forms an intermediate step in the development of words into prefixes.[8]

---

[8] See also Neeleman and Weerman (1992) and van der Auwera (1999) for an analysis of the history of SCVs.

6.4.5. *SCVs with adjectives and nouns*

As pointed out above, adjectives may also function as part of an SCV. For instance, the adjective *open* 'id.' functions as such. The difference from a 'normal' adjective such as *groen* 'green' can be seen in the Verb Raising construction:

(70) ...dat ik de deur wilde open maken/open wilde maken '...that I wanted to open the door'
 ...dat ik de deur *wilde groen verven/groen wilde verven '...that I wanted to paint the door green'

Since *groen* does not form a verbal constituent with *verven*, the modal verb *wilde* cannot be adjoined to the word sequence *groen verven* because it does not form a SCV. On the other hand, the grammaticality of the sequence *wilde open maken* shows that *open maken* is a verbal unit. Thus, we must assume a constructional idiom [[*open*]$_A$ [x]$_V$]$_{V'}$, with the left terminal node fixed. The constructional idiom approach enables us to account for the productivity of SCVs with the word *open*. This is indeed a productive category. The *Van Dale Woordenboek van het Hedendaags Nederlands* (1991) lists thirty-six SCVs with *open*, for example:

(71) openbarst 'to burst open', openbreek 'to break open', openscheur 'to tear open', openschiet 'to burst open', openschop 'to kick open'

Actually, intuitions of native speakers of Dutch with respect to the SCV character of *open* + verb combinations may differ, because there are two potential sources of such a combination: the syntactic construction with a secondary predicate, and the constructional idiom with *open*. Both interpretations are possible because there is no semantic irregularity involved.

In many other cases, the SCV nature of the adjective–verb sequence which can be determined on the basis of its behaviour under Verb Raising, is also proven by its unpredictable meaning, because the adjective does not allow for modification:

(72) blootsta 'to be exposed to'   < bloot 'naked', sta 'to stand'
 goedkeur 'to approve of'   < goed 'well', keur 'to judge'
 grootbreng 'to raise'   < groot 'big', breng 'to bring'
 vreemdga 'to sleep around' < vreemd 'strange', ga 'to go'

6.4. SEPARABLE COMPLEX VERBS

In these SCVs, the adjectives cannot be modified. For instance, sentences such as

(73) *Hij ging heel vreemd 'He slept around a lot'
*Hij bracht zijn kind heel groot 'He raised his child very big'

are ungrammatical. This follows from the proposed structure since the left constituent of such SCVs will be specified as a bare adjective, not as an AP. Hence, it is impossible to modify the adjective in that position.

Most of the SCVs with adjectives are cases of lexicalization; only a few, such as the *open*–V combination is productive, and will be represented as constructional idioms, with an open V-position.

There are quite a number of adverbs that can productively be used in SCVs. The set of these adverbs also comprises a number of complex locational and temporal adverbs such as *omlaag* 'down' and *achtereen* 'continuously'. The examples below are SVCs with simplex adverbs:

(74) heenga 'to leave'   < heen 'away', ga 'to go'
     neerkom 'to descend'   < neer 'down', kom 'to come'
     samenkom 'to convene'   < samen 'together', kom 'to come'
     terechtwijs 'to reprimand' < terecht 'right', wijs 'to point'
     thuisbreng 'to identify'   < thuis 'home', breng 'to bring'
     voortga 'to go on'   < voort 'further', ga 'to go'
     wegga 'to go away'   < weg 'away', ga 'to go'

SCVs with nouns are not productive across the board. The nouns that are used are typically non-referential, as is expected since SCVs are lexical units that function as verbal expressions. Some of these nouns can also occur independently without a determiner (for instance the mass nouns *adem* 'breath' and *bier* 'beer'), whereas other nouns are count nouns (*huis*, *college*) that require a determiner if they function as independent NPs:

(75) ademhaal 'to breathe'   < adem 'breath', haal 'to fetch'
     bierbrouw 'to brew beer'   < bier 'beer', brouw 'to brew'
     collegeloop 'to take classes'   < college 'class', loop 'to walk'
     deelneem 'to participate'   < deel 'part', neem 'to take'
     huishoud 'to run the household'   < huis 'house', houd 'to hold'
     koffiezet 'to make coffee'   < koffie 'coffee', zet 'to set'

paardrijd 'to ride horse'   < paard 'horse', rijd 'to ride'
pianospeel 'to play the piano' < piano 'id.', speel 'to play'

Generally, these separable NV combinations can be considered as idioms: there is no general productivity of SCVs with nouns. There are, however, productive cases, in particular for the domains of games and sports. For instance, in the construction diminutive noun + *spelen* 'to play', all sorts of function nouns can be used in the first position, and therefore, we might assume a constructional idiom [[N + diminutive][*spelen*]$_V$]$_V$ with the meaning 'to act as N':

(76) doktertjespeel 'to play doctor', vadertje-en-moedertjespeel 'to play father and mother', domineetjespeel 'to play reverend'

The following word combinations pose a specific analytical problem because they do not easily occur in main clauses:

(77) mastklimmen 'mast climbing', hardlopen 'fast-running', wadlopen 'shallow-walk', wedstrijdzwemmen 'competition swimming', zeezeilen 'sea sailing'

These words are given here in their infinitival forms because speakers of Dutch have problems in forming finite forms of such verbs, in particular in main clauses. For instance, of the following sentences with the meaning 'My brother likes sea-sailing' the first two are usually felt to be ungrammatical:

(78) (a) *Mijn broer zeezeilt graag
     (b) *Mijn broer zeilt graag zee
     (c) ... dat mijn broer graag zeezeilt

Sentence (78a) in which the verb is not split, presupposes that *zeezeilen* is a verbal compound of the NV type. As oberseved by van Marle (2000b), the more frequent such verbs are, the better they can be split up in main clauses. For instance, a sentence such as *Mijn vrouw spreekt buik* 'My wife ventriloquizes' does occur (de Vries 1975: 97). In the light of the ungrammaticality of (78a), we have to conclude that *zeezeilen* is not a verbal compound (as we saw in Chapter 4, this category of compounds is unproductive), but an SCV, because real verbal compounds such as *stofzuigen* 'to vacuum-clean' can appear in Verb Second Position:[9]

---

[9] As we saw in Chapter 4, it is also possible to coin nominal compounds of which the head is an infinitive, e.g. *niveaulezen* which therefore look like verbal compounds. However,

(79) Mijn broer stofzuigt het hele huis 'My brother vacuums the whole house'

We therefore need a separate explanation for the ungrammaticality of (78b). The question is therefore: why cannot *zee* in the sentences (78) be stranded?

As pointed out by Ackema (1999b), stranding of the noun of an SCV is awkward if that noun does not function as an argument of the verb. This is what distinguishes the verbs in (75) from those in (77): those in (75) take object-NPs, whereas a verb like *zeilen* 'to sail' is intransitive, and does not take an object-NP like *zee* 'sea'. In other words, it appears that SCVs can only be used if they lead to canonical surface structures, i.e. those surface structures that are allowed for independently by the syntax. This is the case for stranded particles, adjectives, and nouns that can function as arguments: they occur in the same positions as secondary predicates and object nouns. On the other hand, a verb such as *zeilen* 'to sail' is intransitive, and does not allow for a direct object; hence, a sentence like *Mijn broer zeilt de zee* 'My brother sails the sea' is ungrammatical.

The idea that it is the stranding of the non-verbal constituent of the SCV that can be the source of the ungrammaticality can also be used to account for the behaviour of a special class of SCVs, those to which the prefix *her-* 're-' is prefixed. An example of such an SCV is *heropvoeden* 'to re-educate', derived from the SCV *opvoeden* 'to educate'. As has also been observed in Koopman (1995), such verbs do not allow being split in main clauses nor appear unsplit in that position, but can be inflected in embedded clauses:

(80) (a) *Mijn ouders heropvoeden ons kind 'My parents re-educate our child'
(b) *Mijn ouders voeden ons kind herop
(c) Ik zie niet graag dat mijn ouders ons kind heropvoeden 'I do not like it that my parents re-educate our child'

The constituent *herop* cannot be stranded, probably because the prefix *her-* cannot occur in combination with a non-lexical element as its base: its occurrence must be licensed by a word of a lexical category (in fact, a verb or a noun).

---

such an analysis implies that these words cannnot be inflected, which is not the case in the examples discussed here: they do have finite forms, but only in embedded clauses (van Marle 2000b).

Splitting SCVs in non-embedded clauses can also be avoided by means of another strategy, the use of the periphrastic progressive construction *aan het V*. Thus, we can make grammatical sentences like:

(80)   Mijn broer is aan het zeezeilen 'My brother is sea-sailing'

Actually, the occurrence of SCVs like *zeezeilen* underscores the point that NV is a productive constructional idiom, in particular for verbs that mention a sport: if the noun is not an argument of the verb, the NV-combination cannot be created by the syntax, and hence it must have another, lexical source, and that is the lexical construction $[N\ V]_{V'}$.

7

Conclusions: The Architecture of the Grammar

One of the goals of linguistic theory is a proper characterization of the architecture of language systems, and thus of that of the human language faculty. In-depth studies of the grammars of individual languages form the empirical foundations for this kind of theoretical research, and this is one of the reasons why it is worthwhile to study the details of a subsystem of one language, the morphological system of Dutch, as we have done in the preceding chapters.

A number of general conclusions concerning the architecture of the grammar can be drawn from the analyses presented in the preceding chapters.

First, we have seen that word formation cannot be fully understood in terms of syntagmatic operations: the paradigmatic relations between existing words and between words and lexicalized phrases play an important role in the formation of new words (Sections 1.3, 4.2.2). Paradigmatic relations also play an essential role in making correct generalizations about the inflection of strong complex verbs (Section 2.4) and about allomorphy patterns (Section 5.3.3). In other words, it is quite clear that the morphology of a language cannot be fully captured in terms of a 'syntax of morphemes', as syntax beneath the X^0-level (contra Lieber 1992 and Ackema 1999a). Both the syntagmatic axis and the paradigmatic axis of language structure are essential for a proper account of morphology.

A concept that appeared to be enlightening when dealing with the formation of new lexical expressions is that of 'construction'. Productive word-formation patterns can be represented in the form of templates, in which at least one position is open. If the use of one word-formation process presupposes that of another, this can be expressed by having templates with more than one open position (Section 4.3.2). Expressions that function semantically as words can also be larger than a syntactic word: periphrastic constructions (Section 2.4.2), the partitive and possessor construction (Sections 2.2.2 and 2.3.4), constructions with the causative verb *laten* and other verbs (Section 6.3), and in particular separable complex verbs (Section 6.4). The implication of assuming constructions of this type is that the lexicon becomes the constructicon of the grammar, the module that not only lists the existing words and word-like expressions, but also specifies how this fund of expressions can be extended by means of morphological and syntactic constructions.

In a number of places in this book we came across evidence that the internal structure of complex words, once coined, remains accessible. This is quite obvious in cases of paradigmatic word formation such as affix substitution, which presupposes that the language user has access to the internal structure of words. Another clear case is the formation of perfect participles (Section 2.4.3): we need to know whether the first syllable of the verbal stem is a prefix, because in that case the prefix *ge-* is omitted. Thus, we found evidence against the hypothesis of A-morphous Morphology, which denies morphological processes any access to the internal morphological structure of the input words.

Another general issue concerning the architecture of the grammar is the relation between form and meaning in morphology. As shown in particular in Chapters 3 and 4, there is a lot of regular, explainable polysemy in the realm of word formation. The apparent diversity in the meaning contribution of a word-formation process can often be reduced by invoking general principles of interpretation of rather vague and general basic meanings, and extension schemata that specify how one can shift from one concept to a related one. Thus, there is no reason to make a radical separation of form and meaning in morphology, at least not as far as derivational morphology is concerned, contrary to what has been suggested by Beard (1995).

The facts of Dutch word formation discussed in this book show that syntax may feed morphology in that certain syntactic constructs such as NPs of the type A + N can appear in the non-head position of compounds (Section 4.2). Similarly, separable complex verbs, which also have phrasal status, feed derivation and compounding. Therefore, the morphology of Dutch cannot be conceived of as a presyntactic component that applies before syntax only. Rather, it is a module of the grammar that defines the wellformedness of morphological constructs. These constructs may contain phrasal subparts whose wellformedness in their turn is accounted for by the syntactic module of the grammar or constructional templates.

A second area of interaction between morphology and syntax is the effect of morphological processes on the syntactic valency of words. Our main conclusion was that it is primarily the semantics of a word-formation process that is involved here. Since semantic structure determines syntactic valency to a large extent, a word-formation process may have syntactic valency effects. This implies that a thorough investigation of the semantics of a word-formation process is necessary in order to determine how its syntactic valency effects should be accounted for. This approach appeared also to be the correct one for a proper account of the syntactic valency of SCVs.

Another issue concerning the architecture of the grammar is that of the position of inflection versus derivation. The hypothesis of Split Morphology claims a radical separation of inflection (post-syntactic) from word formation (pre-syntactic). On the basis of Dutch evidence, we were able to conclude that the Split Morphology hypothesis is incorrect because it does not allow for (certain kinds of) inflection feeding word formation, which does takes place. Instead, I argued for a functional distinction between inherent and contextual inflection; this distinction allows us to specify which kind of inflection can feed word formation, namely inherent inflection, and also highlights the functional differences between the different kinds of inflection (Section 2.5).

The way in which morphology and phonology interact in Dutch also bears upon the architecture of the grammar. In particular, it appeared that the choice between competing affixes cannot exclusively be modelled in terms of different, phonologically defined, classes of input words, that is, in terms of phonological input restrictions. In some cases it is crucially the set of ranked output conditions of the phonological module of the grammar that makes the correct choice. This appeared to be the case both in the realm of inflection where two nominal plural suffixes compete (Section 2.2), as in that of derivational morphology (Section 5.3.1).

In sum, the detailed study of one subsystem of one language gives us insight into the kind of conditions of adequacy that any theory of the architecture of the grammars of natural languages must meet.

REFERENCES

Abbreviations

FdL   *Forum der Letteren*
JL   *Journal of Linguistics*
Lg   *Language*
LIN   *Linguistics in the Netherlands*
LI   *Linguistic Inquiry*
NLLT   *Natural Language and Linguistic Theory*
Ntg   *De Nieuwe Taalgids*
Sp   *Spektator, tijdschrift voor Neerlandistiek*
YoM   *Yearbook of Morphology*. Edited by Geert Booij and Jaap van Marle. Dordrecht: Foris (1988–90), Dordrecht, Boston, and London: Kluwer Academic Publishers (1991–).

ACKEMA, P. (1999*a*), *Issues in Morphosyntax*. Linguistik Aktuell, 26 (Amsterdam and Philadelphia: Benjamins).
—— (1999*b*), 'The Non-Uniform Structure of Dutch N-V Compounds', *YoM 1998*: 127–58.
—— and SCHOORLEMMER, M. (1994), 'The Middle Construction and the Syntax–Semantics Interface', *Lingua*, 93: 59–90.
—— (1995), 'Middles and Non-movement', *LI*, 26: 173–97.
ACKERMANN, F., and LESOURD, P. (1997), 'Towards a Lexical Representation of Phrasal Predicates', in A. Alsina, J. Bresnan, and P. Sells (eds.), *Complex Predicates* (Stanford: CSLI), 67–106.
—— and WEBELHUTH, G. (1998), *A Theory of Predicates* (Stanford: CSLI).
ANDERSON, S. R. (1982), 'Where's Morphology?', *LI*, 13: 571–612.
—— (1992), *A-morphous Morphology* (Cambridge: Cambridge University Press).
ARONOFF, M. (1976), *Word Formation in Generative Grammar* (Cambridge, MA: MIT Press).
—— (1994), *Morphology by Itself* (Cambridge, MA: MIT Press).
AUWERA, J. VAN DER (1999), 'Dutch Verbal Prefixes. Meaning and Form, Grammaticalization and Lexicalization', in L. Mereu (ed.), *Boundaries of Morphology and Syntax* (Amsterdam and Philadelphia: Benjamins), 121–36.
BAAYEN, R. H. (1991), 'Quantitative Aspects of Morphological Productivity', *YoM 1991*: 109–50.
—— (1992), 'On Frequency, Transparency and Productivity', *YoM 1992*: 181–208.

BAAYEN, R. H. and LIEBER, R. (1994), 'Verbal Prefixes in Dutch: A Study in Lexical Conceptual Structure', *YoM 1993*: 51-78.

—— and NEIJT, A. (1997), 'Productivity in Context: A Case Study of a Dutch Suffix', *Linguistics*, 29: 801-43.

—— DIJKSTRA, T., and SCHREUDER, R. (1997), 'Singulars and Plurals in Dutch. Evidence for a Dual Parallel Route Model', *Journal of Memory and Language*, 37: 94-119.

BAKER, M. (1988), *Incorporation* (Chicago: Chicago University Press).

BAUER, L. (1988), 'A Descriptive Gap in Morphology', *YoM 1988*: 17-27.

—— (1990), 'Be-heading the Word', *JL*, 26: 1-31.

—— (1997), 'Evaluative Morphology: In Search of Universals', *Studies in Language*, 21: 533-75.

BEARD, R. (1991), 'Decompositional Composition: The Semantics of Scope Ambiguities and "Bracketing Paradoxes"', *NLLT*, 9: 195-229.

—— (1995), *Lexeme-Morpheme Base Morphology* (Albany: SUNY Press).

BECKER, T. (1994), 'Back-Formation, Cross-Formation, and "Bracketing Paradoxes" in Paradigmatic Morphology', *YoM 1993*: 1-26.

—— (1997), 'Was wir von Aristoteles über die Bedeutung deutschen Wörter lernen können: Über konversationelle Implikaturen und Wortsemantik', in E. Rolf (ed.), *Pragmatik. Implikaturen und Sprechakte* (Wiesbaden: Westdeutscher Verlag), 51-71.

BENNIS, H. (1991), 'Theoretische aspekten van partikelvooropplaatsing II', *Tabu*, 19: 89-96.

—— and WEHRMANN, P. (1990), 'On the Categorial Status of Present Participles', in P. Coopmans and R. Bok-Bennema (eds.), *LIN 1990* (Dordrecht: Foris), 1-13.

BERKUM, J. J. A. VAN (1996), *The Psycholinguistics of Grammatical Gender* (Nijmegen: Max Planck-Institut für Psycholinguistik; Univ. of Nijmegen, doct. dissertation).

BLOM, A. (1994), 'Het ondoorgrondelijk bijvoeglijk naamwoord', *FdL*, 35: 81-94.

BLOOMFIELD, L. (1933), *Language* (London: Allen and Unwin).

BOOGAART, R. (1999), *Aspect and Temporal Ordering. A Contrastive Analysis of Dutch and English* (The Hague: Holland Academic Graphics; Vrije Universiteit Amsterdam, doct. dissertation).

BOOIJ, G. E. (1977), *Dutch Morphology. A Study of Word Formation in Generative Grammar* (Dordrecht: Foris).

—— (1979), 'Semantic Regularities in Word Formation', *Linguistics*, 17: 985-1002.

—— (1985), 'Coordination Reduction in Complex Words: A Case for Prosodic Phonology', in H. van der Hulst and N. Smith (eds.), *Advances in Non-linear Phonology* (Dordrecht: Foris), 143-60.

—— (1986), 'Form and Meaning in Morphology: the Case of Dutch "Agent" Nouns', *Linguistics*, 24: 503-17.

—— (1988a), 'Polysemie en polyfunctionaliteit bij denominale woordvorming', *Sp*, 17: 268–76.

—— (1988b), 'The Relation between Inheritance and Argument Linking: Deverbal Nouns in Dutch', in: Everaert *et al.* (eds.), 57–74.

—— (1989), 'Complex Verbs and the Theory of Level Ordering', *YoM 1989*: 21–30.

—— (1990), 'The Boundary between Morphology and Syntax: Separable Complex Verbs in Dutch', *YoM 1990*: 45–63.

—— (1992), 'Morphology, Semantics, and Argument Structure', in I. Roca (ed.), *Thematic Structure, Its Role in Grammar* (Berlin and New York: Foris), 47–63.

—— (1994), 'Against Split Morphology', *YoM 1993*: 27–50.

—— (1995), *The Phonology of Dutch* (Oxford: Clarendon Press).

—— (1996), 'Inherent versus Contextual Inflection and the Split Morphology Hypothesis', *YoM 1995*: 1–16.

—— (1997), 'Allomorphy and the Autonomy of Morphology', *Folia Linguistica*, 31: 25–56.

—— (1998a), 'Phonological Output Constraints in Morphology', in W. Kehrein and R. Wiese (eds.), *Phonology and Morphology of the Germanic Languages* (Tübingen: Niemeyer), 143–63.

—— (1998b). 'The Demarcation of Inflection: A Synoptical Survey', in R. Fabri, A. Ortmann, and T. Parodi (eds.), *Models of Inflection* (Tübingen: Niemeyer), 11–27.

—— (1998c), 'Samenkoppelingen en grammaticalisatie', in Hoekstra and Smits (eds.), 6–20.

—— (1999a), 'Lexical Storage and Regular Processes: Comments on Clahsen 1999', *Brain and Behavioral Sciences*, 22: 1016.

—— (1999b), 'The Role of the Prosodic Word in Phonotactic Generalizations', in Hall and Kleinhenz (eds.), 47–72.

—— (2000a), 'From Syntax to Morphology: Separable Complex Verbs in Dutch', in C. Schaner-Wolles, J. R. Rennison, and F. Neubarth (eds.), *Naturally! Linguistic Studies in Honour of Wolfgang Ulrich Dressler on the Occasion of his 60th Birthday* (Torino: Rosenberg and Sellier), 59–64.

—— (2000b), 'Inflection and Derivation', in Booij *et al.* (eds.), 360–69.

—— (2000c) 'The Phonology–Morphology Interface', in L. Cheng and R. Sybesma (eds.), *The First Glot International State-of-the-Article Book* (Berlin: Mouton de Gruyter), 287–306.

—— (in press), 'Adjectival Inflection and Dialectal Variation', in J. Berns and J. van Marle (eds.), *Present-Day Dialectology: Problems and Findings* (Berlin: Mouton de Gruyter).

—— and HAAFTEN, T. VAN (1988), 'On the External Syntax of Derived Words: Evidence from Dutch', *YoM 1988*: 29–44.

—— and SANTEN, A. VAN (1995), *Morfologie, de woordstructuur van het Nederlands* (Amsterdam: Amsterdam University Press; second revised and expanded edition 1998).

BOOIJ, G. E., LEHMANN, C., and MUGDAN, J. (eds.), (2000), *Morphology. An International Handbook on Inflection and Word Formation. Vol 1* (Berlin: De Gruyter).

BÖRJARS, K., VINCENT, N., and CHAPMAN, C. (1997), 'Paradigms, Periphrasis and Pronominal Inflection: A Feature-Based Account', *YoM 1996*: 155-80.

BOROWSKY, T. (2000), 'Word-Faithfulness and the Direction of Assimilation', *The Linguistic Review*, 17: 1-28.

BOTHA, R. P. (1968), *The Function of the Lexicon in Transformational-Generative Grammar* (The Hague: Mouton).

—— (1984), *Morphological Mechanisms. Lexicalist Analyses of Synthetic Compounding* (Oxford: Pergamon Press).

BRESNAN, J., and MCHOMBO, S. A. (1995), 'The Lexical Integrity Principle: Evidence from Bantu', *NLLT*, 13: 181-254.

BYBEE, J. (1985), *Morphology. A Study of the Relation between Meaning and Form* (Amsterdam and Philadelphia: Benjamins).

CALUWE, J. DE (1990), 'Complementariteit tussen morfologische en in oorsprong syntactische benoemingsprocédé's', in id. (ed.), *Betekenis en produktiviteit. Gentse bijdragen tot de studie van de Nederlandse woordvorming*. Studia Germanica Gandensia, 19 (Gent: Seminarie voor Duitse Taalkunde, Universiteit Gent), 9-23.

—— (1991), *Nederlandse nominale composita in functionalistisch perspectief* (The Hague: SDU Uitgeverij).

—— (1992), 'Deverbaal -er als polyseem suffix', *Sp*, 21: 137-48.

CARSTAIRS-MCCARTHY, A. (1992), 'Morphology without Word-internal Constituents: A Review of Stephen Anderson's *A-Morphous Morphology*', *YoM 1992*: 209-34.

CETNAROWSKA, B. (2000), 'On Inherent Inflection Feeding Derivation in Polish', *YoM 1999*, 151-81.

CHAPMAN, C. (1996), 'Perceptual Salience and Affix Order: Noun Plurals as Input to Word Formation', *YoM 1995*: 175-84.

CHRISTOFIDOU, A., DOLESCHAL, U., and DRESSLER, W. U. (1990), 'Gender Agreement via Derivational Morphology in Greek', *Glossologia*, 9-10, 69-79.

CLAHSEN, H. (1999), 'Lexical Entries and Rules of Language: A Multidisciplinary Study of German Inflection', *Brain and Behavioral Sciences*, 22: 991-1013.

CLARK, E. V. (1993), *The Lexicon in Acquisition* (Cambridge: Cambridge University Press).

—— and CLARK, H. (1979), 'When Nouns Surface as Verbs', *Lg*, 55: 767-811.

COOPMANS, P., and EVERAERT, M. (1988), 'The Simplex Structure of Complex Idioms: The Morphological Status of *laten*', in Everaert et al. (eds.), 75-104.

CORBETT, G. (1991), *Gender* (Cambridge: Cambridge University Press).

Van Dale Groot Woordenboek van het Hedendaags Nederlands (1991), 2nd edn, edited by Piet van Sterkenburg (Utrecht: Van Dale Lexicografie).

DON, J. (1993), *Morphological Conversion* (Utrecht: LED/OTS; University of Utrecht, doct. dissertation).

—— ZONNEVELD, W., DRIJKONINGEN, F., EVERAERT, M., TROMMELEN, M., and ZWANENBURG, W. (1994), *Inleiding in de generatieve morfologie* (Bussum: Coutinho).

DOWNING, P. (1977), 'On the Creation and Use of English Compound Nouns', *Lg*, 53: 810–42.

DRESSLER, W. U. (1989), 'Prototypical Differences between Inflection and Derivation', *Zeitschrift für Phonetik, Sprachwissenschaft und Kommunikationsforschung*, 42: 3–10.

EVERAERT, M., EVERS, A., HUYBREGTS, R., and TROMMELEN, M. (eds.), (1988), *Morphology and Modularity, in Honour of Henk Schultink* (Dordrecht: Foris).

FAST, P., and MARLE, J. VAN (1989), 'Nogmaals de inwoonstersnamen: verdere evidentie voor -*se*', *Sp*, 18: 423–30.

FLEISCHER, W. (2000), 'Die Klassifikation von Wortbildungsprozessen', in Booij *et al.* (eds.), 886–97.

FLEISCHMANN, S. (1977), *Cultural and Linguistic Factors in Word Formation* (Los Angeles: University of California Press).

FLETCHER, W. H. (1980), '*Blood-hot, Stone-good*: A Preliminary Report on Adjective-Specific Intensifiers in Dutch', *Leuvense Bijdragen*, 69: 445–72.

GOLDBERG, A. E. (1995), *Constructions. A Construction Grammar Approach to Argument Structure* (Chicago and London: The University of Chicago Press).

GREENBERG, J. H. (1963), 'Some Universals of Grammar, with Particular Reference to the Order of Meaningful Elements', in id. (ed.), *Universals of Language* (Cambridge, MA: MIT Press), 73–113.

HAAS, W. DE (1990), 'Restricties op de opeenvolging van prefixen in het Nederlands', *Ntg*, 83: 2–18.

—— and TROMMELEN, M. (1993), *Morfologisch Handboek van het Nederlands* (The Hague: SDU Uitgeverij).

HAEGEMAN, L., and RIEMSDIJK, H. VAN (1986), 'Verb Projection Raising, Scope, and the Typology of Rules Affecting Verbs', *LI*, 17: 417–66.

HAERINGEN, C. B. VAN (1940), 'De taaie levenskracht van het sterke werkwoord', *Ntg*, 34: 241–55.

—— (1947), 'De meervoudsvorming in het Nederlands', *Mededelingen der Koninklijke Nederlandse Academie van Wetenschappen, Afdeling Letterkunde, Nieuwe Reeks, Deel 10, No. 5* (Amsterdam). Reprinted in G. E. Booij (ed.), *Morfologie van het Nederlands* (Amsterdam: Huis aan de Drie Grachten), 1979, 19–38.

—— (1971), 'Het achtervoegsel -*ing*, mogelijkheden en beperkingen', *Ntg*, 64: 449–68. Reprinted in G. E. Booij (ed.), *Morfologie van het Nederlands* (Amsterdam: Huis aan de Drie Grachten), 1979, 77–100.

HAESERYN, W., ROMIJN, K., GEERTS, G., ROOIJ, J. DE, and TOORN, M. C. VAN DEN (1997), *Algemene Nederlandse Spraakkunst* (Groningen: Martinus Nijhoff and Deurne: Wolters Plantyn).

HALL, T. A. (1999), 'The Phonological Word: A Review', in Hall and Kleinhenz (eds.), 1–22.

—— and KLEINHENZ, U. (eds.), (1999), *Studies on the Phonological Word* (Amsterdam and Philadelphia: Benjamins).

HALLE. M., and MARANTZ, A. (1993), 'Distributed Morphology and the Pieces of Inflection', in K. Hale and S. J. Keyser (eds.), *The View from Building 20. Essays in Honor of Sylvain Bromberger* (Cambridge, MA: MIT Press), 111–76.

HASPELMATH, M. (1995), 'The Growth of Affixes in Morphological Reanalysis'. *YoM 1994*: 1–30.

—— (1996), 'Word-Class-Changing Inflection and Morphological Theory', *YoM 1995*: 43–66.

HEUVEN, V. VAN, NEIJT, A., and HIJZELENDOORN, M. (1994), 'Automatische indeling van Nederlandse woorden op basis van etymologische filters', *Sp*, 23: 279–91.

HEYNDERICKX, P. (1992), 'Relationeel adjectief-substantief-combinaties en concurrerende constructietypes', *Sp*, 21: 149–60.

—— (1994), 'Relationele adjectieven in het Nederlands' (University of Gent, unpublished doct. dissertation).

—— and MARLE, J. VAN (1994), 'Over het hybride karakter van -*isch*: op de grens van inheems en uitheems', *Sp*, 23: 229–39.

HOEKSEMA, J. (1984), *Categorial Morphology* (New York: Garland Press, 1988; Rijksuniversiteit Groningen, doct. dissertation).

—— (1988), 'Head-Types in Morpho-syntax', *YoM 1988*: 123–38.

—— (1991*a*), 'Theoretische aspekten van partikelvooropplaatsing', *Tabu*, 21: 18–26.

—— (1991*b*), 'Complex Predicates and Liberation', *Linguistics and Philosophy*, 14: 661–710.

—— (1998), 'Adjectivale inflectie op -*s*: geen geval van transpositie', in Hoekstra and Smits (eds.), 46–72.

—— (2000), 'Compositionality of Meaning', in Booij *et al.* (eds.), 851–6.

HOEKSTRA, E., and SMITS, C. (eds.), (1998), *Morfologiedagen 1996*. Cahiers van het Meertens Instituut 10 (Amsterdam: Meertens Instituut).

HOEKSTRA, T. (1984), *Transitivity. Grammatical Relations in Government and Binding Theory* (Dordrecht: Foris).

—— (1986*a*), 'Passives and Participles', in F. Beukema and A. Hulk (eds.), *LIN 1986* (Dordrecht: Foris), 95–104.

—— (1986*b*), 'Deverbalization and Inheritance', *Linguistics*, 24: 549–84.

—— (1999), 'Auxiliary Selection in Dutch', *NLLT*, 17: 67–84.

—— and PUTTEN, F. VAN DER (1988), 'Inheritance Phenomena', in Everaert *et al.* (eds.), 163–86.

—— LANSU, M., and WESTERDUIN, M. (1987), 'Complexe verba', *Glot*, 10: 61–78.

HOPPER, P., and TRAUGOTT, E. (1993), *Grammaticalization* (Cambridge: Cambridge University Press).

HORST, J. VAN DER, and HORST, K. VAN DER (1999), *Geschiedenis van het Nederlands in de twintigste eeuw* (Den Haag: SDU Uitgeverij).

HÜNING, M. (1992), 'De concurrentie tussen deverbale nomina op *ge-* en *-erij*', *Sp*, 21: 161–72.

—— (1999), *Woordensmederij. De geschiedenis van het suffix -erij* (The Hague: Holland Academic Graphics; University of Leiden, doct. dissertation).

—— and SANTEN, A. VAN (1994), 'Produktiviteitsveranderingen, de adjectieven op *-lijk* en *-baar*', *Leuvense Bijdragen*, 83: 1–29.

IACOBINI, C. (2000), 'Base and direction of derivation', in Booij *et al.* (eds.), 865–76.

JACKENDOFF, R. S. (1975), 'Semantic and Morphological Regularities in the Lexicon', *Lg*, 51: 639–71.

—— (1990), *Semantic Structures* (Cambridge, MA: MIT Press).

—— (1995), 'The Boundaries of the Lexicon', in M. Everaert, E. van der Linden, A. Schenk, and R. Schreuder (eds.), *Idioms. Structural and Psychological Perspectives* (Hillsdale, NJ: Lawrence Erlbaum Ass.), 133–66.

—— (1997a), *The Architecture of the Language Faculty* (Cambridge, MA: MIT Press).

—— (1997b), 'Twistin' the Night Away', *Lg*, 73: 534–59.

JORDENS, P. (1998), 'Defaultformen des Präteritums. Zum Erwerb der Vergangenheitsmorphologie im Niederländischen', in H. Wegener (ed.), *Eine zweite Sprache lernen* (Tübingen: Narr), 63–91.

JURAFSKY, D. (1996), 'Univeral Tendencies in the Semantics of the Diminutive', *Lg*, 72: 533–78.

KAGER, R. (1999), *Optimality Theory, a Text Book* (Cambridge: Cambridge University Press).

KESTER, E. P. (1996), *The Nature of Adjectival Inflection* (Utrecht: LED/OTS; University of Utrecht, doct. dissertation).

KIPARSKY, P. (1971), 'Historical Linguistics', reprinted in id., *Explanation in Phonology* (Dordrecht: Foris), 1982, 57–80.

—— (1982), 'From Cyclic to Lexical Phonology', in H. van der Hulst and N. Smith (eds.), *The Structure of Phonological Representations. Part 1* (Dordrecht: Foris), 131–76.

KLAMER, M. A. F. (to appear), 'Semantically Motivated Lexical Patterns: A Study of Dutch and Kambera Expressives'. *Lg*.

KLOOSTER, W. G. (1972), *The Structure Underlying Measure Phrase Sentences* (Dordrecht: Reidel).

KNOPPER, R. (1984), 'On the Morphology of Ergative Verbs and the Polyfunctionality Principle', in H. Bennis and W. U. S. van Lessen Kloeke (eds.), *LIN 1984* (Dordrecht: Foris), 119–27.

KOEFOED, G., and MARLE, J. VAN (1987), 'Requisites for Reinterpretation', in W. Koopman, O. Fischer, F. van der Leek, and R. Eaton (eds.), *Explanation and Linguistic Change* (Amsterdam and Philadelphia: Benjamins), 121–50.

KOOPMAN, H. (1995), 'On Verbs that Fail to Undergo V-second', *LI*, 26: 137–63.
KOSTER, J. (1975), 'Dutch as an SOV Language', *Linguistic Analysis*, 1: 111–36.
KROTT, A., SCHREUDER, R., and BAAYEN, R. H. (1999). 'Complex Words in Complex Words', *Linguistics*, 37: 905–26.
KURYŁOWICZ, J. (1964), *The Inflectional Categories of Indo-European* (Heidelberg: Carl Winter Universitätsverlag).
LAPOINTE, S. (1980), 'A Theory of Grammatical Agreement' (University of Amherst, doct. dissertation).
—— (2000), 'Allomorph Selection and OT'. *YoM 1999*: 261–94.
LASS, R. (1990), 'How to Do Things with Junk: Exaptation in Language Evolution', *JL*, 26: 79–102.
LEFEBVRE, C., and MUYSKEN, P. C. (1988), *Mixed Categories. Nominalizations in Quechua* (Dordrecht: Kluwer).
LEVIN, B., and RAPPAPORT HOVAV, M. (1998), 'Morphology and Lexical Semantics', in Spencer and Zwicky (eds.), 248–71.
LIEBER, R. (1980), *On the Organization of the Lexicon* (New York: Garland Press, 1994; MIT, doct. dissertation).
—— (1983), 'Argument Linking and Compounds in English', *LI*, 14: 251–85.
—— (1989), 'On Percolation', *YoM 1989*: 95–138.
—— (1992), *Deconstructing Morphology* (Chicago: Chicago University Press).
—— and BAAYEN, R. H. (1997), 'A Semantic Principle of Auxiliary Selection', *NLLT*, 15: 789–845.
LOEY, A. VAN (1976), *Scheidbare en onscheidbare werkwoorden hoofdzakelijk in het Middelnederlands, analytische studiën* (Gent: Secretariaat van de Koninklijke Academie voor Nederlandse Taal en Letterkunde).
LÜDELING, A. (1999), *On Particle Verbs and Similar Constructions in German* (Arbeitspapiere des SFB Sprachtheoretische Grundlagen für die Computerlinguistik, Bericht no. 133), (Stanford: CSLI (in press); University of Tübingen, doct. dissertation).
MCCARTHY, J. J. (1986), 'OCP-effects: Gemination and Anti-gemination', *LI*, 17: 207–63.
—— and PRINCE, A. (1993), 'Prosodic Morphology I. Constraint Interaction and Satisfaction'. University of Amherst and Rutgers University, MS.
—— —— (1994), 'Generalized Alignment', *YoM 1993*: 79–154.
MACKENZIE, J. L. (1985a), '*Ge*-nominaliseer'. *TTT, Interdisciplinair Tijdschrift voor Taal- en Tekstwetenschap*, 5: 177–99.
—— (1985b), 'Nominalization and Valency Reduction', in M. Bolkestein, C. de Groot, and J. L. Mackenzie (eds.), *Predicates and Terms in Functional Grammar* (Dordrecht: Foris), 29–47.
MARCHAND, H. (1969), *The Categories and Types of Present-Day English Word-Formation*. 2nd edn. (München: Beck).

MARLE, J. VAN (1978), 'Veranderingen in woordstructuur', in G. A. T. Koefoed and J. van Marle (eds.), *Aspecten van taalverandering* (Groningen: Wolters-Noordhoff), 127-76.

—— (1981), 'Over de dynamiek van morfologische categorieën', *FdL*, 22: 51-63.

—— (1984), 'A Case of Morphological Elaboration: The History of Dutch *-baar*'. *Folia Linguistica Historica*, 9: 213-34.

—— (1985), *On the Paradigmatic Dimension of Morphological Creativity* (Dordrecht: Foris; University of Utrecht, doct. dissertation).

—— (1986), 'The Domain Hypothesis: The Study of Rival Morphological Processes, *Linguistics*, 24: 601-27.

—— (1988), 'On the Role of Semantics in Productivity Change', *YoM 1988*: 139-54.

—— (1990*a*), 'Rule-Creating Creativity: Analogy as a Synchronic Morphological Process', in W. U. Dressler, H. C. Luschützky, O. E. Pfeiffer, and J. R. Rennison (eds.), *Contemporary Morphology* (Berlin/New York: Mouton de Gruyter), 267-73.

—— (1990*b*), 'De *eur/euse/trice* trits', *Sp*, 19: 254-64.

—— (1992), 'The Relationship between Morphological Productivity and Frequency: A Comment on Baayen's Performance-Oriented Conception of Morphological Productivity', *YoM 1991*: 151-63.

—— (1994), Morphological Adaptation', *YoM 1993*: 255-66.

—— (1995), 'On the Fate of Adjectival Declension in Overseas Dutch (with Some Notes on the History of Dutch)', in H. Andersen (ed.), *Historical Linguistics 1993* (Amsterdam and Philadelphia: Benjamins), 283-94.

—— (1996), 'The Unity of Morphology: On the Interwovenness of the Derivational and Inflectional Dimension of the Word', *YoM 1995*: 67-82.

—— (2000*a*), 'Paradigmatic and Syntagmatic Relations', in Booij *et al.* (eds.), 225-33.

—— (2000*b*), 'Morfologisch-syntactische grenskwesties: scheidbaar samengestelde werkwoorden, verbale defectiviteit, en het probleem van de scheidbaarheid', in H. den Besten, E. Elffers, and J. Luif (eds.), *Samengevoegde woorden. Voor Wim Klooster bij zijn afscheid als hoogleraar* (Amsterdam: Leerstoelgroep Nederlandse Taalkunde, Universiteit van Amsterdam), 193-200.

—— and KOEFOED, G. (1988), 'Herinterpretatie: voorwaarden en effecten', *Sp*, 17: 488-511.

MATTENS, W. H. M. (1970), *De indifferentialis. Een onderzoek naar het gebruik van het substantief in het algemeen bruikbaar Nederlands* (Assen: Van Gorcum).

MATTHEWS, P. H. (1991), *Morphology*. 2nd edn. (Cambridge: Cambridge University Press).

MEIJS, W. J. M. (1981), 'Synthetische composita: voer voor morfologen', *Sp*, 10: 250-91.

MOERDIJK, A. (1987), 'Lexicale semantiek en compositavorming', *FdL*, 28: 194-213.

MOORTGAT, M. (1981), 'Subcategorization and the Notion "Lexical Head"', in S. Daalder and M. Gerritsen (eds.), *LIN 1981* (Amsterdam etc.: North Holland Publishing Co.), 45-54.

NAUMANN, B., and VOGEL, P. (2000), 'Derivation', in Booij *et al.* (eds.), 929-42.
NEELEMAN, A. (1992), *Complex Predicates* (Utrecht: Led/OTS; University of Utrecht, doct. dissertation).
—— and SCHIPPER, J. (1993), 'Verbal Prefixation in Dutch: Thematic Evidence for Conversion', *YoM 1992*: 57-92.
—— and WEERMAN, F. (1992), 'Case Theory and the Diachrony of Complex Predicates in Dutch', *Folia Linguistica Historica*, 13: 189-217.
—— —— (1993), 'The Balance between Morphology and Syntax: Separable Complex Verbs in Dutch', *NLLT*, 11: 433-76.
NESPOR, M., and VOGEL, I. (1986), *Prosodic Phonology* (Dordrecht: Foris).
NORDE, M. (1997), The History of the Genitive in Swedish. A Case Study in Degrammaticalization (Amsterdam: Scandinavian Department, University of Amsterdam, doct. dissertation).
ODIJK, J. (1992), 'Uninflected Adjectives in Dutch', in R. Bok-Bennema and R. van Hout (eds.), *LIN 1992* (Amsterdam and Philadelphia: Benjamins), 197-208.
PAULISSEN, D., and W. ZONNEVELD (1988), 'Compound Verbs and the Adequacy of Lexical Morphology', in Everaert *et al.* (eds.), 281-301.
PEETERS, R. J. (1999), 'The Adjunct Middle Construction in Dutch', *Leuvense Bijdragen*, 88: 355-401.
PERLMUTTER, D. (1988), 'The Split Morphology Hypothesis: Evidence from Yiddish', in M. Hammond and M. Noonan (eds.), *Theoretical Morphology* (San Diego etc.: Academic Press), 79-100.
PINKER, S. (1998), 'Words and Rules', *Lingua*, 106: 219-42.
—— (1999), *Words and Rules. The Ingredients of Language* (New York: Basic Books).
PLAG, I. (1999), *Morphological Productivity. Structural Constraints in English Derivation* (Berlin: Mouton de Gruyter).
PLANK, F. (1994), 'Inflection and Derivation', in R. E. Asher (ed.), *The Encyclopedia of Languages and Linguistics*, Vol. 3 (Oxford: Pergamon Press), 1671-8.
POLLARD, C., and SAG, I. A. (1994), *Head-Driven Phrase Structure Grammar* (Chicago: The University of Chicago Press).
POSTHUMUS, J. (1991), 'Hoe komen wij tot "namaak-buitenlands"? Het Engels als inspiratiebron', *Onze Taal*, 61: 11-13.
PUSTEJOVSKY, J. (1993), 'Type Coercion and Lexical Selection', in id. (ed.), *Semantics and the Lexicon* (Dordrecht: Kluwer), 73-94.
—— (1995), *The Generative Lexicon* (Cambridge, MA: MIT Press). [2nd edn 1996]
RAIDT, E. H. (1968), *Geskiedenis van die Bijvoeglike Verbuiging in Nederlands en Afrikaans* (Cape Town etc.: Nassou Beperk).
RAINER, F. (1988), 'Towards a Theory of Blocking: The Case of Italian and German Quality Nouns', *YoM 1988*: 155-85.
—— (1996), 'Inflection inside Derivation. Evidence from Spanish and Portuguese', *YoM 1995*: 83-92.

—— (2000), 'Produktivitätsbeschränkungen', in Booij et al. (eds.), 877-85.
REULAND, E. (1988), 'Relating Morphological and Syntactic Structure', in Everaert et al. (eds.), 303-38.
—— (1990), 'Head Movement and the Relation between Morphology and Syntax', YoM 1990: 129-61.
RIEHEMANN, S. Z. (1998), 'Type-Based Derivational Morphology', The Journal of Comparative Germanic Linguistics, 2: 49-77.
RUBACH, J., and BOOIJ, G. E. (2001), 'Allomorphy in Optimality Theory: Polish Iotation', Lg, 77.
SADLER, L., and SPENCER, A. (1998), 'Morphology and Argument Structure', in Spencer and Zwicky (eds.), 206-36.
SANTEN, A. VAN (1986) 'Synthetic Compounds: Syntax or Semantics?', Linguistics, 24: 645-60.
—— (1992a), 'Produktiviteit in taal en taalgebruik. Een studie op het gebied van de Nederlandse woordvorming' (University of Leiden, doct. dissertation).
—— (1992b), 'Semantische factoren bij de vorming van denominale persoonsnamen op -er'. Sp, 21: 189-201.
—— (1997), 'Hoe sterk zijn de sterke werkwoorden?', in A. van Santen and M. van der Wal (eds.), Taal in tijd en ruimte (Leiden: Stichting Neerlandistiek Leiden), 45-56.
—— and LALLEMAN, J. (1994), 'Gaat zwak anders dan sterk? Over de produktie van Nederlandse regelmatige en onregelmatige verleden-tijdsvormen', FdL, 35: 1-22.
—— and VRIES, J. DE (1981), 'Vrouwelijke persoonsnamen op -ster', FdL, 22: 115-25.
SASSEN, A. (1981), 'Morfologische produktiviteit in het licht van niet-additieve woordafleiding', Fdl, 22: 126-42.
—— (1992), 'Meervoudloosheid en indeling van Nederlandse zelfstandige naamwoorden', in H. Bennis and J. de Vries (eds.), De binnenbouw van het Nederlands (Dordrecht: ICG Printing), 329-42.
SCALISE, S. (ed.), (1992), The Morphology of Compounding. Special issue of Rivista di Linguistica, 4: no. 1.
SCHREUDER, R., NEIJT, A., WEIDE, F. VAN DER, and BAAYEN, R. H. (1998), 'Regular Plurals in Dutch Compounds: Linking Graphemes or Morphemes?', Language and Cognitive Processes, 13: 551-73.
SCHULTINK, H. (1961), 'Produktiviteit als morfologisch fenomeen', FdL, 2: 110-25.
—— (1962), De morfologische valentie van het ongelede adjectief in modern Nederlands (Den Haag: Van Goor Zonen; reprinted by Hes Publishers, Utrecht 1980).
—— (1964), 'De bouw van nieuwvormingen met her-', Tijdschrift voor Nederlandse Taal- en Letterkunde, 80: 151-84.
SCHULTINK, H. (2000), 'History of Morphological Research: The Netherlands', in Booij et al. (eds.), 162-9.

SELKIRK, E. O. (1982), *The Syntax of Words* (Cambridge, MA: MIT Press).
SMITS, C. (1994), 'Resistance to Erosion in American Dutch Inflection', *YoM 1993*, 27–50.
—— (1996). *Disintegration of Inflection. The Case of Iowa Dutch* (The Hague: Holland Academic Graphics; Vrije Universiteit Amsterdam, doct. dissertation).
SPENCER, A. (1988), 'Bracketing Paradoxes and the English Lexicon', *Lg*, 64: 663–82.
—— (1991), *Morphological Theory* (Oxford and Cambridge, MA: Blackwell).
—— and ZWICKY, A. M. (1998), *The Handbook of Morphology* (Oxford and Malden, MA: Blackwell).
STEINMETZ, D., and RICE, C. (1989), 'The Gender of Inanimate Nouns in German and Dutch'. *Texas Linguistics Forum*, 31: 157–89.
STIEBELS, B. (1996), *Lexikalische Argumente und Adjunkte: Zum semantischen Beitrag von verbalen Präfixen und Partikeln* (Berlin: Akademieverlag).
—— and WUNDERLICH, D. (1994), 'Morphology Feeds Syntax: The Case of Particle Verbs', *Linguistics*, 32: 919–68.
TAELDEMAN, J. (1990), 'Afleidingen op -*sel*: semantiek, produktiviteit en integratie in een globale verantwoording van deverbatieve nomina', in de Caluwe (ed.), 77–115.
TOORN, M. C. VAN DEN (1981*a*), 'De tussenklank in samenstellingen waarvan het eerste lid een afleiding is', *Ntg*, 74: 197–205.
—— (1981*b*), 'De tussenklank in samenstellingen waarvan het eerste lid systematisch uitheems is', *Ntg*, 74: 547–52.
—— (1982), 'Tendenzen bij de beregeling van de verbindingsklank in nominale samenstellingen, I en II', *Ntg*, 75: 24–33, 153–60.
—— (1997), 'Nieuw-Nederlands (circa 1920-nu)', in M. C. van den Toorn, W. J. J. Pijnenburg, J. A. van Leuvensteijn, and J. M. van der Horst (eds.), *Geschiedenis van de Nederlandse Taal* (Amsterdam: Amsterdam University Press), 479–562.
TREFFERS-DALLER, J. (1994), *Mixing Two Languages. French–Dutch Contact in a Comparative Perspective* (Berlin: Mouton de Gruyter).
TROMMELEN, M. (1984), *The Syllable in Dutch* (Dordrecht: Foris; University of Utrecht, doct. dissertation).
—— and ZONNEVELD, W. (1986), 'Dutch Morphology: Evidence for the Right-hand Head Rule', *LI*, 17: 147–69.
VERKUYL, H. J.(1993), *A Theory of Aspectuality* (Cambridge: Cambridge University Press).
VRIES, J. DE (1975), *Lexicale morfologie van het werkwoord in modern Nederlands* (Leiden: Leiden University Press).
WATKINS, C. (1964), 'Preliminaries to the Reconstruction of Indo-European Sentence Structure', in H. G. Lunt (ed.), *Proceedings of the 9th International Congress of Linguists* (The Hague: Mouton), 1035–44.

WEERMAN, F., and WIT, P. DE (1999), 'The Decline of the Genitive in Dutch', *Linguistics*, 37: 1155–92.

WEGGELAAR, C. (1986), 'Noun Incorporation in Dutch', *International Journal of American Linguistics*, 52: 301–5.

WILLIAMS, E. (1981), 'On the Notions "Lexically Related" and "Head of a Word"', *LI*, 12: 245–75.

ZAENEN, A. (1993), 'Unaccusativity in Dutch: Integrating Syntax and Lexical Semantics', in Pustejovsky (ed.), 129–61.

ZUBIZARRETA, M.-L. (1987), *Levels of Representation in the Lexicon and in the Syntax* (Dordrecht: Foris).

—— and HAAFTEN, T. VAN (1988), 'English *-ing* and Dutch *-en* Nominal Constructions: A Case of Simultaneous Nominal and Verbal Projections', in Everaert *et al.* (eds.), 361–94.

ZWICKY, A. M. (1990), 'Syntactic Words and Morphological Words, Simple and Composite', *YoM 1990*: 201–16.

INDEX OF SUBJECTS

Ablaut 2, 10, 11
acronym 13, 38, 123–4
adjective:
   geographical 181
   qualitative 109, 131
   relational 108–9
adverb 48–9, 133
affix:
   competition of 24–32, 58, 101, 104, 128, 184–6, 227
   extraction of 9
   homonymous 91
   negative 93
   order of 83
   phrasal 35
   polyfunctional 89–91
   polysemous 90–1
   root 100
   substitution of 7–9, 15
   syntactic 51
affixoid 100, 111
Afrikaans 25, 39, 45, 93
agent noun 106, 122
agreement 34, 56, 83
   gender 36–7, 43, 82
   semantic 37
Aktionsart 67
allomorph:
   competition of 58
   subcategorization of 46
allomorphy 126–7
   affix 174–6
   stem 176–8
   syntactically conditioned 58
American Dutch 20, 45
A-morphous Morphology 32, 74, 226
apocope 46
appendix 170

argument reduction 196
argument structure 188–201
argument suppression 75
aspect 67
   durative 189, 203
   grammatical 67
   imperfective 68
   inchoative 203
   lexical 67
   perfective 68
   telic 67, 117, 189
auxiliary selection 66–7

back formation 7, 112, 163
bleaching 203, 217
blending 13
blocking 11–12, 101
   of types 11–12, 102
   of tokens 11–12, 101, 177
borrowing 14, 29, 30, 38–9, 63, 96, 100, 126
bracketing paradox 8, 65–6, 101

case 36
categorial morphology 160
clipping 13
closing morpheme 92, 129, 130
combining form 100, 141
comparative 39–42, 80, 84, 115, 156
complex word:
   formally 15, 75, 100, 115, 118
   native 96
   non-native 96
   possible 9, 94
   probable 94
compositionality 105, 195–6
compound 141–66
   adjectival 153–60

compound (*cont.*)
  adjective-noun 12
  bahuvrihi 143–4, 151
  copulative 144, 155
  endocentric 143
  exocentric 143
  formal 173
  nominal 142–53
  numeral 165–6
  synthetic 158–61
  verbal 161–5, 222–4
confix 100
conjunctive 58
coordination 148–9, 166, 172
construction 35, 72
construction grammar 202
constructional idiom 202–4, 213–21
conversion 63–4, 76, 77, 134–40, 160, 162, 164, 211, 215
cranberry morph 16, 155

d-deletion 177
de-deletion 177
default conjugation 62
default rule 56
definiteness 44
degemination 27, 185–6
determiner 33, 35
deverbalization 71
diminutive 37, 89, 92–4, 107, 175, 222
dual mechanism theory 10

endearment suffix 93, 107
English 4, 7, 11, 19–21, 29, 34, 35, 64, 66, 68, 88, 90, 95, 101
Estonian 207
event structure 188–9
extension schema 106
external argument 189

feature:
  diacritic 65
  morphosyntactic 19
female personal noun 6, 102–4, 107

First Order Projection Condition 199
Flemish 206
French 14, 20, 29, 39, 64, 90, 126
future 70

gapping 50, 51, 171–2, 180
gender 36–9, 43
  assignment of 38, 88, 138, 142
  default 38
German 4, 12, 19–20, 23, 56, 64, 70, 74–5, 96
grammaticalization 14, 35, 47, 111, 117, 153–4, 216–19
Greek 8, 14, 29, 100

hapax legomenon 12
haplology 185
Head-Final Filter 49
head operation 65
Hungarian 34, 207

iconicity 154
imperative 58
impersonal agent noun 106
indifferentialis 145
Indonesian 141
infinitive 70–73, 85
  as part of compound 148, 162–4, 222–4
inflection:
  adjectival 39–54
  category-changing 52
  contextual 19–20, 34, 45, 55
  inherent 19–20, 34, 41, 55, 77, 80–2
  irregular 162
  nominal 21–39
  regular 162
  verbal 54–80
Ingvaeonic 23
inhabitant names 109–20, 181–2
inheritance 52, 54, 65
  of argument structure 192, 194–200
  of irregularities 64

INDEX OF SUBJECTS

of syntactic valency 200–1
instrument noun 106, 124
intensifiers 155–6
internal argument 189
IPP effect 70
Italian 20, 29, 30, 56, 88

Laryngeal Spreading 58
Latin 8, 14, 29, 81, 100
layers, *see* stratum
level ordering 101, 162
lexeme 4
lexeme-based morphology 4
Lexical-Conceptual Structure 188–92
Lexical Integrity 206
lexical storage, *see* storage
lexicalization 14–15, 79, 198, 221
Lexical Phonology 167
lexicon 13
   mental 2, 10, 13
   non-native 8–9, 94–101
link phoneme 179
linking phoneme, *see* link
   phoneme
linking rule 189

measure phrase 34
metaphony 2
metaphor 108
metonymy 108, 143
Middle Dutch 219
middle verb 139–40, 191
Morpheme Identity 27
morphosyntactic category 19

No Empty Onset 186
nomen actionis 125
nominalization 125, 194–200
noun:
   abstract 128
   action 125
   agent 106, 122
   personal 121, 123
   number 21

object name 123–4
Obligatory Contour Principle 182–6
Optimality Theory 25–7, 185
output condition 24–5, 40, 46, 58, 104, 184–6
overcharacterization 116, 124

paradigm:
   gap in 21, 40, 42–3
   verbal 55–70
paradigmatic relation 6, 8–9, 17, 132, 178, 181, 225
paradigmatic word formation 7, 66, 77, 96, 115, 152, 164, 178
participle:
   passive 68–9, 75–6, 84, 190
   perfect 15–16, 57–66, 73–8, 157
   present 78–80, 157, 160
   pseudo- 77–8, 159
particle verbs 138, *see also* separable complex verb
passive 68–9
   formation of 75–6
   impersonal 75
percolation 5, 44, 65, 88, 101
periphrasis 42–3, 66–7, 69, 202
phonological word, *see* prosodic word
pluralia tantum 22
pluralization:
   double 30
   of nouns 21–34, 84, 143, 179
Polish 93
polyfunctionality 90–1
polysemy 90–1, 105–8, 123, 194
possessive pronoun 35–7
praesens historicum 56
predicate:
   complex 204–24
   phrasal 207
   secondary 217–18, 220, 223
Predicate-Argument Structure 188–91
prefix:
   boundary of 170
   category changing 88, 113

prefix (*cont.*)
   category determining 88
   category-neutral 111
   native 98–101, 111
   non-native 98–101, 176
   verbalizing 88, 113, 116
preverb 117, 207, 219
Prevocalic Schwa-Deletion 25, 45, 55
productivity 10, 12, 81, 132
   quantitative 11, 101, 110
progressive 72, 203–4, 206, 224
Projection Principle 210–11
Prokosch's Law 59
Prosodic Phonology 168
prosodic word 31, 100, 129–30, 168–74

qualitative adjective 131
quantifier 44–5, 52–4

reanalysis 50, 77, 164–5, 218
recursivity 92, 142
redundancy rules 2
register 11, 95, 118
reinterpretation 17, 49, 54, 89, 174
relational adjective 8, 41
reversative meaning 193–4
rewriting rule 5
rhoticization 177
Righthand Head Rule 5, 87–8, 141
Romance 95–6, 141, 202

samenkoppeling, *see* separable complex verb
schwa apocope 177
schwa deletion, *see* Prevocalic Schwa-Deletion
schwa loss 45
separable complex verb 164, 204–24
sequence of tense 56
serial verb 202
Small Clause analysis 207–8, 212
spelling reform 179
split morphology 83–5, 227

stem allomorphy 145–5, 154, 176–82
stem-based morphology 4
stem extension 120, 145–6
storage 10, 30, 33, 64, 82–3, 177, 209
stratum 94–101
subject name 122, 124, 196–200
suffix:
   closing 92
   cohering 169–70
   Germanic 11
   hybrid 96
   native 11, 95–8
   non-cohering 169–74, 180
   non-native 11, 95–101
   plural 21–4
   root 96, 98
superlative 39, 41–3, 156
suppletion 42, 60
syllabification 168
synaffix 9, 115, 119, 127
systematization 116, 124

template 112–13, 159–60
tense 85
   past 55, 57–66
   present 55–6
   sequence of 56
transcategorial construction 51, 71–2, 75, 79
trochee 24, 46
truncation rule 15
Turkish 34
type coercion 41, 84, 109, 190

unification 69–70
Uniform Base Hypothesis 91
uniform valency effect 113, 191–3

vagueness 108
valency change 139, 188–201
verb:
   Ablauting 59
   causative 114, 120, 139, 193
   durative 213

inchoative 114, 120, 193–4
irregular 58–9
middle 139–40, 191
modal 62
non-accusative 125
regular 58
semi-regular 61
stem-alternating 59–62, 64–5
strong 59
telic 192, 213
weak 59
Verb Raising 70, 206, 220
Verb Second 67, 206
Vietnamese 141

voice assimilation 58
Von Humboldt's Principle 116
vowel lengthening 28, 59

word:
  existing 112
  grammatical 4
  phonological, *see* prosodic word
  possible 112
  prosodic 31, 100, 129–30, 168–74
word-based morphology 3, 4

zero-affix 135, 138
zero-allomorph 46

INDEX OF AUTHORS

Ackema, P. 69, 139–40, 162, 191, 208, 225
Ackerman, F. 75, 202, 207
Anderson, S. R. 32, 74, 82–3, 103
Aronoff, M. 2–5, 15, 16, 91, 132
Auwera, J. van der 219

Baayen, R. H. 10–11, 13, 67, 83, 92, 139, 188, 193
Baker, M. 189
Bauer, L. 9, 88, 107
Beard, R. 8, 40, 66, 105, 159, 226
Becker, Th. 8, 104
Bennis, H. 78, 80
Berkum, J. van 38–9
Blom, A. 44, 47, 48
Bloomfield, L. 4, 95
Boogaart, R. 68
Booij, G. E. *passim*
Börjars, K. 69
Borowsky, T. 58
Botha, R. P. 158
Bresnan, J. 206
Bybee, J. 80, 83

Caluwe, J. de 12, 123, 142
Carstairs-McCarthy, A. 74
Chapman, C. 69
Christofidou, A. 82
Clahsen, H. 10, 65
Clark, E. 136
Clark, H. 136
Coopmans, P. 202–3
Corbett, G. 37–8

Dijkstra, T. 10, 13, 83
Don, J. 1, 135, 138
Dressler, W. U. 81

Everaert, M. 202–3

Fast, P. 103
Fleischer, W. 86
Fleischmann, S. 90
Fletcher, W. H. 156

Goldberg, A. 35, 202
Greenberg, J. H. 83

Haas, de W. 1, 92, 104, 139
Haeften, T. van 72, 188
Haegeman, L. 206
Haeringen, C. B. van 24–5, 63–4, 125
Haeseryn, W. 1, 38, 59
Hall, T. A. 168
Halle, M. 65
Haspelmath, M. 17, 52, 71, 81
Heuven, V. van 98
Heynderickx, P. 12, 96, 108, 137
Hijzelendoorn, M. 98
Hoeksema, J. 42, 46, 53–4, 70, 82, 105, 146, 158, 160, 196, 200, 214
Hoekstra, T. 49, 51, 67, 71–2, 207
Hopper, P. 14, 153, 218
Horst, J. van der 213, 219
Horst, K. van der 213, 219
Hüning, M. 90, 91, 126–7, 132

Iacobini, C. 86

Jackendoff, R. S. 2, 139, 202, 215–16
Jordens, P. 10, 64
Jurafsky, D. 108

Kager, R. 25
Kester, E.-P. 51–2
Kiparsky, P. 45, 162

INDEX OF AUTHORS

Klooster, W. G. 34
Knopper, R. 125
Koopman, H. 206, 223
Koster, J. 67
Krott, A. 92
Kuryłowicz, J. 19

Lalleman, J. 10, 64
Lansu, M. 207
Lapointe, S. 46, 184, 206
Lass, R. 45
Lefebvre, C. 51
LeSourd, Ph. 202
Levin, B. 188
Lieber, R. 5, 65, 67, 88, 139, 188, 193, 197, 225
Loey, A. van 219
Lüdeling, A. 205, 207

McCarthy, J. J. 25, 182
Mackenzie, J. L. 94, 118, 196
Marantz, A. 65
Marle, J. van 6, 12, 17, 45, 50, 52-3, 82, 89-90, 96, 102-4, 116, 124, 132, 163, 222-3
Mattens, W. H. M. 145
Matthews, P. H. 4, 19
Mchombo, S. 206
Moerdijk, A. 152
Moortgat, M. 201
Muysken, P. C. 51

Naumann, B. 86
Neeleman, A. 88, 188, 205, 208, 219
Neijt, A. 12, 98
Nespor, M. 168
Norde, M. 36

Odijk, J. 47

Paulissen, D. 162
Peeters, R. J. 139, 191
Perlmutter, D. 83
Pinker, S. 10, 65, 146-7

Plag, I. 10-12, 139
Plank, F. 81
Pollard, C. 56
Posthumus, J. 164
Prince, A. 25
Pustejovsky, J. 41, 189

Raidt, E. 45
Rainer, F. 11
Rappoport Hovav, M. 188
Reuland, E. 69, 72
Rice, C. 38
Riehemann, S. Z. 2
Riemsdijk, H. van 206

Sadler, l. 188
Sag, I. A. 56
Santen, A. van 1, 10, 64, 90, 91, 94, 103, 110, 123, 132, 158
Sassen, A. 8-9, 21
Schipper, J. 88, 188
Schoorlemmer, M. 139-40, 191
Schreuder, R. 10, 13, 83, 92, 179
Schultink, H. 6, 10, 47, 52, 74, 111, 132, 137
Selkirk, E. O. 197
Smits, C. 20, 45
Spencer, A. 1, 8, 66, 101, 188
Steinmetz, D. 38
Stiebels, B. 205, 207

Taeldeman, J. 124
Toorn, M. C. van den 157, 163, 180
Traugott, E. 14, 153, 218
Treffers-Daller, J. 38
Trommelen, M. 1, 38, 88, 92, 104, 142

Verkuyl, H. J. 68
Vincent, N. 69
Vogel, I. 168
Vogel, P. 86
Vries, J. W. de 103, 113, 211, 215, 222

Watkins, C. 207

Webelhuth, G. 75, 202, 207
Weerman, F. 36, 205, 208, 219
Weggelaar, C. 164–5
Wehrman, P. 78, 80
Westerduin, M. 207
Williams, E. 5, 87
Wit, P. de 36

Wunderlich, D. 205, 207

Zaenen, A. 75–6
Zonneveld, W. 88, 142, 162
Zubizarreta, M.-L. 72, 188
Zwicky, A. 1, 202

INDEX OF AFFIXES

a- 99, 186
-aal 97, 108
aan- 116
-aan 97, 110
-aar 32, 40, 91, 102, 105–6, 110, 121–2, 183–4
-aard 32, 110, 121
aarts- 111
-aat 9, 110
-abel 98
achter- 116
-achtig 84, 90, 105, 108–9, 130–1, 169, 171, 185
-ade 98
-age 31, 98
-air 97, 108–10
aller- 41–2, 155
an- 186
-ans 98
-ant 97, 104
anti- 99–100
-arij 127
-aris 97, 102
-arius 98, 184
-asme 98
-ast 97
-atie 15, 97, 120, 125–8

-baar 17, 18, 87, 89–90, 94, 112, 130–2, 169, 171, 190–1
be- 113–15, 188, 191–3, 201
-boer 153

co- 99
contra- 99

de- 99, 186
-der (comparative) 39–40, 183

-der (nominal) 40, 121–2, 183–4
-derij 127
des- 186
-dom 31, 84, 128, 130, 169, 171
door- 116–17, 193

-e (female) 31, 92, 102–4
-e (nominal) 31–2, 41, 50–4, 92, 121
-eel 97, 108
-een 98, 110
-eer 15, 78, 97, 119–20, 126
-ees 97, 110
-ein 97, 110
-elaar 185
-elijk 112, 130–3
-eling 121, 185
-elings 134
-ement 98
-en (adjectival) 108
-en (infinitive) 70–3
-en (plural noun) 21–34
-enaar 32, 110, 121
-end 78–80, 112, 160
-enij 127
-enis 125–6
-ent 98, 104
er- 113
-er (adjectival) 108
-er (comparative) 39–42, 183–4
-er (nominal) 3, 6, 7, 31, 38, 90–1, 102–7, 110, 121, 124, 161, 183–4, 196–200
-erd 31, 121, 184
-eren (plural noun) 22–3, 64
-erie 126–7
-erig 130–3
-erij 91, 125–7
-erik 121, 185

INDEX OF AFFIXES

-ernij 127
-erwijs 134
-es 102
-esk 97
-esse 97, 102
-et 98
-etje 175
-etjes 133
-ette 31, 97
-eur 32, 102, 106
euro- 100
-eus 97
-euse 102-3, 106
ex- 99-100, 174

ga- 119
ge- (nominal) 88, 94, 106-7, 117-18, 126, 139, 201, 207
ge- (participial) 15, 74-5, 77, 117-18, 207
ge- (verbal) 113
ge-...-te 119
-gewijs 134

-halve 134
-heid 12, 13, 17, 31, 84, 95, 108, 128-9, 169, 171, 201
her- 111, 174, 210, 223
hyper- 99

-iaan 97
-ica 98, 102
-icus 98, 102
-ide 97
-ie 98, 128
-ief 97, 100, 108, 128, 137
-iek 98, 100, 108, 137
-iel 108
-ier 32, 97-8, 102, 110, 121
-iër 110
-ière 102-3
-iet 97, 110
-ieus 97
-ig 17, 91-2, 108, 128-33, 158-60, 185

-igheid 17, 128-9
-ij 106, 110, 127
-ijn 98
in- 99
-in 102
-ine 97
infra- 99
-ing 37-8, 106-7, 125-6, 194-5
-ioen 98
-isch 97, 108, 181-2
-iseer 95, 97, 120, 139
-isme 8, 32, 95, 97
-ist 8, 31, 97-8, 104, 109-10
-istisch 8-9
-iteit 12, 95, 97, 101
-iter 133
-itis 98
-ix 102

-je 175
-jes 133

-kje 175
kut- 153

-lijk 108, 130
-lijks 159
-ling 31, 108, 110, 121, 169, 171
loco- 99
-loos 93, 130-1, 169, 171

macro- 100
meta- 99
micro- 99
mis- 116
mono- 99

neo- 99
niet- 108, 111-12
-nij 127
-nis 31, 125-6
non- 94, 99, 108

oer- 111

INDEX OF AFFIXES

-oir 97, 108
om- 116, 193
on- 17–18, 80, 84, 93–4, 99, 108, 111–12, 116
onder- 116–17
ont- 113–14, 116, 194
-oot 95, 97, 110
opper- 111
-or 102, 106
oud- 111
over- 116–17, 193

-pje 175
-pjes 133
pre- 99
pro- 99
pseudo- 99

re- 100
-rice 102–3

-s (adjectival) 108, 181–2
-s (nominal) 52–4
-s (partitive) 52–4
-s (plural) 21–34
-s (possessive) 34–6
-schap 31, 85, 90, 128–9, 169, 171, 174
-se 103
-sel 31, 106–7, 124

semi- 99
-st (nominal) 125–6
-st (superlative) 39, 41–3
-ster 6–7, 9, 31, 102–4
sub- 99
super- 99–100

-t (nominal) 125–6
-te 92, 128
tele- 100
-tenis 125
-tig 174
-tje 31, 92, 107, 133
-tjes 133
turbo- 99

ultra- 99

ver- 41, 113–16, 138, 188, 193, 201, 210
vice- 99
vol- 116

-waarts 134
weer- 116
-weg 134
wereld- 153

-zaam 112, 130–1, 169, 171

Printed in Germany
by Amazon Distribution
GmbH, Leipzig